PRAIS...   D0978120   ...n a

ᴇDUCATIONAL TRAVᴇ...   fam

"Travel has always been considered an essential aspect of a fine education. Unfortu... ...primitive costs have put distant locales beyond the reach of most far... That is why the publication of this encyclopedic work is such ...opedic work is such welcom... ...re. Practical, frugal, witty, ar... ...of those rare books folks wi... ...using. Don't leave home w...

...thor of *Just Visiting*

"This b... ...s, and seniors who want to... ...e. It's a treasure of details a... ...ng travel for those with spe... ...ell. Best of all, it's a book ab... ...r the destination— providin...

...rd-winning author *...hat Once We Loved*

"Did yo... ...ld nuts and berries to save ... ...ionaries to see the world? in... ...laminated souvenir place mats to teach geography, or testing the science of box springs at cheap motels? Thousands of tips, heroic tales, and great creativity from two inventive moms make *Educational Travel on a Shoestring* an indispensable guide to living, learning, and traveling the world as a family for just pennies a day."

—Kʏʟᴇ McCᴀʀᴛʜʏ, editor of Family Travel Forum.com
and author of twelve *Frommer's* budget guides

"Some books are filled with great ideas, others major on practicalities. this book does both. If you can't find an idea for a quality family vaction at a price you can afford, you aren't looking!"

—JANET AND GEOFF BENGE, authors of several titles
in the Christian Heroes series of biographies

"*Educational Travel on a Shoestring* is chock-full of great ideas and helpful resources for traveling familes. This book makes you want to grab the kids and hit the road because afte reading it you'll be able to make any trip educational and fun! It addresses one of the toughest questions of all: how to finance family trips, whether a short getaway or extended travel. And last but not least is the valuable resource guide, which places a wealth of information at your fingertips and saves you valuable research time."

—SHELLY ZOELLICK, editor of *Families on the Road* newsletter
and the Web site, www.FamiliesOnTheRoad.com

EDUCATIONAL TRAVEL

on a Shoestring

EDUCATIONAL
TRAVEL
on a Shoestring

FRUGAL FAMILY FUN & LEARNING AWAY FROM HOME

JUDITH WAITE ALLEE
AND MELISSA L. MORGAN

SHAW BOOKS
an imprint of WATERBROOK PRESS

Educational Travel on a Shoestring
A Shaw Book
Published by WaterBrook Press
2375 Telstar Drive, Suite 160
Colorado Springs, Colorado 80920
A division of Random House, Inc.

ISBN 0-87788-204-5

Library of Congress Cataloging-in-Publication Data
Allee, Judith Waite, 1949–
  Educational travel on a shoestring : frugal family fun and learning away from home / Judith Waite Allee and Melissa L. Morgan.
    p.   cm.
  ISBN 0-87788-204-5
  1. Family recreation—United States. 2. Education—Parent participation—United States.
3. Home schooling—United States.   I. Morgan, Melissa L., 1958–   II. Title.
  GV182.8.A44 2001
  790.1'91—dc21   2001049599

Printed in the United States of America
2002—First Edition

10 9 8 7 6 5 4 3 2 1

To Hugh, my beloved husband and best friend, in this, our twenty-fifth year of marriage. I appreciate your uncomplaining encouragement and support—it takes a special kind of person to live with a writer! We've traveled together with the help of the Lord through trials, tears, joys, and laughter. You're my adventurous, energetic explorer, always willing to feast on unusual sights and jump into rare experiences. Thanks for gently pulling me out of my refuge and taking me on field trips, ministry trips, and vacations that have enriched our lives.

—Melissa

To Nancy Cynthia Allee—my daughter, my friend. You saw a lot of the back of my head, backlit by the glow of a computer screen while I was writing this book. Here's hoping for many more miles together over the years on our journey into lifelong learning.

—Judith

Contents

ACKNOWLEDGMENTS

Our heartfelt thanks go to the many travelers that we have met, both in person and on the Internet, who graciously shared their time and experiences with us to make this a better book. Although we can't list all of you by name here, you'll find the book sprinkled liberally with your trips, freebies, and tips. We feel richer and wiser from knowing you.

To Elisa Fryling, Robert Bittner, Joan Guest, and Jennifer Lonas from Shaw Books: Thanks for your encouragement, patience, and wisdom through the long process of finishing (finally!) this book.

From Judith, thanks to:

Growing Without Schooling Magazine, which connected my family with new friends across the country; and Shelley Zoellick's *Families on the Road* discussion list members, who contributed resources, stories, and friendship.

The Berry-Hellers, Merrions, Camerons, Boyds, Prestons, and all the other families who changed the face of travel for us by sharing their homes, becoming our friends away from home.

Friends and online buddies who volunteered to critique the manuscript at various stages, especially Stephanie Bernhagen, Diana Blowers, Collette Carlisle, Cafi Cohen, Jim Foreman, the whole Goza family (Kimberly, Dennis, and Zephyr), Jaimie Hall, Bruce Humphrey, Dave Levingston, Dee Packard, Greg Robus, Billy Romp, Charleen Skalski, Hope Sykes, Coleen Sykora, and Barbara White.

My parents, Helen and Leonard Waite, who didn't know I was paying attention when they introduced me to the joys of camping and educational travel.

My sister, Cindy Waite, and Marylin Nyros, a sister in spirit, both fellow writers and honest critiquers.

Melissa, whose creative ideas, endless patience, unfailing friendship, and fearless dedication to deadlines have been an inspiration to me.

My husband, John Allee, whose loving support made this endeavor possible in a thousand ways. If every child could have such a father and every woman could have such a mate, this world would be a better place.

From Melissa:

Thanks to my Lord and Savior Jesus Christ, my Creator and my Good Shepherd, who has led me through the authorship of this book and has traveled with me through life's twists and turns.

Mom and Dad—Thanks for your encouragement. You have rejoiced at my successes and have always been there during times of tears. I also thank my older children, John Morgan and Lori Morgan, for sharing their experiences and even editing some of my bloopers. And I appreciate my littlest, Susie Morgan, for keeping me from getting too distracted by the computer. She reminds me of the important things in life.

I am grateful for friends from the PATHWAYS (Pataskala Area Teaching Homes with Able Young Students), New Song Community Church, and Whitehall Christian Community Church, who have stood in the gap for my family during difficult times, health crises, and the transition from country to city life. The Iannis, Trumpowers, and Harringtons, in particular, have gone far beyond the call of friendship. These families and others literally helped put a roof over our heads as we raised our city home.

Judith—Thanks for traveling with me through thick and thin to the end of our writing journey together. I am a better writer for knowing you, and I'm glad I can call you friend.

PREFACE

When we joined forces to write our first book, we were barely acquainted. That book, *Homeschooling on a Shoestring*, took six years to finish and was written in stops and starts between the ups and downs of family life. This book took another two years. During the eight years we have been writing together, we have each gained a precious friend en route. There's simply no better way to bond than to give birth (to a book) jointly!

In our first book we described ourselves as "two unabashed penny pinchers, compulsive recyclers, and unflinching trash pickers." We discovered during the writing process that we aren't as frugal when it comes to words and ideas. The first draft of our first book was over five hundred pages long! We had to cut a chapter on educational travel.

That already-written chapter gave us the idea for a second book—this one. It turns out we had a lot more to say. And virtually all of it applied to families of all descriptions, not just homeschoolers. Nearly all the books we found on educational travel were geared toward high-school students taking foreign exchange trips, college students backpacking around Europe and other exotic destinations, and ElderHostel programs for retirees. Few were about families traveling with school-age children, especially those traveling on a tight budget.

Our own real-life adventures with educational travel have made us passionate about this topic, and this book project gave us "permission" to take time from our own busy lives to research something we both love. The more we learned about educational travel through our own experiences and the experiences of others, the more we wanted to share the resources we've discovered and the real-life "tales from the road" we've collected. In addition to our personal insights on the topic, our research involved reading, surfing the Internet, and interviewing numerous families who have generously shared their insights about learning and saving money while traveling. Their experiences range from volunteering to earning money while traveling to long-distance bicycling to kayaking and many other activities.

Our own families have changed and faced new challenges since the writing of our first book. The Morgans, whose two older children are now age ten and thirteen, have added a baby girl to their family. Susie, who was born medically fragile, is now a nonstoppable toddler.

During the time this book was written, the Morgan family moved from the country to the city and built a new house as a family project. John, their oldest child, is keen on basketball and woodworking, while Lori, their oldest daughter, likes nature study and crafts. They both enjoy music, reading, writing, and drawing.

The Morgans learned firsthand about some of the difficulties of special-needs travel during their daughter Susie's first year. During that time most of the family's field trips involved hospitals and doctors' offices. Now that Susie is more "portable," the family is always equipped to go, whether on overnight trips or local field trips. The kids keep their book bags packed with activities to keep them busy in the car and during waiting times.

Judith, long accustomed to the flexibility of a home-based business, started working full time for her local Mental Health Association (MHA), facilitating parent support groups and presenting workshops like "Parenting Without Losing Your Cool." In addition, she continues to assist with the family business, Allee Photography. With Judith's job comes a traditional two-week vacation. These days, family "working vacations" with the photography business have become less impromptu and less frequent. Judith's daughter, Nancy, now a college student, volunteers with middle-school students, presenting skits about preventing violence (for an MHA program). Sometimes she travels to build homes with Habitat for Humanity or to visit relatives as a solo traveler. Although their schedules rarely mesh, Nancy occasionally goes camping with her parents.

Our families' struggles during our work on this project (including both our husbands enduring major medical crises) have reinforced the true premise of the book: Time with your family is precious. Don't wait until "someday" to travel or to do other things that are important to you. Don't wait a decade for Paris when you can go to the Adirondacks today.

Although travel comprises a relatively small percentage of our lives, we find that it represents a disproportionately large chunk of our special moments. Those special moments reflect how traveling takes us away from daily routines. Travel offers us a glimpse of our lives, and of one another, from a fresh perspective.

Wanderlust (or as RVers call it, "hitch itch") has long influenced the contours of human history. Our history books honor explorers from Marco Polo to Neil Armstrong. Nameless prehistoric travelers presumably crossed the Bering Straits on ice floes to become the first North Americans. Whatever drives this impulse for discovery, we find that most people are either travelers or wannabes—or occasional travelers who wanna travel more.

You don't have to stay in the ranks of the wannabes. Lack of money and time can force you to decide what is truly important. If you, like us, have made financial mistakes in the past, we hope this book will encourage you to take stock of your finances and make some important changes. These changes, small or large, can bring form and substance to your travel dream.

Now that the book is finished, we want to grab our families and take off for the horizon as often as we can. Through our research, we have learned about so many adventures that we would like to try as well as travel mistakes to avoid. We don't know what we'll find around the next bend in the road, but our families are ready to learn and rarin' to go.

Happy trails!

Chapter One

The Great Adventure

"It's like they were just here yesterday," Danny, age twelve, whispered in awe to his foster mom, Judith Allee. He was talking about the battle at Devil's Den that took place on July 2, 1863, at the base of a rocky hill called Little Round Top. The site, just outside the little village of Gettysburg, Pennsylvania, overlooked an ordinary wheat field and a hillside tumbled with boulders that a young soldier could hide behind. During the course of battle, the wheat field changed hands six times, from Union to Confederate and back again. Eighteen thousand soldiers were killed or injured that day.

A history buff at Gettysburg gave Judith's family a personal tour of the battlegrounds, sharing stories—some funny, some touching, some agonizing—about the people who were at Little Round Top during that terrible time.

Danny used to think history was boring.

Do you want to try something different this year instead of the same old sunburn? Make your family travels educational. Educational opportunities are everywhere—and many of them are inexpensive or free.

Although most people think of travel in connection with vacations, there are other ways to make travel—especially educational travel—a part of your family's lifestyle. Judith's husband, John, travels to photograph conferences and reunions. When Judith and their daughter, Nancy, traveled with him over the years, those trips became working vacations and getaways for a family that could not afford traditional vacations.

For me, adult-only travel versus traveling with kids is like cooking for yourself versus cooking for your family. When you cook for yourself, you tend to say, "Oh, I'll just grab a sandwich." But if you're cooking for your family, you're more likely to fix roast beef and mashed potatoes, carrots, a salad—and dessert! When you travel with kids, you tend to go the extra mile to make your travels more educational and exciting.

A year or two ago I embarked on my first extended trip without children since my honeymoon. We missed Nancy's company. As a family, we'd take time to explore caverns and go on factory tours. We tend not to bother when it is just the two of us. New sights, new people, new experiences are all richer and more meaningful somehow when you have a young person to share them with. It's more fun!

With kids along, even a trip to the doughnut shop or to drop off film for processing can be an exciting—and free—field trip. This book is not only about formal vacations. It's also about being alert to educational opportunities in your own neighborhood and in your daily activities.

Melissa and Hugh Morgan have tried to make learning a seamless part of daily life wherever they roam. They feel children absorb important information from being involved in the adult world rather than always being with other children their own age. Melissa includes the children in her activities whenever she can.

We are so used to bringing the children with us that it takes us by surprise when we find that children are excluded from an activity. They are with us when we are helping out at a mission, sitting in at a business seminar, or watching construction at a home building site. Our children have journeyed with us to business training in Virginia, and they have seen government in action in Washington, D.C. We have prayed together in front of the Supreme Court building. We find that real experiences help our children understand what they have studied in books.

Taking a child's interests seriously helps him or her to think seriously about the future. Learning has more meaning when there is a goal. At age twelve, John Morgan had expressed an interest in the air force, so the family stopped at the Dayton Air Museum in Ohio. There a display of a historic biplane caught John's imagination. He pointed out that it had "all-natural wood and three engines, one on each wing and one on the front. Its body resembled a boat, and it had a machine gun mounted in front of the copilot's seat. It looked so out of place among the metallic single-wing planes. I might have liked to fly in it, if it had any seat belts!"

The family also visited Sunwatch, a re-created Native American village near Dayton, Ohio. Ten-year-old Lorianna "felt sad to learn that many of the village children died at the age of five. A normal life span for an adult was only forty years. They were missing nutrients, because they mainly ate corn and meat."

Travel can help a family absorb more than just facts. It can help people empathize with the experiences of others.

In recent years, the Morgan family has encountered new challenges. Susanna, now age two, was born medically fragile, so most of their "field trips" have been to medical facilities—which were educational but not pleasant! "It is not what we planned, but our older children, John and Lorianna, have indeed learned a lot—about medical procedures, therapies, and equipment. They've also learned about coping with emergencies and what is truly important in life."

A Family Is…

For convenience, we use the term *family travel.* You may be single or married parents, grandparents, favorite aunts and uncles, or Big Brothers or Big Sisters with your Littles. This book is intended for anyone with a sense of adventure and a school-age child or teenager (or more than one) to share it with.

Travel, by definition, takes us outside our normal experiences and into new frontiers. We call it the "sauna effect." Children, it seems, soak up knowledge through their pores. Just being away from home and away from the normal routine opens up those pores like a Swedish sauna. Starting with the excitement of dreaming, planning, and preparing, an excursion makes learning come alive, whether the journey is crosstown or cross-country.

The sauna effect is even more dramatic for parents. Children are always ready to respond to something that fascinates them, no matter what they are doing, but we parents are often too busy, too pressured, too caught up in our daily responsibilities. Once on the road, we can put away all our to-do lists. We can take the time to step back and discover new things about our family and our world.

Aren't Vacations Supposed to Be Fun?

The idea of educational family travel does not sit well with some folks. Their concern is that relaxing is undervalued in our society and that both children and adults need downtime. After all, what is wrong with simply having fun together?

Not a thing. We are all for family fun. And, yes, we agree that too many children today have every moment scheduled, darting from one after-school activity to another.

But let's be open-minded about fun. In our experience, learning together as a family is great fun. Sometimes we share our knowledge with our kids, but just as often, we learn right alongside them, asking our own questions and learning our own lessons. A shared sense of awe and discovery is just as much fun as our former exhausting trips to theme parks, and often less expensive. Keep in mind that any activity you choose can offer educational opportunities. Are you going to the beach? Lounging in the sun? Sea and sun are equally fun—and more exciting—when you learn something about sea life. A child who finds an unusual shell might be thrilled to pull out the sea-life guidebook in her backpack so she can learn more about it.

A *Calvin and Hobbes* cartoon by Bill Watterson shows this connection between learning and fun. Young Calvin and his buddy, Hobbes, a stuffed tiger, have found a snake. They get to wondering how the snake glides along so easily, how it smells with its tongue, and whether it has eyelids. They dash off to see if Mom would get them a book—until Calvin remembers it is summer vacation. He doesn't want to *learn* anything on summer vacation, does he? But Hobbes says, "If nobody makes you do it, it counts as fun." In the final panel, the two buddies are poring over a snake book and having a grand time.

We are not talking here about replicating school on the road. The last thing we want to encourage parents to do is to turn their family time into lectures and lessons, complete with quizzes to make sure everyone is paying attention. Kids will surely resist our efforts to force-feed them facts and figures in the guise of a vacation.

You can help a child understand that history is made up of events that happened to real people and that people today are making history. You can relate events in today's newspaper to events in history. A visit to Abraham Lincoln's modest home and offices in Springfield, Illinois, can lead to a discussion of current political leaders and help children make a connection back to the tall, shy representative from Illinois who became president.

"Travel has always been a component part of a well-rounded education," write George and Karen Grant, authors of *Just Visiting: How Travel Has Enlightened Lives and Viewpoints Throughout History.*

> In times past, travel was seen as far more significant than just fun and games. It was for more than mere rest and relaxation. It was intended to be more than simply a vacation or a getaway. Instead, it was a vital aspect of the refined instruction in art, music, literature, architecture, politics, business, science, and divinity. It was, according to Benjamin Franklin, "the laboratory where theory meets practice, where notion encounters application."

Planet Talk **Newsletter**

Write for a free subscription to *Planet Talk,* a quarterly print newsletter. The newsletter, from Lonely Planet Publications, contains information about the publisher's products, but the majority of the publication is about exotic destinations and cultures. You can also subscribe to their monthly electronic newsletter, *Comet.* Check out their "shoestring" series of guides for traveling around the globe. Lonely Planet Publications, 150 Linden Street, Oakland CA 94607; (800) 275-8555; *http://www.lonelyplanet.com/comet.*

The Grants' book explores a small sampling of the great cities of the world—cities that have inspired some of the brightest minds, the clearest observers, the greatest leaders, and the best writers through the ages. Our children are some of the brightest minds and clearest observers—aren't yours?

FAMILY TRAVEL AND SCHOOL

Most often, families plan their travel around their child's school schedule. Some families take their children out of school to travel, though. Their reasons vary:

- A parent may be available to travel only when school is in session—for example, during the "slow season" at work.
- An opportunity may arise for travel that does not fit into the school schedule—perhaps the family can accompany a parent on a business trip.
- Some destinations are better in the winter. Who prefers going to Florida in the summer?
- For some families, a dream vacation may be affordable only by taking advantage of off-season savings.

With help, your children can keep up their schoolwork in spite of missed school time. You can help a child get ahead on his schoolwork before the trip, catch up when he gets back, keep up during your travels, or a combination of these.

Some teachers and schools are more open-minded about travel than others. Some see it as an opportunity at least as valuable as the time spent in a classroom, and they encourage families to take advantage of travel opportunities. Others are rigid about attendance requirements.

High-school students are most vulnerable to school pressures, because more is at stake concerning grades, credits, college admission, and graduation. Do not assume, though, that you cannot work out a reasonable solution. One young man, a gifted high-school honor-roll student, had difficulty getting permission to go to Italy on a work-related trip with his parents. His mother was so convinced of the importance of this opportunity, she took her dilemma to the school board and won her case.

It is unlikely you would have to go to such lengths. Start by planning ahead with the teachers. If problems arise, make an appointment to discuss your concerns with the principal. For high-school students, visiting prospective colleges during your trip may add weight to the legitimacy of the absence and add value to your travel.

If you plan extended travel, you might want to consider registering as a homeschool family and then reenrolling your child on your return. Homeschooling is a legal alternative in all fifty states; however, the requirements and paperwork vary from state to state. To investigate this option, contact local, state, or provincial homeschool support groups, which your librarian can help you find. You can often find them yourself by searching the Internet with the keywords "home schooling," "homeschooling," or "legal" and the name of your state or province.

Do your research before contacting your school district. If you do, you may find that you know more about the legal requirements for homeschooling than school officials. Without that preparation, the response you get may be based on faulty assumptions and inaccurate information.

If you homeschool temporarily, be aware that while the school probably has to reenroll your children, they may not get credit for the work they have completed independently. Some schools have policies to cover homeschooled students returning to school. For example, a high school may give standard course credit if the student passes the same exams given to the rest of the class. Another school may refuse credit for homeschool work under any circumstances.

If you are planning extended travel with an older teen but are concerned about school requirements, here's a more radical idea: Consider the option of taking the GED (General Equivalency Diploma), which obviates the need for a high-school diploma altogether. The GED hotline is (800) 626-9433.

But a GED is not as highly valued as a high-school diploma, right? Perhaps, but in general, a high-school diploma is more important for a teen who does *not* go to college. In that case, a diploma may make a difference with some employers. If your child wants a career in the armed forces, she should check their requirements.

Travel experiences, combined with significant independent learning, such as internships or volunteer work, might make more difference on a college application than whether a student has a diploma or a GED. Selective colleges seek students with unique skills and experiences. If your child has good grades and is college-bound, her scores on her entrance exams will matter more than missing a semester of high school.

As an alternative, if the school will not give her credit for keeping up her studies while she is away, she can still go back and finish her classes after your trip. Not getting credit may not matter much in the long run. She will, however, still get the education. What your children learn while traveling is also valuable—even if it is not exactly the same material covered in school—and they will be more likely to remember it.

WHEN YOU HOMESCHOOL YOUR CHILDREN

If you educate your children at home, how will family travel be different than before? Let's see:

- Your children are with you more, so you go more places together than most families.
- Freed from school schedules, you are more likely to travel with your children. If one spouse has to go out of town on business, the whole family is more likely to come along.
- A small business or a sideline business is a common financial strategy for homeschool families. Thinking creatively, you may be able to find a way to earn money while you travel, making more travel possible.
- Taking advantage of discounted off-season rates may make it possible for you to travel more often.
- Instead of travel being extracurricular, you can make travel part of your curriculum. You can involve your children in preparing for trips and researching your destinations to an extent that would be difficult if they were in school.

When Judith had children in school, she helped with homework, served as a room mother, and attended all the parent-teacher conferences and meetings. Homeschooling caused her to look at education in a different way. "Work, education, and recreation used to seem like separate ways to spend time. Then the lines started to blur. I used to think that my job as parent was to help my children do well in school, and the school's job was to plan for their overall education. I didn't realize that I thought this way until my children's education became my responsibility. Then I started to think of education as being a part of life."

SPIRITUAL JOURNEYS FOR FAMILIES

In John Bunyan's *Pilgrim's Progress,* the young hero set off on a spiritual journey to escape from the City of Destruction. Pilgrim found hardship, adventure, and, eventually, salvation. Families can grow spiritually when the members experience a new environment and new challenges.

The desire for a deeper investigation of history, science, archaeology, or other studies from a biblical perspective can motivate a family to travel. The Morgan family traveled to a creation science seminar sponsored by Answers in Genesis. This organization also offers workshops and tours of natural landmarks such as Dinosaur Ridge in Colorado and the Grand Canyon.

Religious organizations sponsor conferences and camps for families and youth. Conferences frequently offer low-cost opportunities for learning, for meeting people with whom you share a common interest, and for family fun. Many offer low fees for camping or renting a cabin. For instance, Maryland-based Sandy Cove Ministries offers a family camping vacation with "eternal impact." Their cabin fees are minimal—about the same as tent camping in a public or private campground, but with more amenities, including cabins with air conditioning and full utilities. Add on about the same amount for conference fees, and you have lodging and activities for your whole family at a reasonable cost.

TAKING A SPIRITUAL INVENTORY

Our society admires nonstop action. We discourage contemplation. At times, however, we need to digest information in order to move on to the next step in life.

New surroundings can help us reassess the quality of our lives and take spiritual inventory. When a significant educational decision looms—such as what subjects will lead to a preferred career, which mission field is the right one, or what school to go to—it pays to change your environment and to think and pray in surroundings that will bring rest from stress without straining your pocketbook.

Even a day trip can help. A nearby church may offer parks or gardens that are free and open to the public. (If you're not sure, ask first. Make sure that you will be recognized as a pilgrim and not an invader.) A Mount Vernon, Ohio, church spent years cultivating a stone garden that illustrates Bible concepts and New Testament events through the use of stone. The garden is open to the public year-round, and admission is free. The church invites visitors to walk through the garden at any time before dusk "for prayer, solitude, and personal meditation."

Finding Your Life's Path

Discovery Trail: A Pathway to Find Your Spiritual Gifts is a pocket-size booklet that can help teens and adults find their life paths. Answer *Discovery Trail*'s 102 questions to inventory your spiritual gifts and to get help determining your direction in life and ministry. You can take the booklet and a pencil along with you on the trail. Request a free sample of *Discovery Trail* as well as samples of other tracts, from the American Tract Society, P.O. Box 462008, Garland, TX 75046; (800) 548-7228; *http://www.gospelcom.net/ats*.

Parents and children can find a place to be together, but they can also find time for each person to be alone for a while. You don't have to go far, and it doesn't need to cost money. Some time alone outside under the stars can lead to life-changing revelations for kids or adults.

Bible wax museums, available across the country, can bring scenes from the Bible to life. A spiritual dance, musical, or outdoor play can bring inspiration. A concert can touch children and adults, prompting a commitment to service or ministry. In many cases, an event with a spiritual message will be free or inexpensive, or it may be offered on a "free-will offering" basis.

While traveling, check hometown newspapers for listings of church-sponsored events in your area. Christian bookstores can offer leads on nearby events as well and usually stock publications that list events. If you are a member of a specific denomination, you can also check your church publications before your trip.

You might like to look into retreat facilities in your area of geographic interest. Most retreat centers will take in lodgers regardless of religion or denomination. (Inquire first, to be sure.) A retreat facility could be an ancient abbey or a brand-new building. Often the price for lodging is inexpensive and may include meals. At Retreats Online you can search for a retreat facility by geographic location or by category. It includes facilities from all faiths as well as listings by areas of interest. You could also look in the yellow pages for your destination under the category "Retreats." Remember to ask about a retreat's policy regarding children.

CHANGING YOUR ENVIRONMENT

Despite popular belief, the Pilgrims did not come from Holland to America to escape religious persecution. (That is, indeed, why they originally fled from England to Holland.) They withstood deprivation and hardship during their journey to America to escape "the great licentiousness of youth in that country," which influenced their children.

Do you feel financially trapped in an urban jungle or a suburban wasteland? Today a new land may mean a new start in another state or moving to a small town with a lower cost of living. It may mean a complete lifestyle change, from employment to self-employment on the road. It may mean a shift to a different school district or to homeschooling.

Even if you can only temporarily travel to a different environment, the trip may bring a new perspective and strengthen a child's relationship with the family. Once in a new setting, children often feel relief from the pressure to conform to values that conflict with those shared by their family and church.

STRENGTHENING YOUR FAMILY

Every trip, even a short one, gives you a chance to create special memories. Those memories cement learning. Real-life travel adventures can help families grow closer in close quarters. Travel can help families find time to talk to one another away from work, school, sports, church, or other commitments. Severed from routines and demands, you may develop closer relationships through family bonding.

Because she was medically fragile, Melissa's youngest daughter, Susanna, was sheltered from the outside world for the first year or so of her life.

Now that Susie is stronger, we've discovered how to include her in our educational travels. We travel closer to home and for shorter periods than we used to, but we can still learn about the real world.

On our first overnight trip with Susie, we stayed in a state park cabin overlooking Lake LaGonda and took the kids on nature walks. A short getaway from home, it was very different from our previous tent-camping trips. The cabin had a larger kitchen than we have at home.

Being in new surroundings and away from our usual routines helped John and Lori to develop as a big brother and big sister. They delighted in showing Susie new things—a dandelion, a worm. We rejoiced in watching her with her older siblings, gingerly touching her first caterpillar, squishing sand between her toes, and observing birds feathering their nests.

Many families today see their children increasingly influenced by negative peer pressure. Family members, adults as well as children, drift away from family values, beliefs, and morals. One way to explore and reinforce your family's values is through shared experiences in educational travel. For instance, we can talk about how we value diversity and are concerned about racial justice. Then we visit a university that has a predominantly African American student body so we can learn about its historical struggles and its famous graduates. This way we can experience living history, and our children can understand our values on a different level.

MEMORIES WITH TEENS

Traveling with a teenager can be a special challenge. It also gives you a chance to have some fun together and to get to know each other again. Here are some suggestions:

- Don't have an agenda for closeness. Just let intimacy happen.
- Don't rush. Allow for relaxed time together for talking, walking, and having leisurely meals.

- Share an adventure. Share something awesome—something that puts you on equal footing because you are all beginners. Learn something your teen knows more about than you do.
- Leave criticisms and old business at home.

Moving Forward

In this book we provide a smorgasbord of ideas so you can pick and choose a few that fit your children's personalities, interests, and abilities. When we offer nitty-gritty suggestions like mileage math or historical fiction, we hope those activities will make your travel more fun and educational.

At the same time, however, we hope such details won't sidetrack you—educational travel is about far more than traditional academics. Through travel, you have the chance to enrich your child's education in a way that school cannot. A child can look at a map in school, but only through travel will he understand how endless and flat the prairies are and how majestic the mountains. Travel brings geography, history, literature, and math to life in concrete and meaningful ways that no textbook can compete with.

Travel is not a "product," although it is often packaged and sold in the form of a cruise, an attraction, or an airfare deal. It is not a "consumable," like food or clothing. Travel is an experience, and its essence is the memories you can build with your family.

Chapter Two

Researching Your Destinations

Long before you leave your driveway, your family starts to reap the educational benefits of travel. They are still learning long after the last suitcase is unpacked. A short trip might be the start of a long fascination.

Although a spur-of-the-moment trip can be a great adventure, planning ahead has its advantages. It can save you money—lots of it. You can develop valuable research skills along with your children while locating low-cost fares, food, lodging, entertainment, and educational activities. You can investigate the pros and cons of off-season travel, which may be the difference of a single day. You can also protect your wallet by avoiding scams, and you can teach your children to be educated consumers in the process. Before you can scrounge up the funds to travel, you can begin daydreaming and brainstorming for your trip—and that may give your family the inspiration to save enough money to go.

Advance research can multiply the learning and the fun. Visiting Fort Sumter is more meaningful if you have read about the people involved in the battle. Through research you can find out about little-known educational side trips, such as a Passion play at an area church or a small town's annual honey festival.

Playing with Your Interests

What are your children interested in? Go beyond asking them about their favorite subjects in school. Instead, observe what they like to do in their free time. One of your children may enjoy video games. What about a trip to a software company? For a child who loves the movies, why not visit a movie set or the location where a favorite movie was filmed?

Can you guide each of your children to develop a new interest and then bring it out through travel? Does one child have an interest in construction equipment? Perhaps you could arrange a trip to a plant where the equipment is manufactured or visit a construction site. Go where the action is and see if any sparks fly. If you are concerned about gaps in your children's education and experience, think about ways to fill them. What are their gifts and talents? What fascinates each of them?

By All Means, Paint

"If you hear a voice within you say, 'You cannot paint,' then by all means paint, and that voice will be silenced." —Vincent van Gogh, artist

---

You may increase a child's interest in music by attending a symphony performance in a city you are visiting, especially if you familiarize the child with the music before the performance and meet the musicians or the conductor afterward.

Or follow up on the interest. "We saw the opera *La Bohème* in Reno, Nevada, then bought a recording of it in Salt Lake City," says Kimberly Goza, who travels with her husband and eleven-year-old son. "We've listened to it countless times while driving since then." The tape means more to them because they saw the opera in person.

Find a niche. Perhaps you can attend a writers' workshop or visit an author to help a young person see that writers are ordinary people who write one page at a time.

This real-life, hands-on kind of learning is more a matter of attitude than money. It can change a child's perspective on his abilities, even if he has special needs academically or physically—especially if he does. Perhaps in your travels he can meet a successful person who has overcome a similar challenge.

The ideal is to have at least one facet of your travel that holds special interest for each person. Do not neglect your own interests. Is there something you have always wanted to see or experience? If you have always wanted to learn Asian cooking, and you follow through, your children will see for themselves that adults can take their own interests seriously. Think about how much more fun it is to be with an enthusiastic parent than one who "endures" an entire vacation of child-oriented activities.

Everybody Wins!

All the Best Contests for Kids by Joan and Craig Bergstrom lists hundreds of unusual contests all around the country, ranging from the offbeat (the art of frog jumping or duck calls) to the sublime (writing stories and poems) and back to the even more offbeat (the Tom Sawyer Fence Painting Contest in Hannibal, Missouri).

The Encyclopedia of Associations (available at many larger libraries) lists over twenty-two thousand organizations involved with every topic imaginable. To research the possibilities, look up associations that relate to your family's interests. Many of these organizations host conferences, workshops, shows, or other events, and those events are often mentioned in the listings.

The ABCentral Web site maintains links to national and international organizations for an amazing variety of special interests. Seriously. Under "Arts" you can find the International Guild of Swordsman and Swashbucklers. Interested in history? You might be curious enough to explore the Web site of the North American Vexillological Association, which is devoted to the study of flags and flag history. Is someone in your family interested in writing? Wouldn't you know, there is a link to the American Amateur Press Association, which has no minimum (or maximum) age limit? How about gardening? There are twenty-seven organizations listed for lovers of bonsai (the horticulture of weathered-looking miniature trees) and seven organizations for alpine and rock gardeners. You can look for a group in the area you will be visiting if you would like an entrée into their unique worlds.

You can build confidence, encourage positive social skills, and stretch your child's abilities when you travel to a contest such as a National Spelling Bee, Special Olympics, a science fair, a chess tournament, or a horseshoe competition. You do not have to enter the competition to attend; enthusiastic audience members are welcome. Attending may make entering seem less formidable the next time.

Be creative. Everyone is—or can be—good at something.

CONNECT-THE-DOTS ROUTE PLANNING

When we will be traversing several states, we find it helpful to make a photocopy of that portion of the map, enlarging or reducing it on the photocopier so that it fits on a sheet of letter-size paper. While we are at it, we make several copies for our backseat drivers. Next, we use a highlighting marker to show all the sites we would like to see and the locations of all the people we would like to visit. Then we plot our route by playing "connect the dots"— but not necessarily connecting *all* the dots. We try not to pack too much into our trip. We have found that too much activity is worse than not enough. However, by investigating until we have "too much" information, we then have backup plans in case of bad weather, traffic problems, unforeseen closings, or changes in our agenda.

wiseguy

Be Where You Are

"There are people who want to be everywhere at once…and they get nowhere."
—Carl Sandburg, poet

Jim Foreman travels by bicycle and recreational vehicle (RV) with his wife. Here is his suggestion for planning a route with each person's interests in mind: "Nearly every state puts out a vacation travel guide. Let each person sit down with the travel guide, a map, and a highlighting pen. When they find something of particular interest to them, they can note it on the map, perhaps with the page number out of the guide. Then each day's travel can be planned to let as many people in the group as possible see their particular thing. My wife and I are going to New England this fall, and she is already working on her list. I'll do the same, and then both of us will get to see the things that interest us most."

Not sure where you want to go? Check out sources in print and online for offbeat destinations, like the Henson International Festival of Puppet Theatre in New York (see resource guide for chapter 3) or the Rodale Experimental Farms in Pennsylvania, with a daily tour of organic gardens and farming methods. Perhaps your family will enjoy planning several imaginary trips before deciding where to go.

We found eighty-three books when we searched an online bookstore for the keywords "travel" and "children." Many of them were about specific destinations, like *The Lobster Kids' Guide to Exploring Montreal* by John Symon or *Kids Culture Catalog: A Cultural Guide to New York City for Kids, Families and Teachers,* edited by Randall Bourscheidt and Maria Asteinza (Alliance for the Arts). Be sure to look up your own city (or the nearest metro area) while you are at it. You will probably learn a lot from a book that explores your own region, even if you are a lifelong "local."

For additional travel ideas, you can turn to travel videos and educational television programs. Rick Steves's travel show on public television might inspire you. You can find your local PBS travel program schedules online by going to *http://www.pbs.org* and linking to your local station.

Learning about your destination can help you plan your route and keep you from arriving at the right place at the wrong time. Melissa sheepishly relates that her family really did visit Amish country on a Sunday. Surprise! Everything was closed, except for the tourist traps.

FACTORY AND MILITARY TOURS

Learn about real-world manufacturing processes in friendly businesses across the country, many of which offer free or inexpensive tours. You may find that a tour at a bicycle factory is more memorable for your kids than the obligatory amusement park visit. Or maybe they'd like to know how a teddy bear, a kazoo, or a teabag is made. What companies are related to your children's career interests? Who makes their favorite bicycles, books, food, or toys?

LEGOLand, a theme park built of (what else?) LEGO-brand plastic bricks, is located halfway between Los Angeles and San Diego and has additional parks in England, Denmark, and Germany. Aside from tours and activities for the general public, special services are available to educational groups. For a guide to factory tours across the United States, check out Karen Axelrod and Bruce Brumberg's book *Watch It Made in the U.S.A.* The Thomas Registry, available in the reference section at most libraries, lists manufacturers of everything from doll eyes to solar-powered appliances to water garden supplies.

When Judith's daughter, Nancy, said she wanted to go to Hershey, Pennsylvania, Judith thought she meant the huge amusement park there, which would have taken an entire day—an exhausting and expensive day—out of their itinerary. Judith was in for a surprise.

"It turned out what Nancy really wanted was to take the Hershey's Chocolate World tour, a simulated factory tour that takes an hour or so (including waiting time) and is free of charge. You can find the factory by following your nose—the fragrance of chocolate wafts along West Chocolate Avenue as you cruise through the little town of Hershey."

If you are interested in touring a military base or other military facility, call the public affairs office at each facility to find out the tour schedule and what is available.

The U.S. Air Force Web site is searchable and lists facilities and programs worldwide, including the performance schedules of the U.S. Air Force Band at Bolling Air Force Base in Washington, D.C., and fourteen other air force bands stationed around the globe. A highlight for those interested in the U.S. Air Force is the F-16 Demonstration Team, known as the Thunderbirds, featuring distinctive red, white, and blue F-16 fighter jets. The Thunderbirds show off air force mission capabilities in performances around the world. To see their schedule, go to *http://www.airforce.com/thunderbirds*. If you visit the Las Vegas area, you can tour the Thunderbirds' home base, which includes a museum, a film with the history of the Thunderbirds, and a flight demonstration if the Thunderbirds are in town.

Maps usually designate military facilities, so check to see what facilities are on your route. In addition, the Department of Defense has links to each of the service branches (Army, Navy, Air Force, Marines, National Guard, Reserves, and Coast Guard) at *http://www.defenselink.mil/faq/pis/sites.html.*

Look up the base you are interested in to find contact information for the public affairs office there.

If you have a valid Department of Defense ID card—which can include military personnel, retired military, DoD civilians, and their families—you may be eligible to use campgrounds and other lodging facilities at military installations along your route. Policies are determined by each base, and military personnel and their dependents have first priority. Rarely are facilities available to the general public, and then only on a limited basis.

Finding the Path

In his heart a man plans his course, but the LORD determines his steps. —Proverbs 16:9

Visiting a College Town

College towns are especially rich in low-cost educational opportunities. Larger towns are likely to have a variety of shops, ethnic restaurants, and inexpensive entertainment. Colleges often sponsor free programs that are open to the public, such as festivals, lectures, art shows, visiting artists, and demonstrations in science, archaeology, or other fields. Universities sometimes have their own museums that are open to the public free of charge or for a nominal admission fee.

Take, for example, New Haven, Connecticut, home of Yale University. Located between New York City and Boston, but with cheaper accommodations, New Haven and the surrounding area offer boat rides, beaches, carousels, nature centers, biking and hiking trails, historic homes with guides in costume, and many free attractions. All ages can enjoy the Peabody Museum of Natural History at Yale and its outstanding permanent collection of dinosaur fossils. By train, New Haven is about an hour from New York City and about two and a half hours from Boston, making it a good home base for short trips to both cities. Since most kids love trains (including many of us big kids), the ride itself is worth writing home about.

Specialized colleges have activities you may not find elsewhere. The Julliard School in New York City, for example, is a choice school for young musicians. Its operas and concerts are inexpensive—some performances are free—but topnotch.

At many colleges, you can arrange a visit with professors in subjects that especially interest you or one of your children, such as astronomy or cinema.

There is no need to wait until your child is a high-school junior or senior to visit college campuses. One family we know started when their twins were ten years old. Visiting a variety of campuses over the years gave them a sense of comparison for the diverse makeup of campus life—large versus small schools, urban versus bucolic, competitive versus relaxed. The visits also helped the children develop goals and understand why they needed to study such remote-sounding subjects as physics or trigonometry.

To locate colleges on your route and identify the ones that are the best match for your students, check with your library, a school guidance counselor, or the Web sites listed in the resource guide.

Finding the Road Less Traveled

For a free sample issue of an offbeat quarterly newsletter called *Two Lane Roads,* produced by Loren Eyrich, send one dollar (for postage) or three first-class stamps for a copy by mail, normally $4.95 at press time. This is a special offer to our readers, so mention this book, and allow four to six weeks for delivery. You can view a sample issue online. (Contact information for this and nearly all other resources mentioned in this book can be found in the resource guide.)

RESEARCH STRATEGIES FOR SAVING MONEY

Your destination is calling you, but how can you make your trip a reality? While you're researching your trip, try the following tricks of the trade.

1. *Book your trip on the spur of the moment.* You may actually have been planning this for a long time—you just didn't know the day or the hour. Target underbooked transportation and accommodations for on-the-spot savings.

2. *Try the opposite: Plan your vacation up to a year in advance, and plan to travel at off-peak times when prices are low.* Traveling during the off-season,

you may get substantial savings on accommodations and attractions. Judith stayed at a seashore hotel that was fifty-five dollars a night on March 31 and eighty-nine dollars on April 1. Same hotel, same seashore, next day.

Angie Zalewski, coauthor of *Cheap Talk with the Frugal Friends,* travels with her husband and two boys, ages six and eight. Although they sometimes travel frugally in the off-season, she says there are disadvantages too. "The trade-off is that many attractions are open only during tourist season. Also, some of the 'flavor' of the trip may be lost in the off-season—such as street vendors and entertainers, seasonal native animal activity, trees or flowers in bloom, etc."

3. *Ask if a scholarship or financial assistance is available for special activities, whether or not a formal financial aid program is in place.* Nancy Allee applied to attend a YMCA-sponsored archaeology camp several hours from home, and Judith asked about a scholarship. No camper had ever inquired about financial aid before, so the question bounced through the chain of command to the director, who approved it the same day.

4. *Take advantage of any discounts you may be eligible for through your membership in the American Automobile Association (AAA) or other organizations.* Some states offer a special card for "seniors," who might be as young as fifty-five. In Ohio, it is a Golden Buckeye Card, and most Ohio restaurants offer cardholders a discount for the entire family. If a parent is over fifty, consider a membership in AARP, which provides discounts on lodging, prescriptions, and other benefits. Usually, grandparents traveling with grandchildren can include their little guests in their discount.

5. *If you homeschool, take advantage of educator discounts, often available at museums and other attractions.* Also ask about signing up for an educator's card to buy tourism books, atlases, and other resources at many stores, such as Half Price Books, Zany Brainy, and Media Play.

TRAVEL SHOWS AND TRAVEL AGENCIES

Travel and vacation shows offer an inexpensive peek at multitudes of trips and options. In our area, the Sports, Vacation, and Boat Show is a charity fund-raiser, complete with clowns and a magic show. Topical events range from tips on how to organize a group cruise, fly-fishing for beginners, talks by various travel writers, and the chance to meet a Royal Canadian Mounted Police officer.

Although many of the exhibits feature overpriced resorts, cruises, or RVs, others could prove economical and educational. Certainly, you will need to bring a strong dose of sales resistance if you attend a travel show. One good rule—absolutely no unexpected purchases or commitments. If the offer won't be good tomorrow, there is probably something wrong with it.

Don't overlook travel agencies as a resource. A savvy agent may be able to help you tailor your trip in ways you would never think of on your own. Call several travel agencies and compare a package trip with what you would pay to purchase everything separately. Because a package can include many discounts, you usually save more than if you purchase the airfare, hotel, and car rental (and sometimes meals) separately.

How to Avoid a Tourist Trap

How can you spot a legitimate educational attraction and avoid wasting hard-earned travel cash on a tourist trap?

- Use travel guidebooks, such as those provided by AAA.
- Network. Get personal recommendations before taking your trip.
- Check affiliations. Is the attraction accredited by a legitimate professional or scientific organization?

Kids Are Great Bargain Hunters

It takes time to search for bargains, so consider using free labor: your kids! In return, your children learn how to research a subject and become savvy consumers.

Public education goals now include a category of becoming a "lifetime learner," which includes knowing how to find information. With guidance from you, older children and young adults can find information for your trip by themselves if you teach them the strategies and tricks of the trade. Writing for information can help kids polish grammar, spelling, and business skills. Older kids can learn to make business phone calls, send e-mail, and use reference books and the Internet for research. Bargain hunting involves practical, hands-on math.

Try to oversee their progress and be available for questions. If you wish, you can provide incentives, such as a celebration party, when the research is done. Or you could allow the bargain hunter a percentage of the money saved to be used for spending money on the trip.

Hang On to Your Wallet

The Better Business Bureau (BBB) recommends dealing with businesspeople you personally know and have confidence in, or checking out businesses with the BBB or a recognized travel organization.

- See if the travel agent or service has membership in the American Society of Travel Agents. If so, the society may be able to mediate any disputes that arise.
- Contact the National Fraud Information Center and ask for the free booklet *Telemarketing Travel Fraud.* The booklet, produced in conjunction with the American Society of Travel Agents, offers guidelines to help you avoid fraudulent travel schemes.
- The BBB offers a brochure to assist consumers in evaluating travel and vacation offers. Included is information on travel packages, vacation certificates, "red flags" that indicate vacation scams, steps to take to protect yourself from a vacation or travel scam, and a quick checklist to follow when finalizing your vacation plans.

Finding the Information You Need

Remember the saying, "Give a man a fish, and you feed him for a day. Teach him to fish, and you feed him for a lifetime"? Teach your children more than facts. Teach them how to find the information they need—whether through reading books, contacting people, or surfing the Internet—and they will benefit for the rest of their lives.

Beyond the Library Card Catalog

You may want to start with your local library. If it is small, consider visiting the main branch of a metropolitan library. Some public libraries allow you to have a library card even if you live in another town (possibly for an annual fee); most allow anyone to use their resources on-site.

You can take advantage of Internet access at the library if you do not have access at home. Many attractions and cities have their own Web sites with links to related information. You can also make a quick stop at a public library while you are traveling. Judith decided to visit a Toastmasters International club while traveling in Missouri, so she stopped at a library, pulled up the Toastmasters site, and found three clubs that meet in St. Louis on Tuesday nights.

Travel Research Facts

- About three out of four family travelers decide on their destination within three months of their travel departure. Of those, half decided within a month, 20 percent within a week, and 10 percent on the very day they traveled.
- Most family travelers collected travel information prior to their trip (65 percent). About half of those collected and filed travel information throughout the year. The other half gathered information only when planning for a specific trip. Baby boomers were more likely to collect information throughout the year; younger people typically collected it only when they were planning the trip.
- One out of four indicated that they didn't need information because they always went to the same place.

—Travel Industry Association of America, 1998 study, *http://www.tia.org*

Here are some library services, beyond the stacks and videos your children probably are already familiar with, that could be helpful as you start researching your trip. Pick a few you think your family might enjoy.

The Reference Section
- Look through the vertical files (usually filing cabinets) for maps, travel brochures, articles, and other loose items.
- Look in the subject volume of *Books in Print* (BIP) to find current books that the library does not carry. You can request an interlibrary loan for books that are more than a year old. For newer books, you can fill out a purchase request form, and the library will consider

buying the book (eventually). In addition, many out-of-print books are available through interlibrary loan.

- Look for telephone directories for your destination. Even small libraries will have telephone books for a few major cities. Look up yellow pages listings for museums, recreation, factories, colleges, and universities. You can also locate businesses that pertain to your family's interests. Nancy Allee designs water gardens. A highlight of the family's Pennsylvania trip was a huge water garden retail center near Pittsburgh, which they found in the phone book. (You can also access the yellow pages on the Internet at www.att.com/directory.)
- Look up your destination in an encyclopedia. Compare several encyclopedias on the same topic, such as a state, city, or attraction you want to visit, or a historical event or famous person from that locale.
- Browse the *Encyclopedia of the States,* which has detailed information listed state by state, including photos of parks, museums, and points of interests. *The Junior Worldmark Encyclopedia of the States* is written for children grades four to ten. For travel outside the United States, check the *Worldmark Encyclopedia of the Nations.*

The Stacks

- Look at both the juvenile and adult travel sections, no matter what ages your children are. Juvenile books often provide a well-illustrated, understandable introduction to a complex topic, suitable for any age. Likewise, an adult book also can be interesting to a child, if only for the pictures. Children can understand higher-level material better when it is read aloud to them than when they read it themselves.
- Check out biographies of famous people from your destination. *The Traveler's Reading Guide: Ready-Made Reading Lists for the Armchair Traveler,* edited by Maggy Simony, includes background reading. That is one way to find authors who write about certain locales—for example, *The Rainbow Chasers* by Ervin J. MacDonald, set in the Canadian wilderness, or *Joshua, Then and Now: A Survey of Joshua's Life from Montreal Slum Childhood to Current Fame* by Mordecai Richler. You can also search the Internet for authors, such as "Wisconsin authors."

Worldmark Encyclopedia of the States lists famous people by the states they were born in or lived in. We have found reading more than one biography about the same person to be an eye-opening experience—you learn not to believe everything you read, because you find discrepancies. Authors from each state are also listed.

- Ask if the library has any special collections, such as a local, state, or provincial section. These collections may be for reference only and may be in a private room that you can access only with permission.

Periodicals

- Look through the list of magazines that the library stocks, including travel-oriented publications, such as the *Consumer Reports' Travel Tips* newsletter, as well as hobby magazines that list events.
- The larger the library, the larger the selection of newspapers you can expect to find. Look for local attractions, upcoming events, and lodging and restaurant specials. More and more newspapers and radio stations also have Web sites listing local news and events.

Be sure to stop back at the library after your trip, while the experience is fresh, to follow up on what you learned from your travels. While you are at it, how about offering to fill a library display case with interesting mementos of your trip along with related library books?

MORE FREE AND CHEAP INFORMATION SOURCES

Private libraries offer specialized information that may not be available anywhere else. Our historical society, for example, has information on the Underground Railroad in Ohio and maps showing local geology. Other groups that may have private libraries include genealogical societies, Civil War round tables, and industry associations. Some private libraries are for members only, although they may allow the general public to use the materials on-site.

Many organizations have their own directories and publications. Your local hobby club may have access to a list of upcoming shows and events in the area you will be visiting. If you are a member of a local service club such as Kiwanis, Rotary, or Lions, you can get information on clubs to visit as you travel.

If you are a member of AAA, you can get free maps, tour guidebooks, customized trip guides, and club discounts.

Use toll-free numbers for tourism offices to order coupon books, event calendars, and free state or local maps. They also may be called convention and visitors bureaus or vacation and visitors bureaus, depending on the location. In some areas, the chamber of commerce serves the same purpose.

If you get a friendly and helpful person on the phone, take a few minutes to chat and describe what your family likes to do. That is a good way to find out about an offbeat activity, interesting restaurant, or little-known site. It does not have to be considered a tourist attraction to be perfect for your family. For an online listing of tourism offices, including the toll-free numbers and Web sites for all fifty states, Canadian provinces, and Mexico, visit the Families on the Road Web site (see resource guide).

Stop at the first interstate rest stop when you enter a state for free maps and racks of information about events and educational outings. That first rest stop often has the largest quantity and variety of tourist materials. You will find fliers on museums, parks, restaurants, and tourist information. Watch for discount coupon books for hotels and restaurants. File information obtained on your trip and use it the next time, or ask the library if they would like it for their vertical files.

LET YOUR KEYBOARD DO THE WALKING

Many families who once used mail, books, magazines, and telephones for making travel plans not very long ago are now using the Internet. We have found the Internet quick, handy, and cost-effective—or time-consuming and frustrating, depending on the task.

The Internet is both the boon and the bane of modern research. It is a boon if you are looking for a needle in a haystack. When the Allees photographed a conference in Branson, Missouri (a mecca of country music entertainment), Judith searched for "Branson," visited the Branson tourism Web site, found out what shows were available, got a toll-free number, and called for reservations—all within about fifteen minutes.

If you're looking for the haystack, however, the Internet can provide an overwhelming amount of information—some of it helpful, most of it not.

Don't even bother using a search engine to look for "educational travel" unless you would rather surf the Web than travel. (A search at *www.google.com* pulled up over a million pages with that word combination.) You would probably be better off looking through travel books and magazines at the library. Or you might want to start with a few of the top sites at your favorite search engine (two of our favorites are *http://www.copernic.com* and *http://www.ask.com*), and link from those sites to other recommended sites.

Internet access comes with a cost. For one thing, there is so much to see and explore that a simple information search can swallow up many hours. The Internet also requires newer, speedier computers, so you will need to upgrade your equipment as Web sites escalate their requirements for speed and memory. Safe use of the Internet for children is another concern. We keep our computers in our main living areas, making it easier to monitor their use.

If you spend much time surfing the Internet for travel bargains, save those Web addresses for later use. Start a travel folder in your browser's "Favorites" or "Bookmarks" file, and create subcategories as needed, such as "destinations," "hotel discounts," or "car rentals."

wiseguy

Turn Right

"Why stress over a dangerous left turn onto a busy street when you can turn right instead? Two wrongs may not make a right, but three rights make a left."
—Judith Allee

You can also create a travel folder in your e-mail box. For example, if Judith wants to visit relatives in Tampa and Los Angeles, she can sign up for free "e-zines" at travel Web sites, such as *www.air-fare.com, www.bestfares.com,* and *www.SmarterLiving.com*. She drags all the e-mails to her travel folder, and then when she is ready to travel, she can search the folder for "Tampa" and "Los Angeles" to get an overview of current airfare discounts.

Take the time to become proficient at searching with at least one favorite search engine. Often, though, you do not need to use a search engine to find a site. With a large company or brand name, try using their name as their Web address. (For example, you could find American Airlines by simply trying *http://www.AmericanAirlines.com.*) Chances are, you will find what you are looking for.

Families pick destinations for different reasons. What experiences are most important to your child's development? Every family will answer differently. Just asking the question, however, may change how you spend your vacation dollars. You can tailor your educational travel destination to teach and reinforce what is important to your family. Then do more than wish: Make it happen!

Chapter Three

Low-Cost Learning

According to the Travel Industry Association of America, the four most popular activities that parents participate in when they travel are as follows:

- Shopping—33%
- Outdoor recreation—20%
- Historic sites and museums—15%
- Beaches—12%

Which of these activities and locations can be educational? All of them. Historic sites and museums are formally designed for learning, of course, but our children are learning all the time. Certainly they can learn by exploring beaches, the outdoors, and yes, even the shopping arena. You can also journey beyond the top four and choose from a rich array of real-world educational adventures—perhaps exploring outside of your family's usual comfort zone.

Give Me Some Credit!

Real-world adventures can give the adults or the teens in your family an opportunity to earn college credit at a bargain price. The Council for Adult and Experiential Learning publishes *Earn College Credit for What You Know* by Lois Lamdin, which shows how to document what you have learned through your life (and travel) experiences. This is a cost-saving way to acquire some credits and jump-start your future. *College Degrees by Mail & Internet* by John Bear has related information, such as finding organizations that will help you evaluate foreign academic experience or educational travel.

Talk to an archaeologist and participate in a dig. Explore a rock quarry. Meet a museum curator and find out how she got interested in her work and what her day-to-day job is like. Your trip's educational experiences will make your vacation all the more memorable—and not necessarily more expensive. You can take advantage of learning opportunities everywhere you go.

Learning and Loving It

When you travel, every "educational subject" comes into play (literally). While "subjects" are a handy way for us to categorize information, math is not separate from reading or writing or science in real life. We offer an assortment of ideas in this chapter in the hope everyone will find something useful and fun here. (For convenience, we have listed the subjects alphabetically.)

Art

Experience a wide variety of exhibits, including art galleries. If a particular painting in a museum captures your attention, try drawing it. You will probably not be the only one, since this is a common practice for artists who want to develop their skills. Most museums allow artists to post themselves and set up their drawing materials.

Bring along a few art supplies for young artists to use during downtime—waiting time, travel time, rainy time. Be aware of aesthetic designs in your travels, from sculpture in public places to sculpture gardens. Every city has architecture you can learn from, from pueblos to Frank Lloyd Wright to castles in Kentucky.

Family History

With our mobile society, our extended family may be strangers to our children. We can take opportunities while traveling to develop relationships as well as to learn from our genetic or adopted links with the past. Children can create a family recipe book that will be sure to engender a warm welcome from family members far and wide. Gather family recipes and ask Grandmother or other family members to let your family make dinner, under her or their supervision, to make sure you fully understand the process and can carry on traditions.

Ask older relatives to help you fill out a genealogy chart, and distribute the information to others in the family. Is there a box of photographs that have not been labeled? How about sitting down with your relatives and labeling the photographs, recording the stories that go along with them? This is history in its most personal and meaningful form. It is one thing to read in a history book about the Great Depression. It is another to hear what it was like from someone who lived through it, especially when that someone is your own great-grandfather.

Learn about other eras by asking questions. Tape-record the answers if it is all right with the person being interviewed; a microphone turns a kid into a news reporter. What did Uncle George do when he was bored as a child and didn't have video games? How did Grandmother and Grandfather meet? Any embarrassing stories they would care to share about their children (you)?

For family gatherings, do not forget a camera—and film and batteries!

Foreign Languages in Real Life

If someone in your family (or the whole family) is studying another language, why not seek out opportunities to use the language in your travels? French is spoken in the province of Quebec, Canada, and Spanish is the language of Mexico, both destinations within easy driving distance for millions of people in the USA.

You do not have to go far from home to find native speakers, however. Travel to any major city in North America, and you will find a sizable Spanish-speaking community as well as many other smaller ethnic communities. What is your heritage? Whether it is Hungarian, Russian, Somalian, or Ugandan, you can probably find native speakers if you take the time to look. You might be able to obtain resources from them to help your family learn about its heritage.

Subscribe to magazines or newsletters, such as *Hola* and *Buenhogar* (Spanish) or *Nouvel Observateur* and *Figaro* (French). You may be able to find them at a large city library. You can also find French- or Spanish-language editions of American publications, such as *Good Housekeeping, People,* and *Newsweek.*

Attend ethnic events or international festivals in your own area to make contact with people who speak the language you are learning. Then tell those people you are looking for contacts in the area you will be traveling to and ask for referrals. Check the index under "festivals" for ways to find festivals by city, state, or type of festival.

For more about learning foreign languages, see chapter 6, "Are We There Yet?"

Esperanto

As you travel, you can speak to people from any country in the world without language barriers if you learn Esperanto, an invented international language. Granted, the Esperanto community is small, but you can find it anywhere you travel, in every major city (and numerous small ones) worldwide. Esperanto clubs sponsor family-friendly conferences that tend to attract an international crowd and give you a chance to practice speaking. As with most languages, children tend to learn quickly and will likely be chattering away sooner than you are.

Incredibly easy to learn compared with other languages, Esperanto has absolutely no irregularities in spelling or grammar—which was the point of having an invented language. You can learn enough Esperanto to communicate on a rudimentary level in just a few weeks. To find fellow Esperantists and clubs and to learn about events your family might enjoy, contact the Esperanto League for North America. You might also want to visit Esperanto pen pals or e-mail pals. As a fringe benefit, Esperanto helps its speakers understand the parts of speech in English and other languages—for example, all nouns end in the letter *o*—and it makes other languages easier to learn as well. Enthusiasts believe an international language helps promote world peace. The league offers free lessons by mail or e-mail.

American Sign Language (ASL)

Your travels can give your family experiences with ASL, another invented international language, this one designed for people with hearing impairments. ASL is accepted as a foreign language at some colleges and high schools.

If you notice people using ASL, you may want to politely introduce yourself by signing "hi" after they have finished their conversation. We have found that most people who use sign language are delighted to chat and are welcoming even if you are just learning to sign.

Each major city has events for the hearing impaired, and beginners may be welcome to observe or join in. Learning to sign has a side benefit for parents, according to the *Special Signs* video. The video teaches parents fifty-five signs "to be used in training children before they are able to verbally communicate themselves, and, then, to help communicate forgotten manners or give reminders 'quietly' in public for years to come!" If you would like to locate a church that provides sign language interpreters during services, call the chamber of commerce or check the local papers under the religion section.

HISTORY FOR TRAVELERS

If we could travel via time machine, we could experience living history. Since that's not possible, we can try the next best thing. Families can participate in events such as a one-room schoolhouse reenactment in a living-history village or visit a historical town such as Colonial Williamsburg, Virginia. Most states have re-created Native American villages or Revolutionary War forts. Many are little known, even to locals. The Morgan family visits several such sites every year, all in their home state. They still haven't visited all of them.

The best textbook on the market cannot compete with real experiences. See, touch, smell, and even taste history. Take a hike along Boston's 2.5-mile Freedom Trail. The trail boasts sixteen historic sites, including the site of the Boston Massacre. Most of the historic sites are free. Read about the history of slavery, then experience life as a slave. Visit a full-size reproduction of the slave ship *Amistad,* which makes a series of calls along the East Coast. A sampling from the Ohio Historical Society schedule included these:

- Civil War encampment at the statehouse
- frontier kitchen featuring foods from the early nineteenth century
- driving tour along the Miami-Erie Canal
- vintage baseball festival
- fall flower hike
- art of preserving food
- flint Knap-In, a campout about flint knapping (the art of making Native American flint points and blades)

One way to find living-history sites is to subscribe to state or local historical society mailing lists. For local societies, contact the chamber of commerce or state tourism bureau in your destination area, or check the yellow pages under "associations" or "museums." The Web site for the Association for Living History, Farm and Agricultural Museums (ALHFAM) has links to over one hundred living-history museums at *http://www.alhfam.org*.

Extra! Extra! Read All About It!

The *Civil War News* features over seventy pages of historical articles about the war and information about reenactments around the country. A free sample copy is available for families interested in subscribing. Call (800) 777-1862 or contact *The Civil War News*, 234 Monarch Hill Rd., Tunbridge, VT 05077; *http://www.civilwarnews.com*.

Historic Trails

Many children enjoy reading books about historic trails, such as the Oregon Trail. You can also borrow or buy software about it. Trace the route on maps and follow a part of it. Traveling the historic Cherokee Trail of Tears can help children learn how greed and prejudice can cause injustice and suffering.

Make a Time Line

The dates you hear when visiting historical sites may not have a lot of meaning to your children. A string of dates can be meaningless without anything to compare it to. Show your children how to draw a time line for your destination. Bring a favorite history book or tour book and help your kids write dates and events in the time line. Children can illustrate their time line book with pictures of famous people, inventions, and events.

"We hang a clothesline around the perimeter of our van, and we add index cards with historical information," says Kimberly Goza, a traveling homeschool mother. Plain paper or a roll of adding machine tape works well too. Judith's family kept their time line on their fifty-foot-long front porch, using a string the entire length of the porch. They started the time line with the prehistoric people who lived in the area and added events or people as they traveled or read about other civilizations. They marked off each century with a colored bead and each millennium with a different color. This required some computation and measurement to make all the centuries the same length!

They soon found they needed separate time lines for recent centuries because the scale on their first time line was too small to go into detail on events, including wars, the Great Depression, and the years that various presidents served. You can include dates that are important to your family, such as birth and wedding dates of family members. You can create an even smaller scale time line to document your travels and other events in your immediate family—the births of your children, their personal milestones— and update it as you gather family history in your travels.

Keep adding to your time line. If you visit the John F. Kennedy Library and learn about his life, add the years of his presidency and the significant events of his life. If you visit Grandpa and discuss World War II, add that to the time line. The time line puts history into context.

It's the Byway or the Highway

Call (800) 4-BYWAYS or visit *http://www.byways.org* for a free map and directory of federally designated National Scenic Byways. When you call the toll-free number, you can also access a list of publications related to scenic byways.

Ask your librarian about historical fiction about the locale you will be visiting. For example, if you plan a trip to Kentucky, you could read Harriet Beecher Stowe's *Uncle Tom's Cabin*. Borrow some audiobooks and take them with you on your trip. Your family might enjoy the My Name Is America series or its counterpart, the Dear America series, which is aimed at girls. Historical fiction often is far more engaging than a history book. Our children can learn critical thinking skills as they compare several sources of information. You may enjoy *Critical Thinking in United States History* as a conversation starter in the car.

Check your library's reference department for *American Historical Fiction: An Annotated Guide to Novels for Adults and Young Adults.* The book provides geographical listings, state by state and city by city, of historical fiction. You might also want to check *World Historical Fiction: An Annotated Guide to Novels for Adults and Young Adults,* which contains place and time indexes.

Explore Your Heritage

The *African American Heritage Directory* highlights the 240 cultural and educational institutions affiliated with the Association of African American Museums. You can pick up a free copy at any Howard Johnson hotel or motel worldwide, or in the future, it may also be posted at *http://www.hojo.com.* If you do not have easy access to a Howard Johnson hotel (not the restaurant), you can request a copy by writing: Free *African American Heritage Directory,* Howard Johnson International, 1 Sylvan Way, Parsippany, NJ 07054. Include a self-addressed, stamped envelope.

Sacred Spaces

When you travel, you have the opportunity to discuss religious artifacts and beliefs in the context of your own beliefs. Most well-known prehistoric and historic sites have religious significance; religious practices give us some insight into a civilization. Aside from the well-known sites such as the Vatican, the Pyramids, the Wailing Wall, or the Taj Mahal, there are numerous lesser-known places that you might overlook unless you do some research. For example, we live near a magnificent earthwork believed to be an astronomy observatory that was used for religious purposes. It was created by the Mound Builders, a prehistoric civilization. You could drive right by it without realizing its historical and scientific significance.

In the United States and Canada, lesser-known historic sites are cataloged by the state or provincial historical societies. Most of the societies are online, and many of the sites are free or low-cost.

The Pilgrim's Guide to the Sacred Earth is a travel guide to over 150 sites around the world considered sacred, including 13 in the continental United States, 13 in Canada, and 9 in Hawaii. Written by Sherrill Miller, who traveled around the world with her husband, photographer Courtney Milne, the book includes practical information: how to get there, availability of parking and car rentals, and information about local customs and legends.

Some of the sites are places of worship built by the area's inhabitants, such as the Ohio Serpent Mound and the Christian church at Glastonbury, thought to be Britain's first Christian church, which was built among older Celtic religious remains. Other sites are natural, like Bryce Canyon in Utah, with its hoodoo stone formations.

MATH MADE USEFUL

Kids can understand math through real-life travel experiences. It just makes sense: Arithmetic, after all, is more than numbers on a page.

Money is math that gets kids' attention—and since shopping was listed as the number one activity that parents participate in when they travel, why not include your kids in the fundamentals? Teach your children to ferret out the best travel bargains, and you will not only save money, you will also give your children skills for successful adulthood. Will coupons actually save money—or do the coupons require you to buy the more expensive option, thereby costing more overall? Saving up for the trip, handling spending money, and budgeting give your children a better understanding of math concepts and why they are important to learn.

As you travel, you may pass through various time zones. This gives you an opportunity to help your children learn to switch back and forth between zones and understand why the zones were created. You can also track your elevation and compare it with your elevation at home. We have more math ideas in chapter 6, "Are We There Yet?"

Keep in mind that many people we think of as scientists, such as Thomas Edison and Albert Einstein, were mathematicians. In real life, science and math are interwoven. The theory of relativity was born on paper, not in a laboratory. If you study scientists, you may be able to learn more about how math was involved in their work.

The Performing Arts

Travel gives you a chance to expose your children to the performing arts without spending a lot of money. You can meet actors, dancers, jugglers, mimes, storytellers, circus performers, and musicians ranging from classical to bluegrass styles. To find out what performances are available, contact the chamber of commerce, peruse newspapers at your destination, or do an Internet search under the name of your destination. Music centers such as Nashville and Memphis have special events, including songwriters' nights, when known and unknown songwriters share their creations. In the summer, many cities have open-air concerts, usually free and often at a public park.

If your family is interested in learning one of these skills, you can plan to take advantage of training and events for fellow enthusiasts. Any form of the performing arts you can think of has a community, organizations, a newsletter, Internet resources, and a conference. Music societies organize special events for every instrument. Many are open to serious music students. Some music events are more family oriented and include beginners, especially those having to do with country music and folk music. Some of the reenactment groups (Civil War and Revolutionary War) have music groups that play period music, and they often welcome families, since teenagers were actually involved at the time.

Historical dramas dot the countryside, with such diverse topics as the Underground Railroad and *Daniel Boone: The Legend and the Man.* Some are held outdoors, such as *Tecumseh!* a drama about the chief of the Shawnee nation, defeated in his attempt to unite the indigenous tribes so they could defend their homelands from the settlers. The drama features real horses and plenty of action.

Try an Internet search using the keywords "historical drama" plus the name of the state or province you will be visiting. You can purchase a low-cost directory for a few dollars from the Institute of Outdoor Drama or view the directory at their Web site *http://www.unc.edu/depts/outdoor,* which is sponsored by the University of North Carolina, Chapel Hill. The institute's Web page has audio clips and photographs from a number of the shows.

To find dramas, concerts, and plays sponsored by churches, check the religion section of newspapers in the area you will visit, or contact churches of your denomination ahead of time. The cost is usually on a donation basis to cover expenses.

Everyone can enjoy storytelling—ranging from family stories and personal experiences to tall tales and traditional folktales. Storytellers are a dedicated clan that welcomes new clan members, both tellers and listeners, of all ages—at least all ages old enough to sit quietly and listen to stories. (Be prepared to remove noisy children.) If you look, you will find events in every state and province. Tellabration, a worldwide annual storytelling event on the third weekend of November, has 320 locations in 42 states and 14 countries *(http://www.tellabration.org)*. There may be one near you or near where you will be traveling. The National Storytelling Festival in Jonesborough, Tennessee, is a three-day event in early October that is dedicated to the art of storytelling and showcases stories from all over America and around the world. (See chapter 5 for more information on storytelling events.)

PERSONAL GROWTH

Your child's history textbook may describe slavery, the antislavery movement, and the Civil War. As you visit former slave quarters or Civil War battlegrounds, you can help your children understand these events within the context of your values and religious beliefs, a perspective they cannot get from a textbook.

To relate topics to the Bible, read about the journeys of the apostle Paul in the book of Acts, and look for *Pilgrim's Progress* in a modern children's edition. You can also use a Bible concordance or a computer program. What does the Bible have to say about slavery? What verses did proslavery Christians use to justify owning slaves? What verses did abolitionists use to justify their participation in the Underground Railroad, even though it was an illegal activity? All of these questions could lead to a discussion of passive resistance in the Civil Rights movement in the twentieth century.

Travel also gives a family the opportunity to strengthen their sense of purpose. Service to others helps children (and adults) see beyond themselves. When you work together as a family to make the world a better place, you "put your money where your mouth is" and make a difference in the world. Some of our family's most memorable learning experiences have been the result of meaningful volunteer work. (See chapter 7 for details on family volunteering.)

Your family can use travel to seek out and broaden fellowship within your faith by visiting other churches. You can also look for opportunities to learn about other faiths and cultures by participating in cultural festivals or visiting other worship services. Churches near campgrounds and resort areas often display a "come as you are" sign to let campers know they are welcome in casual clothing.

PHOTOGRAPHY

Photography is an art, a craft, and a science. You can use it as an art medium or as a tool to document and illustrate, enhancing writing, social studies, and other subjects. Judith's husband, John Allee, a professional freelance photographer and former news photographer, started taking and developing black-and-white pictures at age thirteen and became his high-school yearbook photographer. It led to a lifelong passion. Watch for photography exhibits that can give your budding photographers a sense of what others before them have accomplished. You can also pay attention to news and magazine photography from an artistic standpoint. What makes one picture have more impact than another?

If you live in a small town, perhaps you can visit some big-city photographers in your travels. A newsroom may be willing to let you take a tour and talk with the photography staff. Photography specialties include such esoteric fields as advertising, architecture, fashion, and microphotography (using microscopes). There are photographers who shoot photos of nothing but food or weddings.

Running out of film on vacation is like running out of bait when you are fishing. Film will be cheaper at your local discount store or camera store than at a tourist destination. Bring lots of film if you will be away from a convenient place to pick up more or if you want specialized film available only at camera stores.

Exposed film deteriorates more quickly than unused film, so keep it from getting too hot. One way to protect it is to process it. Use a local one-hour or overnight service while you are traveling. If that is not practical, you might want to consider bringing some prepaid mailers for developing your film.

Be aware that many galleries, museums, and other attractions will not allow photos. You cannot beat the price of their postcards, however. And the attraction's own photographer has the benefit of professional equipment and access to off-limits areas.

Sharing the information you have found with others can give your children an exciting goal and teach them some important skills. Suggest that your child make a presentation to a hobby club, church group, or youth organization about his trip. While attending an archaeology camp on a scholarship, Nancy Allee, then twelve, took photographs of activities and new friends. Back home, she selected which photographs to convert to slides and gave a fifteen-minute slide show and talk to her rock club about her experiences. The grand finish: a view of the seat of a muddy pair of pants of a student working on the "dig," and on the slide were the words "The End."

PHYSICAL FITNESS

Your children's attitude toward physical activity today can affect their health for the rest of their lives. Now is the time when they are forming strong bones and the habit of being active—or being couch potatoes.

According to Project Fit America:

- Over twenty million children are overweight by an average of 8.3 pounds.
- Childhood obesity is up 54 percent in children ages six to eleven and 39 percent in children ages twelve to seventeen.
- Eighty percent of obese teenagers will become overweight adults.
- More than half the girls and one-quarter of the boys six to seventeen years old cannot run a mile faster than they can walk it.

American culture's obsession with being thin, combined with a lack of attention to health, leads to eating disorders such as anorexia and bulimia, which are killing our young people. Some experts believe our nation will face an entire generation affected by osteoporosis, due to a deadly combination of lack of exercise, overconsumption of carbonated soft drinks and sugar, and lack of dietary calcium.

Travel gives you an opportunity to try out a variety of physical activities, such as dancing, hiking, skiing, canoeing, kayaking, rafting, Frisbee, golf, orienteering (finding your way on foot with a map and compass), long-distance bicycling, and table tennis. (Don't laugh. Table tennis can get pretty strenuous the way we play.) Not only do you have more access to different activities when you travel, but you can take more time to try novel activities when you are away from home.

City sports can be a fun and inexpensive change of pace on the road; most large cities have recreational centers and roller rinks. For a fun break from travel on a hot day, check out the city swimming pools to see if a pool is open to visitors. (This is a time-honored way to get a nice hot shower if you have been camping primitively.) YMCA/YWCA pools are another possibility, although they tend to have more limits.

Some hotels have an exercise room that lets your family try out a variety of equipment. Children need supervision to protect them from strangers and from misusing the equipment.

For one friend, sports were the family's main reason for travel during her children's high-school years. She traveled with her daughters' swim team for years as they participated in competitions, spending many hours with them. It gave them an opportunity to see much of the country and meet a wide range of people with a shared interest. If your children are interested in a sport, consider attending an event so they can see topnotch performers in competition.

Finally, you can focus on physical fitness even as you explore other subjects. Children can learn how exercise affects the body by measuring their heart rate and respiration. Sports such as orienteering tie in naturally with geography, geology, and math. You can set physical fitness goals and create a progress chart for each person.

Remember: If we want our children to be physically active for the rest of their lives, we need to keep it fun—and do it ourselves!

Reading for the Road
Reading skills tend to jump ahead when a child is motivated to read something that sparks a genuine interest. If your travels spark an interest in your child, strike while the iron is hot. Find more information at the library, including periodicals, before and after your trip. Take books and tapes with you on the road to study your journey in depth. You can plan a unit of study based on your travels.

Science for Hands-On Kids

Hands-on science museums feature a variety of unique exhibits and activities. For example, children will enjoy the hands-on demonstration area at the Indianapolis Children's Museum, where we experimented with paper aircraft powered by balloons and rubber bands. Such events may occur only once or a few times a day. Going to the museum's Web site or writing ahead for a schedule of events will let you know what special activities are going on and what the event times are.

Another way to learn about science is to study the scientists. You can visit the birthplaces or workplaces of inventors and other famous scientists such as Thomas Edison, the Wright Brothers, or Albert Einstein. Reading their biographies or autobiographies beforehand—or afterward—can enhance your experience and makes a good read-aloud in the car. Biographies from the children's section give you a quick overview, even if your family has moved on to adult-level books. (We'll look at science in the outdoors in the next chapter.)

Social Studies

The field of social studies covers a lot of ground besides history. It involves learning about people and society—careers, business, geography, and current events. You will find many opportunities to learn about the world as you travel. Here are a few related ideas that might interest your family.

Coin and Stamp Collecting

Travel can spur an interest in collecting coins or stamps. As you travel, collect stamps in an inexpensive binder or folder as souvenirs of your adventures along the way.

Around Town with a Map

Map skills can start at home. To learn beginning map skills, help your children make a map of your house, your neighborhood, and the way to the grocery store. For longer trips, use printed maps to teach kids about using a legend and a mileage scale and identifying the symbols for interstates, state highways, and county roads. If they get good at it, they might be able to navigate you through any detours you encounter on the road.

Homemade Passports

Create a postcard-size "passport" for each child, a fun idea from *The Penny Whistle Traveling with Kids Book* by Meredith Brokaw and Annie Gilbar. Card stock (a heavy paper available at copy shops and print shops) makes a good cover. You can make a tracing, rubbing, or drawing based on a real passport cover to decorate it. Lamination adds a nice touch. Add pages for stamps, postcards, snapshots, autographs, ticket stubs, and handwritten entries to show where you've been. Fold and staple it to create a book. With a convincing cover, a small photo album could serve as your "passport."

UNIT STUDIES ON THE ROAD

Travel is a kind of "unit study," which is curriculum based around a topic that ties in various traditional academic subjects. It takes away the artificial separation of history from science, science from math, and reading from everything else. Of course, you can overdo it. The following tongue-in-cheek demonstration of unit studies, adapted from material on the Internet, shows how a parent might get a little carried away.

Question: How do you change a light bulb if you are a family preparing for educational travel?

Answer: Well, first, you go to the library and check out books on electricity, Benjamin Franklin, and Thomas Edison. You have relatives in Detroit, so you plan a side trip to Deerfield Village, Michigan, to visit Thomas Edison's laboratory, after printing out a map at a free Internet mapping service. Back to the library to check the Thomas Register to see if there is a light bulb manufacturer on your route and when the factory tours are. On the way, the children figure out gas mileage and estimate the arrival time based on the speed limit and the distance calculated using the mileage scale on the map.

At Deerfield Village you learn about the times when Thomas Edison and Henry Ford were alive and how the assembly line changed manufacturing. Back home, you construct an electromagnet using wire and batteries, and then you find out where tungsten is made and how it is manufactured. Next you study the history of lighting, dip your own candles, and study by candlelight, just like Abraham Lincoln.

Now the children call stores in the area, practicing their alphabetization skills by using the telephone book, and do price comparisons of light bulbs, then select a product based on price and anticipated hours of light provided. At the store, they figure out the change from a five-dollar bill. On the way home, a discussion develops over the history of money. Finally, after building a homemade ladder out of branches dragged from the woods, the light bulb is installed. And you have light!

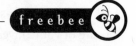
freebee

State Unit Studies

Here's an idea for a unit study: Learn about each state you will be visiting. At *50States.com,* you can find an information sheet for each state. You will find links for each president who came from that state, tourism links for each large city, genealogy links, and others. You can also check out the state unit studies under Education/ Homeschooling at *http://homeschooling.about.com*. Although the site is designed for homeschool families, everyone is welcome! You can print out a map of the United States and color in each state as you study it, or you can print a state information sheet for each state you wish to study.

WRITING IN THE REAL WORLD

Often the only writing children do is connected with school projects. Getting a real letter addressed personally to you is a heady incentive for writing. Having a pen pal costs next to nothing, and having an audience for their writing can bring out the best in your children.

World Pen Pals promotes international friendship and cultural understanding by matching up pen pals among young people ages nine to twenty. When you sign up, you can specify a male or female pal and a geographic region—such as "male–Latin America" or "female-Asia." Currently, the fee is three dollars per pen pal or half that amount for groups of ten or more when coordinated through one individual, such as a teacher.

The staff that serves you at restaurants, hotels, and visitor centers rarely get written thank-yous. Maybe you can think of someone each day to thank or collect names during the day for consideration. Perhaps grandparents, neighbors, or friends would enjoy hearing from the travelers, and you could make copies of the letters later to form an informal journal. Bring mailing labels (addressed to friends and family) for postcards and letters.

It is fun to enclose a memento in your letters back home. If you visit a beach, you can enclose a little sand. In October, enclose a colorful leaf. A clipping from your destination's local newspaper, a colorful stamp, or a sticker is easy to include and adds a little spice to your correspondence.

If you have Web-savvy kids, perhaps they would enjoy creating a family Web site of your travels. To see a sample Web site, visit "Tippecanoe and the Internet Too," a history site developed by a fourth-grade class. Web site space is available free on the Internet, supported by advertising banners.

Journals for Journeys
Jim Foreman and his wife, Frieda, occasionally travel with their grandchildren and have found journaling a low-key way to make their trips more memorable as well as encourage their grandchildren's literacy. According to Jim,

> Bound books of blank pages can be found at all bookstores. One should be given to each person to record daily experiences. We did that on all our extended trips in our motor home, and we occasionally go back and read what we wrote. It's almost like doing the trip again. It's especially fun for the kids because they can look back in a few years and see not only where they went but also how they felt about it.

A family journal, highly recommended for the young writer who needs inspiration, might include the best and worst thing about each day for each family member. How about keeping top-ten lists for each trip? The Best, The Worst, The Most Boring, and The Silliest are all fodder for family memories. Take along a sketchbook and embellish your writing with artwork.

"On one family vacation, we kept a running tally of weirdest moments and most strange encounters," said Kate Redd in *52 Ways to Make Family*

Travel More Enjoyable. "If we experienced a disappointment, it made our list with a laugh!" Kate also suggests keeping lists of first-time experiences and best meals.

Friends Old and New

It is easy to travel across the country on the interstate highways, staying in the chain motels whose signs can be seen from the road. You can eat in versions of the same restaurants you eat in at home, but you'll miss out on a charming but inexpensive ethnic restaurant on a side street or a church supper a few blocks away. Nighttime may find you watching television in your motel room to pass the time rather than going out. If you do any sightseeing en route, you may spend much of your time trying to figure out how to get somewhere.

Now imagine that you have old friends who just happen to live in the same city you are visiting and are delighted to hear that you are coming. They can't wait to tell you about things to do and see in their town. Suddenly, you have an insider's view of the city and the warm welcome of friends.

We may not have old friends at each destination, but we have found ways to meet new ones during our travels. By opening our lives to new friends, we have enriched our children's education as well as our own.

Getting to see some of America's crossroads through the eyes (and from the front porches) of the people who live there has given us a spectacular view we couldn't have gotten from the freeway. Educational travel is more fun when you make new friends or visit old ones.

Our fondest travel memories are of the people we met, whether they were passing acquaintances or became lifelong friends. Our children can learn more about other cultures and languages from people who live in them, and they can continue their contact through cards and letters for years to come. Meeting diverse people and sharing their lives, even for a short time, gives you a chance to experience a place from the inside out, instead of from the outside in.

Can we reconcile meeting new people with Mom's sage advice not to talk with strangers? Caution is needed, of course, but we do not have to live in fear to the point that we stay away from strangers everywhere we go. Friends of friends are safest, but we tend to find a warm welcome from communities of like-minded people, and within those circles there is a measure of safety.

We have made it a mission to meet people in our travels. It is not difficult to do, but it takes some effort and planning. Judith's family makes a point of seeking out friends of friends and people they contact through membership organizations. The family participates in host directories for several organizations, giving the family a chance to meet other families with similar interests as well as save money while traveling:

> We have visited host families in sixteen states, and we hope to include Mexico and Canada in the future. We also hunt up relatives we haven't seen in years or have never met. We save some money on lodging, although traveling more slowly and sometimes going out of our way for a visit offsets those savings. We usually bring a host gift and food to share, and sometimes we take our hosts out to eat.
>
> Even if we didn't save a dime, though, we wouldn't give up our host experiences for anything. Who can forget climbing the bell tower of the oldest church in St. Louis, Missouri? The caretaker, a home-school dad, was our guide. Our daughter still has prize specimens gleaned from the discard pile of rocks and fossils behind the geology building at the University of Wisconsin. New friends showed it to us. In Indianapolis, friends invited us to attend a high-spirited class for American Sign Language, an unforgettable experience. Thanks to our new friends, we have sampled Greek, Mexican, southern, and vegan cooking.

Your children learn networking skills when you contact like-minded individuals in your field of study. Starting a home business? In your travels you may be able to meet others who have successfully started a similar business. If you have a family member with a disability, you can meet other families who are facing similar physical or developmental challenges and share what works and what does not.

In her book *Home Is Where You Park It*, a book about living and traveling in an RV, Kay Peterson says it is easier for her husband to meet new people in a campground because all he has to do is raise the hood of his car, and men from around the campground practically trip over themselves to stop by. Helping your children meet other children at a campground is almost as easy; of course, it needs supervision. One way is to work on a jigsaw puzzle at the recreation center or at your picnic table. Another is to take a pet for a walk through the "neighborhood."

Zephyr Goza, an eleven-year-old boy, makes friends easily as he travels with his parents around the country. His advice applies to people of all ages. "When I make friends," he says, "my method is just to say hi, ask them their names, what kind of things they like, and basically just exchange information." The entire Goza family—Kimberly, Dennis, and Zephyr—travels full time as professional storytellers. Sometimes they stay at hotels and motels, but Kimberly sees a lot of advantages in meeting people at campgrounds.

> First of all, when we stay at campgrounds, Zephyr can ride his bike and Rollerblade to his heart's content. There are common areas available, generally within view of our campsite, where children gather. Because we can see and hear him, he is allowed to visit with new friends at their campsites (outside), and the parents of his friends feel comfortable allowing them to come over to our site.
>
> At one campground in Seattle, the kids all chased wild rabbits and held bicycle races. In Oklahoma City, they put together a band, made a recording of their original songs, and swam in the pool. In Oregon, he organized a kids club with a secret hideout and built a maze through the trees for contests. At the Ute Reservation in Utah, everyone had a blast watching the Fourth of July fireworks together. Many times they get together to play and discuss video games. Or he'll invite kids over to roast marshmallows.

Sandra and Duke Merrion find that camping gets them among real people, where they can make friends, even across the world, as they travel with three of their children. "One five-star hotel is like another five-star hotel," says Duke. "When you go on back roads, you really get a good feel for the country, the culture, and the people. By camping, you meet local people."

Nature programs are another good way to meet people. Duke, Sandra, and their three teenagers toured a glowworm cave, rowing in on a river. "It was like the night sky," remembers Sandra. "Another family, who had children around our kids' ages, told us, 'Well, when you get to Auckland, come stay with us.' We did, and we had a great time. Six years after our visit, they're coming here and staying with us."

"When you find local people, they send you places," says Sandra, which is one of the advantages of being friendly. That is how the Merrions had the opportunity to see early graffiti on the Oregon Trail, with names carved on a rock that was dated 1850.

The Merrions contacted the National Coalition of Alternative Community Schools when they got to Australia. A fellow there told them he was going to the New Edinburgh Folk Music Festival in New Zealand. "He suggested we might want to go if we weren't doing anything," says Sandra. "We camped there for four days." The festival, which featured such things as a tin whistle group and a workshop on flute collecting, was a good way to meet more people.

HOMESCHOOLING ON THE ROAD

If you already homeschool, you will need to decide whether to keep your usual routine or let your travel become one big unit study, leading wherever it may. To some extent, that may depend on how long you are traveling. For a one- or two-week vacation, you will probably leave the workbooks (if you use them) at home. Workbooks, however, can be a good time-filler during long waits and car rides if your children can read and ride without motion sickness.

Do you homeschool with few, if any, textbooks? Do you believe that children learn best when they explore their interests? If so, you may call yourself an "unschooler," or perhaps a "relaxed homeschooler." (You can find more information on homeschooling styles and methods in our earlier book, *Homeschooling on a Shoestring*.) Unschoolers, in general, rely more on real-life experiences than on traditional curriculum. Travel offers an opportunity for more-structured homeschool families to enjoy unschooling on a temporary basis.

For the Allee and Morgan families, homeschooling during travel time was not much different than at home, except that they had opportunities while traveling that they would not have had at home. They do bring along books for each family member and for reading aloud in the car, and they also bring foreign-language tapes and a lap desk with art supplies. However, they don't allow these items to become their main focus when traveling; rather, the journey and the destination are the objects of their attention.

Visiting other homeschool families was especially exciting. Host families exposed the Allee family to activities and sites off the beaten tourist path— the local food co-op, ethnic restaurants, and a class on American Sign Language. They also shared their homeschool projects ranging from origami—which got Nancy started on a three-year origami kick—to raising lambs. Exposure to training draft horses convinced the Allees (if they needed convincing) *not* to try this at home!

Some families start homeschooling specifically because they want to travel. Judy and Gary sold their business and decided to take a year to travel in an RV with their two daughters, ages six and eight, instead of waiting for retirement. Their first day on the road was also their first day of homeschooling. They struggled with how much academic work to require, how to provide some routine in a moving home with an ever-changing "backyard," and how to meet families with children while traveling. As do most first-year homeschoolers, they worried about whether their daughters were keeping up with their peers, since the girls would be going back to school when their extended trip ended. Judy and Gary gradually relaxed as they realized how much their daughters were learning—and how efficient one-on-one tutoring is, compared with classroom time.

Books are heavy and bulky to carry. Extended travelers face some special challenges. Kimberly Goza travels full time with her family in a van, towing a little U-Haul–type trailer for their belongings. She had to find alternatives to carrying lots of books. "Yes, it is hard to leave behind all the books," she says. "Hello, libraries and bookstores! Wonderful places to relax, read, and even drink coffee—they've become our 'living rooms.' We also pick up used *National Geographic* magazines or really cheap used books, so it doesn't bother us to leave them behind at Laundromats for others."

Serendipity: Taking Advantage of Opportunities

You can plan for the unexpected, whether your journey is near or far from home. Sometimes we learn the most from serendipity—the unforeseen but welcome event. An unplanned adventure can provide a needed break, especially if you feel as if your life is too regimented.

Kimberly Goza says that even unexpected and seemingly unwelcome experiences can turn into a learning adventure. "One breakdown led to my son writing a little picture book about a tow truck, and he just loved talking to the mechanic and watching the motor home being fixed. On a separate occasion, a bee that stung him became a specimen for our microscope."

Melissa learned early how serendipity can enrich a family vacation.

My parents took my brother, two sisters, and me on a trip from Ohio to southern Illinois to learn about our roots. I was eight at the time. One memory stands out vividly from that trip—the day my parents decided to follow a tip from an area native and go down back roads to an old slave house. Yes, there really was slavery in the divided state of Illinois. I can still imagine details of that unplanned tour—the wooden pallets, the hardware to attach the chains. I can still feel the chills running down my spine. That one chance visit shaped my understanding of slavery and the American Civil War. It nurtured a lifelong interest in history. I didn't just read about it. In a way, I lived it.

The Trail Is the Thing

"The trail is the thing, not the end of the trail. Travel too fast and you miss all you are traveling for." —Louis L'Amour, author

If every moment is accounted for, you will not have time for serendipity. We have sometimes passed by a cool-looking museum or the chance to attend a cultural event because we were on a tight schedule. But whenever possible, we try to leave some slack in our schedule, to make room for serendipity. Kimberly, her husband, and their son, Zephyr, remember going a little out of their way to go to Zephyr, Texas. "Gee, I wonder why we went there?" she says.

"Spur-of-the-moment travel, in my opinion, is the most enjoyable way to go," says Jim Foreman. "We did that for almost two years in our motor home. We were traveling with no particular destination. We'd know where we were going when we got there."

Now *that* is planned serendipity.

Chapter Four

Discovering the Great Outdoors

Whether we are vacationing, taking a field trip, or becoming more observant in our own backyards, nature is close enough to touch. With our eyes wide open, even a hike around a city block can uncover wriggling insect life under a rotting board or fossils embedded in stone buildings and steps. No matter how limited your budget, you can enjoy God's creation wherever you roam.

A Parent's Duty

"No subject is given shorter shrift than nature. Before college, students will hear little more than a mention of botany, geology, zoology, and natural history. Children grow up with few insights into the natural world or their place in it. From ignorance springs disrespect.... Yet it is wrong to blame teachers. They see our kids only briefly, in crowded classrooms severed from nature. It is parents who must expose children to the great outdoors." —Steven Boga, in *Camping and Backpacking with Children*

When you travel, seek out adventures on land and sea to learn more about the earth. From there, the sky's the limit, offering astronomical delights. Kids can eat, sleep, walk, and breathe science while they explore the outdoors, igniting their sense of awe and wonder. Families can experience the gentle, peaceful side of nature and learn to observe, listen, and contemplate.

They can learn to respect nature's wild and brutal side and practice survival skills that could someday save their lives.

Preparing for Adventure

What will you need for this great natural adventure? Pack a travel book bag with some low-cost learning resources for your young naturalist. With little expense, your family members can easily carry rock collecting or nature guidebooks for reference on the road.

Purchase several guidebooks, such as the Audubon Society's *Pocket Guides,* on topics that interest your children. Some examples include:

- animal tracks
- leaf identification
- birds
- insects
- cloud formations and weather indicators
- the moon
- constellations and other phenomena of the night sky
- flowers
- trees
- seeds
- fossils
- rocks and minerals
- shells
- caves and caverns

Through a Child's Eyes

"'But children are difficult to teach.' 'They will never enjoy being away from the television for more than one night.' 'They will get tired.' 'They will...' I have heard all the excuses. Believe me, taking your kids hiking or camping doesn't require much effort as long as you keep one rule in mind: See everything through a child's eyes."

—Michael Hodgson, *Wilderness with Children: A Parent's Guide to Fun Family Outings*

You might also want to provide your child with a handbook of instructions for practical skills in the outdoors. It takes little space in a suitcase and offers a diversion during travel time. Play "What if?" What if you are lost in the wilderness? What if you need to cook outdoors, forage for natural food, perform basic first aid, or build a shelter? Children can search for the answers in their handbook. One such handbook is a scouting manual, often available at secondhand shops or wherever scouting supplies are sold. You can also purchase an inexpensive handbook from Keepers of the Faith, a Christian youth program. The handbook includes guidelines for independent science and nature study and for developing character and a knowledge of the Bible.

NATURE TOOLKIT

Help your children pack an inexpensive nature toolkit to take along when traveling. Carry it even on neighborhood walks for unexpected finds. Include:

- plastic bags or recycled plastic 35mm film canisters, to carry nature specimens (Include some grocery sacks with handles and some sandwich-size and larger bags to tuck in your backpack. For the car, an empty facial tissue box makes a nice bag dispenser. Use for scientific finds, such as shells from the beach or bags of pond water to study. A bag with holes punched for air makes a temporary home for tiny critters. Your bag collection will come in handy for many things while you are traveling.)
- masking tape—for labels
- a magnifying glass
- an aquarium net
- a pocket-size notebook and pencils (Mechanical pencils are handy for travel, since you don't need to sharpen them.)
- a flashlight for your head, leaving your hands free (Buy one or make your own from a lightweight flashlight and headband.)
- binoculars (Put them on your Christmas wish list or pick them up at a garage sale. Maybe you can borrow a pair for your trip.)
- pocket knife or craft knife, for parents or responsible older children (Use it for activities such as examining bird droppings and dissecting dead insects.)

- work gloves
- disposable wet wipes
- tracing paper, for leaf rubbings and tracing nature pictures
- sketch pad and drawing materials

FINDING FREE EXPERT ADVICE

An inquisitive child can stump well-educated adults with questions like, What do fireflies eat? Are birds cold? What is that black thing in the center of that flower? We have personally fielded all of these questions, but we needed help to get all of the answers. Guidebooks won't answer every question. And we don't expect you to pack an encyclopedia in your backpack.

The solution? Write down all the questions. Then ask an expert.

Many experts love to freely share their knowledge. They've sharpened their expertise because they are passionate about their areas of interest. A park guide, for example, will politely give directions and tell you when the park closes, but watch the guide light up when asked about nature (if you get the right guide). It is amazing and sad how few people take advantage of free lectures, nature exhibits, and guided tours at public and private parks.

Online Resources

Many of us enjoy daydreaming and preparing for a vacation as much as we enjoy the trip itself. Here are some free resources to feed your daydreams.

- *Gorp.com* offers recreation forums for tips and anecdotes from sports enthusiasts. GORP also provides advice on wilderness survival, fishing, adventure stories, travel information, links, expert advice, and shopping.
- *AllOutdoors.com,* founded in 1995 (olden times in Cyberland), hosts about eight thousand pages of gear reviews, travel stories, advice, directory resources, discussion forums, and classified ads.

Park guides aren't the only experts around, of course. A question can break the ice and start a friendship with fellow tourists. You may want to stop at a public library or call and ask the research librarian for help on the phone. Librarians and other guides may steer you to local hobbyists, such as rock hounds or cavers (cave explorers, also known as "spelunkers"), who may welcome your interest.

DIRT CHEAP: EXPLORING LAND ON A BUDGET

Ready for a land adventure? Schools teach kids about various environments, but your kids can gain firsthand knowledge of ecosystems, weather, and animal habitats when they explore cool mountains, arid deserts, farmland pastures, and city parks.

Your kids can dig into earth science and not even realize they're learning. Here are some earth science topics you may wish to explore while visiting with nature. Gather information from the library or Internet before your trip. While sitting around the campfire, find time to talk about what you've seen and learned.

- Learn how animals—and people—thrive in the desert and survive in the snow. Native American languages contain many words concerning nature and weather that have no English equivalent. For example, we have only one word for snow, while some languages have many words for the various types of snow. Distinguishing the types of snow was important for survival.
- Try not to just ask, What is photosynthesis? Delve deeper and ask why. Can you find out why some plants need more light to grow than others? When you travel, find some of those plants.
- Kids may know the difference between a deciduous tree and a conifer from school, but do they know why an evergreen tree keeps its leaves in winter? How plants survive in the desert? Travel to their native habitats, and children can see, touch, and smell the plants. You may use this as an opportunity to remind them to examine nature carefully.

Jim Foreman and his wife, Frieda, found they did not have to travel far or spend a lot of money to make a big impression on their grandchildren with the outdoors. Jim says:

Most kids under twelve years of age have little concept of time, distance, or direction. They can get lost one aisle away from their mother in the grocery store. This can make for a great weekend adventure without getting more than a few miles from the house.

One time my wife and I were visiting our son and his family in California. Being totally self-contained in our motor home, we were at home no matter where we parked. We didn't want to remain on the street in front of their house overnight, so I found a city park a mile or so away where we could stay.

We invited the two oldest grandsons, who were about five and seven, to spend the night with us. On the way to the park we stopped for a few groceries we needed, then picked up takeout for dinner. They played in the playground until dark. Then we roasted marshmallows over a propane camp stove and told stories until bedtime. Next morning, we had breakfast and returned.

Ten years later, they still talk about the time they went on a camping trip with Grandma and Grandpa. We could have gone to Yosemite, and they wouldn't have been any more impressed. A youthful imagination is your greatest asset.

Dave Levingston recommends camping close to home for the first outing or two. "If disaster happens—it rains, the tent blows down, someone gets stung by a bee, they just don't like sleeping in a tent, any of the many things that can go wrong on a trip with young children—you can always jump in the car and take them home," he says. For that matter, a test run in the backyard for a night or two will teach you what to bring on your trip and what you can easily do without.

BARGAIN LAND ADVENTURES IN THE NATION'S PARKS AND PUBLIC LANDS

Ask if the National Park or Bureau of Land Management campground you visit has a Junior Ranger program. For a few dollars per child (the cost varies from park to park), the Junior Ranger program gives children a chance to earn a pin, badge, or sticker for completing nature activities. Youngsters receive a worksheet or workbook with activities, such as a treasure hunt to find certain natural features at the park, or they can attend a free ranger presentation.

The Junior Ranger program is custom-tailored to each park. At Imperial Sand Dunes, operated by BLM, Junior Rangers had a chance to see scorpions, geckos, snakes, and other desert creatures at a program about "Creepy Crawlies of the Desert." At the Eisenhower National Historic Site, children age seven to twelve can become Junior Secret Service Agents instead of Junior Rangers. New agents are awarded a badge and certificate for learning about the Secret Service.

For the winter program at Yellowstone Park, five- to twelve-year-olds attend a program led by a park ranger. The youngsters record wildlife observations, make a record of geyser and hot spring activity, and hike, ski, or snowshoe a trail. For a small fee (about the cost of a fast-food kids' meal), they receive an activity paper and "snowpacks," containing a thermometer, hand lens, and data collection tools. Snowshoes are available specifically for Junior Rangers and their families. After completing the program, children have their work reviewed by a park ranger and receive an embroidered badge.

Twenty-two parks with Junior Ranger programs are linked to the National Park Service Web site's Junior Ranger page *(http://www.nps.gov/interp/jrranger.html)*. Some of the parks have activity sheets online that children can complete at home and submit via the Internet to earn a badge. The activities are designed for children who want to learn about the park before their visit or who cannot visit the park in person.

HIKING HAPPY TRAILS ON A BUDGET

If you visit a state or national park, arboretum, or nature center, check with the naturalist or the bulletin board to see if the park offers any guided hikes. City parks and recreation departments sometimes sponsor hikes. You may need to register, but guided hikes are usually free. They are often geared more toward learning about nature than toward a physically challenging trek.

On the challenge scale, day hiking is a step up from short, guided hikes. *The Boy Scout's Hike Book* by Edward Cave can help you plan for hiking with children ages four to eight. Traditional backpacking, with its heavier load of camping equipment and food, can prove even more challenging, but perhaps too difficult for younger children. You need to be in excellent condition yourself if you plan to carry a child; they get heavier each step of the way. *Camping and Backpacking with Children* by Steven Boga takes you from adventures in your backyard up through adventurous backpacking expeditions with children of all ages.

Happy Trails to You

To find hiking, biking, and canoeing routes, you can search a database of over seventeen thousand trails, complete with topography and weather, at *http://www.trails.com*.

If your family is ready for a physical challenge, consider hiking the Appalachian Trail (AT)—or part of it, anyway! The AT is over twenty-one hundred miles along the Appalachian Mountain ridge lines from Springer Mountain, Georgia, to Mount Katahdin, Maine. There is a small but devout group of AT hikers, called thru-hikers, who aim to hike the whole trail in one session, which usually takes about five or six months. Another group of inspired hikers takes the AT piecemeal, sometimes over a lifetime, picking up each year where they left off the year before. One fellow hiked as a fundraiser for a nonprofit children's organization, asking for per-mile pledges.

The Appalachian Trail Conference is a nonprofit organization that provides state-by-state information about the trail, compiles educational information for teachers and others, and coordinates volunteers to maintain the trail. Their Web site can connect you to trail clubs and an online store that offers trail guides, maps, books about the AT, and supplies.

Best Hikes with Children is a series published by Mountaineer Books, a nonprofit conservation club. The series has editions including sixteen states, ranging from the specific (San Francisco North Bay) to the vast (Vermont, New Hampshire, and Maine).

Have Skis, Will Travel

If you want to learn to ski, you have three main choices: downhill skiing (as in down the side of a mountain), cross-country (you learn to ski uphill as well as down, but the hills are more gentle), and snowboarding, which is a lot like surfing or skateboarding. All three give you a full-body workout. Skiing is one sport your children can continue to participate in long after they become adults.

Make sure you purchase the right type of ski equipment. There is a difference between downhill and cross-country skis (and a snowboard, which accommodates both feet, is shorter and wider than a ski). Renting is a good way to try out equipment to see if skiing is for you and what kind of equipment you like. Buying a pair of used skis may be more economical than renting—especially if you plan to use them more than once; you will pay about one-tenth the cost of new equipment. For used equipment, watch for a ski swap, which may be sponsored by a ski club. Also check at Goodwill and Salvation Army stores. New ski apparel and equipment usually go on sale around Valentine's Day.

Cross-country skiing can be inexpensive and relatively safe. (Melissa says that she handles cross-country skis adequately, even though she claims she has two left feet.) It is free in many parks, and your family can experience nature in its quiet, sleepy winter's rest. If you plan to ski in a public area, call the parks or recreation department before you leave home, as some areas prohibit skiing.

You do not need to travel to the slopes for cross-country skiing, and logic says you are less likely to break a bone going cross-country than going down the side of a mountain. Yet downhill skiing certainly has its enthusiasts. The speed (and the danger that comes with it) is part of what makes it exciting.

Hostels in Ski Country

When you are traveling, consider lodging at a hostel in a ski area. Write to Hostelling International—American Youth Hostels for a free listing of affiliated hostels in ski country. Aside from low-cost lodging, sometimes less than ten dollars a person, hostels may offer special ski packages, a shuttle to the slopes, and snowshoe rentals—and in some cases, fireplaces and hot tubs. Standard rooms are dormitory-style sleeping quarters, with males separate from females, but some hostels offer more expensive family rooms with advance reservations. (For more information, see the resource guide.)

If you live near ski slopes, season passes may allow you to ski at a reduced rate. A homeschool group in Indiana purchases passes with a school group discount, arranging a regular ski date on a weekday, when the slopes are less busy. The school discount is much cheaper than the regular group discount, and it usually includes a lift ticket, ski rental, and a lesson. Having the parents learn alongside the kids has created some comical moments. This is one skill that children tend to pick up faster than adults.

Rock Hounds and Rock Puppies

Judith's daughter, Nancy, collects rocks as free or inexpensive souvenirs from each of the states she has visited. Some she gathered from the yards of people we visited or other places where we had permission. Others she received as gifts or purchased from roadside stands and museum gift shops. As she grew up, she had encouragement from members of the local club for rock hounds (enthusiastic rock collectors), and was pronounced a "rock puppy." Rock clubs scout out good hunting places and get permission to sponsor field trips on farms, quarries, campgrounds, and other sites.

Rock Resources

You may want to join a rock club in your area or find one to visit as you travel. To locate clubs that focus on rocks, minerals, lapidary arts (jewelry making), or fossils, contact the American Federation of Mineralogical Societies at *http://www.amfed.org*. The site also lists rock shows, demonstrations, and other events nationwide. The shows often feature a children's area and a competition for display cases, which includes categories for novices. You can also find out how to join or start a Future Rock Hounds of America, a club for younger rock enthusiasts.

By the time Nancy was nine or ten, her expertise had outstripped that of her parents. The rock club provided her access to experts. No matter what kind of fossil, mineral, or artifact she found, someone at the club knew what it was or how to find out. Nancy created her own display cases for her club's shows with guidance from other members, using her favorite fossils and minerals. Labeling and organizing her specimens gave her an impetus to learn more about their origin and classifications.

Fossils are the earth's scrapbook. Thousands of scientists in the United States and around the world question many tenets of evolutionary theory; however, the evidence supporting intelligent design—rather than "change by accident"—is not usually included in school texts. You can discuss these issues with your children as you explore geology, archaeology, and even paleontology in your travels. Bring along magazine issues of *National Geographic* and *Creation: Ex Nihilo* to aid in discussion. These magazines and others can also inspire ideas for family nature trips, such as a trip to study evidence regarding the formation of the Grand Canyon.

Sand is a nice reminder from the beach or desert area. Tuck a little in an envelope for letters to friends back home, and its gritty confetti conveys the essence of the beach to your correspondents. To cause a surprise spill when the person opens the letter, fold the letter into a packet shape to hold the sand. (Remember to wash hands after handling rocks, dirt, or sand.)

Leave Each Place a Little Better

Many parks and arboretums have the visitor philosophy, "Take nothing but pictures. Leave nothing but footprints." It is a federal crime to remove any natural artifacts from many of our national parks—and that includes lakes, rivers, and ocean coastlines. Be sure to obtain permission before removing rocks, insects, wildflowers, soil, leaves, coral, fallen nuts, shells, or any scientific specimens. No one will mind, however, if you remove trash. If you picnic or hike, take a few minutes to round up all the trash—not only your own, but that left by others. Your children can learn firsthand about their environment, earn a little civic pride, and understand why it is important not to litter. A ritual of leaving each place you visit more litter-free than it was when you got there makes that place a little more your own. Even if you travel on a budget, you will feel rich!

Botany on a Budget

In your travels, you can visit nature centers, wildlife preserves, and arboretums. For national listings of botany-related organizations, see *North*

American Horticulture, which lists organizations by state and province. It is compiled by the American Horticultural Society. For regional information, visit chambers of commerce and tourist information centers.

You can use tracing or art paper to make rubbings of leaves, tree bark, fossils, or other interesting textures you find. Use a piece of chalk, charcoal, pencil, or a wax or pastel crayon without its sleeve. Trace lightly enough so that you don't tear the paper. Watch out for poison ivy and sumac—and if you cannot recognize them, learn! Ask a naturalist to show you a sample, and remember: "Leaves of three, let it be—it's poison ivy!"

Have a science scavenger hunt. At the beach, how many different types or colors of shells and driftwood can you find? In the woods, how many different leaves can you find? (If you are not permitted to collect, use only fallen leaves, and leave them behind.)

BE A "JOHNNY APPLESEED" FAMILY

Johnny Appleseed is a beloved character who, according to stories, was frugal to the bone. Appleseed traveled the country with a cooking pot on his head, carrying and wearing all of his few worldly goods. He planted apple trees and evangelized to the people he met along the way. All it took was a sack of seeds and a committed spirit, and the countryside was forever changed. Although some of the folktales about him are exaggerated, he was a real person: John Chapman.

Just as Chapman was known for accomplishing so much with so little, your family could have a similar mission that would leave an indelible mark as you cross the country. A packet of seeds or bulbs costs very little, but it goes a long way.

Find out what varieties are needed in various planting zones and where you can gather or purchase seeds or bulbs. Check with a naturalist, who will suggest an endangered or threatened species of plant or tree, or maybe a native tree or plant that is needed in greater quantities. You can find a naturalist by contacting one of these sources:

- the county extension office
- the Department of Natural Resources in individual states
- the U.S. Department of Agriculture
- the Department of Environmental Conservation (by state)

- plant preservation societies in each state or province (to find them, check with your reference librarian or search the Internet under "threatened plants")
- an arboretum, botanical garden, or nature center
- the National Arbor Day Foundation, which offers information as well as a source for ordering trees
- a local university

Doug Dudgeon, a horticulturist from Dawes Arboretum in Newark, Ohio, has these suggestions for "Johnny Appleseed" families who want to help the environment while traveling:

1. *Learn to identify pests or weeds, and report your sightings to a naturalist.* Two prime examples of pests that are reaching epidemic proportions are gypsy moths and garlic mustard. "I think that the average person, if educated about them, can be a help in their control," Dudgeon says. He adds that spotting pests like the gypsy moth is critical. They pop up quickly in new areas and, in caterpillar form, are voracious feeders. The moths can devastate landscapes and defoliate trees, especially oaks. Homeowners can help stop the caterpillars by applying sticky strips of tape around trunks of susceptible trees and crushing egg masses on trees in winter. Also check for egg masses on your vehicle. This is how the insects are transported and infect other parts of the country.

Garlic mustard is taking over certain areas, especially the borders of fields and woods. It is crowding out more desirable native species. Pure stands of this weed are forming that choke out all other vegetation. "It is problematic to the point that we had to have an all-staff garlic mustard–pulling day here at the arboretum," says Dudgeon.

2. *Identify and report diseases that affect trees and plants.* Diseases can be catastrophic to plants. Chestnut blight entered the United States from Europe and has killed or severely damaged all of our native chestnuts. What was once the dominant tree in eastern forests is now just a memory. Your homework will tell you what diseases to watch for in the area you are traveling. For example, fire blight, a bacterial plant disease found throughout North America, currently affects pears, cherries, apples, apricots, peaches, and other plants in the rose family. Look for wilting and blackened branch tips that have a scorched appearance.

3. *Plant threatened specimens.* Some advance research will show you how to plant the species you adopt and how to select the right site. Ask for permission, whether on private or public property.

4. *Study threatened plants and watch for them.* In Ohio, for example, the sweet fern once grew in scattered sites throughout northern Ohio. It now exists only near western Lake Erie.

Tree Care and ID Booklets

The National Arbor Day Foundation offers a free booklet of tree-care tips that includes a nursery stock catalog. For a small fee you can also order a pocket-size tree ID guide so you can play "Name That Tree." The guide provides color pictures to help you identify different varieties of trees throughout the eastern and central United States. Contact the foundation at 100 Arbor Avenue, Nebraska City, NE 68410; (402) 474-5655; e-mail: info@arborday.org; Web site: *http://www.arborday.org.*

To find out about endangered species native to your planned destination, consult the telephone directory's blue pages to locate the state division of natural resources. Ask about the Nature Conservancy. The program is available in every state and lists hundreds of endangered plant species. Call or write for information before your trip, or contact the local natural resources department after you arrive. You can also find information about threatened species through the Natural Heritage program. It has divisions in all the states and provides information from other countries.

Finding and identifying rare plants "takes quite a bit of skill. Because they are rare to begin with, even trained botanists often come up unlucky," says Dudgeon. Of course, when you find them, the thrill is that much greater.

Do some thorough research so you can accurately identify truly rare or threatened plants. Looking in a plant guidebook is not enough. A naturalist can guide you to reference materials, or you can find botany textbooks at public libraries as well as major university botany departments. You can also visit the Department of Natural Resources office, if one is nearby, and ask a staff member if you can consult their materials. In some cases, they will allow amateurs to use their libraries but not borrow the books.

If you are still convinced you have a genuine rare plant, report your findings to the nearest naturalist. When a naturalist or horticulturist learns about a rare plant, he or she will document it and get verification from a plant taxonomist (expert in plant identification). Based on the finding, affiliated universities will be informed, and a group of botanists on a decision-making committee will publish the results. It is serious business, and they appreciate the public's willingness to be their "eyes." They are often busy, overworked people, however, so you may need to take a plant specimen to the expert.

freebee

How to Prepare Plant Specimens

For a free handout on how to collect and preserve plant specimens, contact the Ohio State Herbarium at the Museum of Biological Diversity. Curator John Furlow has prepared information on preserving plants for future study, either by expert botanists or on your own, wherever you roam. Contact the herbarium at (614) 292-3296.

You can also beautify the countryside with more common wildflower seeds, flower bulbs, or ornamental shrubs. When visiting friends or family, you can offer to plant some perennial seeds or bulbs in their yard. Bring along some flower and vegetable seeds if you plan volunteer work or mission work on your trip. They are lightweight and easy to pack and can leave a caring reminder of your efforts. If you are visiting relatives, perhaps you can share cuttings from Grandma's favorite forsythias or pussy willows, creating a meaningful tie between family members at a distance.

FEED THE BIRDS—TUPPENCE A BAG?

Like Mary Poppins, you can provide food for the birds on your travels. It may cost a little more than tuppence, but you can find inexpensive sources of seeds and plants that provide a food source for the birds that live where you are traveling. A naturalist can tell you what bird-friendly plants and shrubs are needed if you would like to make planting them your "Johnny Appleseed" project.

Nature centers sometimes sell wildlife packets, inexpensive assortments of plants that provide food and shelter for local feathered friends. Ask about any seed packets or plants at state and county natural resources departments. It pays to do your research in advance. Many inexpensive wildlife packets must be ordered months in advance. In some cases, your order will be mailed to you. Otherwise, you will need to pick up your package in person at a wildlife center. Availability may be restricted to area residents.

Where can you bequeath your plants—on some unsuspecting person's property by dark of night? Nah. Once you get started, you will find lots of possibilities. Again, the Department of Natural Resources may have some ideas, especially for government property. If you are a member of a church or a service club, such as Kiwanis or the Lions Club, you can contact chapters along your route, either in advance or when you get there, for ideas on locations that would welcome your donation.

If you stay at a campground, talk to the staff to get permission and find a good spot. If you visit a host family, you can offer to plant in their yard or ask them if they know of an available spot elsewhere.

Along your route you can visit food pantries and donate seed packets for garden vegetables. (You can also offer to volunteer for a few hours while you are there—you will meet the nicest people.) Seeds are lightweight, and a single packet goes a long way. You can buy a case of seeds at a special price, especially if you coordinate your effort through a nonprofit food pantry or food cooperative back home. Find co-ops and food pantries by contacting the Family Matters volunteer line at (800) VOLUNTEER, or contact the United Way or any other local social service agency. You can also search on the Internet under "food cooperative" or "food pantry" along with the name of your destination state or province. (Families, please remember: You can be a Johnny Appleseed in your own neighborhood, city, and county as well as when you are traveling, helping the environment in bite-size, doable ways.)

Of course, not all the plants will live. Some will grow and prosper, though. Imagine John Chapman, years after lovingly planting a handful of apple seeds in a field, as he strolls through that same field, now an orchard sweet with the scent of apple blossoms. Perhaps your children, too, will return some day to see the fruit of their labors. But even if they don't, they will always carry the seeds of stewardship for our world that you have planted. You nurture those seeds when you spend precious time with your children and show them what you value.

"Backyard" Conservation Packet

Adopt a neglected spot and nurture it back to beauty with the help of a conservation informational packet. Even though it is intended for backyards, you can use the information as you travel. The packet includes nature fact sheets as well as a sign proclaiming that you are a "Backyard Conservationist…doing my part for our environment." Contact the USDA Wildlife Habitat Council at (888) LANDCARE.

ZOOLOGY WITHOUT CAGES

Studying wildlife, from tiny insects and microscopic pond life to the huge remains of dinosaurs from lost eras, teaches us about ecology and our place in it. Learning about the intricacies and habits of various kinds of wildlife gives children some insight into the mysteries of the food chain and life and death in the wild.

You have the opportunity to cultivate respect in handling even the smallest of creatures. Keep human handling to a minimum, however. You can put that tadpole in a specimen container for a minute or two to inspect it closely, then back it goes into its natural habitat.

HELPING HOMELESS BIRDS

If botany is not your bag, perhaps you can follow in John Chapman's footsteps as a bearer of birdhouses. You can bring homemade birdhouses—or bring the pieces, ready to assemble en route—and "plant" the birdhouses as you travel. As an alternative, you can pack a few tools, buy wood as you need it, and build birdhouses as you go. Offer to put on a birdhouse-building workshop at the campground in exchange for a free night's stay.

To find out which birds are likely to be homeless, contact the state

Department of Natural Resources, a nature center, or the nearest chapter of the Audubon Society. You can research how to build birdhouses to suit each species and how to select the right site and height.

Birdhouses make good host gifts for the folks you visit on your trip. Selling birdhouses while traveling could be a way to earn extra money at flea markets, since birdhouses are popular both for birds and for home decor. If you want to give that a try, start with a local flea market to test the water.

Instead of building birdhouses, your children might enjoy growing them to take on your trip. For example, large round gourds with short necks suit the purple martin just fine. Here are some instructions from *The Tightwad Gazette* by Amy Dacycsyn:

> Grow large, round gourds that have short necks. Let them dry on the vine until midwinter. Pick and cut a cut about two inches in diameter on one side. Let dry for another day, then sand the doorway's edges smooth. Clean the inside with a spoon. Drill holes in the bottom for drainage. Cut two more holes in the neck so that you can run a nylon cord through them.
>
> Putting a teaspoon of sulfur in each birdhouse will help keep mites away and will not bother the birds.... Martins are colonial nesters, so in early spring, hang at least two or more gourd birdhouses at least one foot apart on wooden crosspieces fastened to a pole that is at least 12 to 20 feet high. The pole should be at least 40 feet away from trees or buildings, but not more than 90 feet from your home...martins like to be near human beings. Martins live in all states east of the Mississippi River and in several western states.

Bird Treks on a Shoestring

Birding adventures are a little like golf. It is a passion that is difficult to explain to someone who is not infected by it. Some families plan their vacations around bird migrations. If your family is serious about birds, check out *The Traveling Birder: 20 Five-Star Birding Vacations* by Clive Goodwin and Roger Tory Peterson. You can include birding in your vacation and add little or no cost to your trip. Wherever you go—city, country, or woodlands—you can find free resources to learn about birds, their nests, their food, and their distinctive calls.

First, use your eyes. Read up on the birds you see. Study the migration patterns of the birds in your area. Any chance you will be "migrating" to the same place your local birds and animals have gone? Watch for them. What different birds do you see on your travels?

Shelley Zoellick travels full time with her husband and young son. Her husband's job requires extensive travel, and they have found living in an RV preferable to a life of motels and restaurants. Shelley has also found that her son's education has been enriched by real-life nature experiences. In her newsletter, *Families on the Road,* she wrote,

> Recently my son began noticing all the birds around our campsite, so I bought him a field guide and showed him how to use it. Now he bursts into the camper, excitedly describing some new bird he has seen while his little fingers fumble through the pages of color photos. Yesterday he described a black bird with red "shoulders," which I told him was probably a robin, although he insisted it wasn't. Imagine his delight when he identified the bird from the guide and showed it to me—a red-winged blackbird!

Another family purchased a coloring book with a different bird on each page. Each time the child identified a species, she colored that page. The child had a growing sense of accomplishment as page after page erupted into color.

Belonging to a bird-watching club gives you access to enthusiasts and experts. The best way to find birding activities is to check magazines such as *Birdwatcher's Digest, Wild Birds,* and *Birder's World.* Birding has become so popular that some magazines are available at the supermarket checkout, garden stores, or libraries.

Night Hiking—Spooky Fun for Free

Only 15 percent of the world's mammals, including humans, are active during the day. The rest are creatures of the night or twilight, predators and herbivores that come forth to try to fill their empty bellies.

You can join the "night owls" for free. You can also find many other animals in the dark. A night hike can be memorable, spooky, cold, exciting, fun—or all of these. In many areas, the hikes are scheduled year-round in all kinds of weather. This allows the public to see how native flora and fauna change across the seasons.

Without a guided hike, you will need to be your own guide, taking safety precautions so you do not get lost. Let a park ranger know your plans. Ask for tips. Some parks prohibit night hiking—often with good reason (in bear country, for example)—so be sure to follow the rules.

Night Vision

The gleam of a raccoon's eyes reflected by your flashlight is caused by special membranes that help nocturnal animals see better at night. Night-vision glasses, which use infrared or other technology to intensify low-level light, can do the same for you. Some of the lenses can adapt to your 35mm camera. Infrared glasses can cost as much as several thousand dollars. On the low end, night-vision scopes can be found for less than two hundred dollars. A used model might be in the doable range for a family of outdoors enthusiasts.

One advantage of a guided night hike is that the guide is likely to know where to find an owl's nest and a badger's burrow. She can give your family nuggets of information about nightlife in the forest. Check, though, to see how long or arduous the hike is so you can decide if your children are up to it (or if you are up to it, for that matter). If you are in doubt, find out if you would be able to easily find your own way back in the dark. Or will the hike be off the trails in unfamiliar territory?

Try to maintain silence during your night hike; talk only in whispers when necessary. Your guide (if you have one) will probably talk at certain times and then ask for periods of silence. You need not go far on your hike. If you visit the same spot you visited during the day, you'll find a different world there. Sit quietly and be aware of all your senses—sound, smell, sight, and touch.

Be a Scatologist

You can be an animal detective and find out what an animal ate for dinner. Scatology is the study of mammal droppings, also called pellets. They cost a pretty penny in science catalogs, but they are free if you find your own. Why would anyone want them? In his book *Camping and Backpacking with Children*, Steven Boga writes,

> Every young child I've ever hiked with has delighted in pointing out trail poop. By examining droppings for the basic characteristics of size, shape, and content, even laypeople can often identify the responsible animal. Deer, which drop little pellets 13 to 22 times a day, are easily distinguished from moose, but may be confused with rabbits.... One wildlife researcher, Olaus Murie, has a collection of 1,200 scat specimens, dried, varnished, labeled, and wrapped in plastic bags. Murie's collection is in constant demand for classes and seminars.

Young trail detectives, especially those of a certain age (say, five to ten) will delight in identifying animals by their scat and in becoming the expert-on-the-block back home. Scat collections make good microscope specimens and can fit in with your science and health studies. (Those studies need to include lessons on the importance of proper handling and storage of scat for safety and on proper hand washing.)

Animal Tracks

Make a cast of animal tracks. Buy plaster from the hardware store and follow the package directions. If the tracks are in dry earth, lightly moisten the soil with a spray bottle. If you want your cast to be flat on top, smooth it out with a rock or stick. When it's dry (after about fifteen minutes), brush off the dirt and add the cast to your nature collection. Paint it, if you like.

Your studies will have more impact when you see the whole picture by observing nature at work. Scatology fits in with studying the cycle of life.

Animal droppings fertilize the plants and feed earthworms and insects. They help create healthy topsoil that teems with life.

BE A SPIDER SNIFFER

Since small children are close to the ground, they are especially drawn to the smallest of creatures. That makes them the perfect people for spider sniffing!

Actually, it's not so much "sniffing" as it is knowing what to look for. Did you know that a spider's eyes reflect light like a cat's? It's true. But for people to see that reflection, the light source must be no more than four inches from your eyes. So Jim Foreman wears a headlamp (a light strapped to his head, like those used by miners) to look for spiders at night as a game to amaze children—and adults. He says it will also work if you hold a regular flashlight against the side of your head.

A Pound of Webs

"Some spider webs, if straightened out, would extend for three hundred miles. One pound of web would be long enough to circle the globe at its equator." —Steven Boga, *Camping and Backpacking with Children*

"The reflection is a bright blue light, much like a diamond," says Jim. "There are two kinds of spiders, those that spin webs and sleep at night and those that sleep during the day in holes and come out at night. The second kind (nocturnal) is what you are looking for." He uses this knowledge for a trick that is popular with his grandchildren.

"We go out to 'sniff' spiders," he says, pointing out that he dramatizes the event to the nth degree by sniffing like mad and looking like a cartoon hound dog with a weird headlamp. "We walk around for a bit and I announce that I can smell a spider. Then I start sniffing and searching for the elusive spider. With a few changes of direction, I end up with the beam of my light shining down on a spider on the ground."

Since no one but Jim can see the spider's eyes, the kids can easily believe the "sniffing" part. Let your kids in on the secret so they can try it—and amaze their friends! But be sure your children know all the good things spiders do and why we should never hurt them, especially the ones we find in nature. Books on creepy crawly insects fascinate most youngsters and are readily available, new or used.

Exotic Nature for Frugal Families
You can have a truly inexpensive vacation by exploring some of the lesser-known nature preserves. In some cases, you can see exotic wildlife in a natural environment—the closest you may ever come to a trip to Africa or Asia.

The Wilds, for example, is home to twenty-four species of African, Asian, and North American wildlife that roam freely, unencumbered by cages, pens, or bars. Located in southeast Ohio, The Wilds spans nearly ten thousand acres of reclaimed land that once was surface-mined for coal and is now dedicated to advancing the sustainability of wildlife through conservation. Most of the wildlife are endangered or threatened species involved in research and breeding programs.

Admission to The Wilds is roughly one-third the cost of most large amusement parks, and group discount rates are available. The Wilds features guided bus tours and sponsors annual events for biking, horseback riding, and hiking. One event, the EcoAdventure, features over fifty miles of mountain biking, trail running, kayaking, and hiking through remote areas along lakes, wetlands, woods, and meadows. When calling attractions like The Wilds, ask about current discounts.

Adopting a Wild Horse or Burro on Your Trip
If you want a horse or burro, and if you plan to travel out west, this might be the time to plan your vacation around "adopting" a wild horse or burro through the Bureau of Land Management (BLM). They match animals with good homes to control overpopulation and starvation. For information, call toll-free (866) 4MUSTANGS or visit *http://www.wildhorseandburro.blm.gov*. You must be preapproved by your state BLM office if you come from out-of-state to adopt a horse or burro.

Does a wild animal require more horse expertise than other horses? Not necessarily, according to Kristin Schander from the BLM call center in Nevada. "If you get a horse under two years old, it's pretty much like getting any other horse," she says. "They are just as easy to handle. If you don't have much horse experience, we encourage you to get a horse under two years of age." Wild horses do not stay wild if you work with them. One police officer from California adopted a number of wild horses through BLM, and he now uses them for mounted patrol. His teenage daughter is a rodeo queen for her high school and will be competing for state championship—all on formerly wild horses.

Not counting travel expenses, adopting a wild horse will probably be cheaper than buying a horse locally. Currently, BLM charges $125 for a horse at its holding centers (and possibly more where there is competitive bidding). That includes a physical exam, current immunization shots, tests to screen for disease, and health records. Less than half of the male animals are geldings. According to BLM, the cost of caring for and gentling an animal for one year averages between $500 and $1,000 or higher, depending on economic conditions and the locality. You must keep the horse for at least a year before you receive a title for the animal. If an animal is too much for you to handle, you can return it to BLM, but you cannot sell it or give it to someone else.

Many of the wild burros are smaller than standard domesticated burros, but some of the bigger wild burros make good riding animals for children and adults. Burros of all sizes make good pets. Many people get a burro as a friend for their horse. Horses are social creatures and enjoy having a buddy. (As one friend said, "Even my pets have pets.") People often adopt a burro to act as a guard dog to protect their cattle, sheep, or goats from foxes, coyotes, wild dogs, or other predators. Burros are good pack animals, and they can pull a small cart.

Burros tend to have fewer health problems, but they have different needs than horses. They eat less grain and more hay. If they get afraid, they will stop and just stand there, while a horse will take off for the hills. A burro needs a five-foot fence, versus a six-foot fence for full-grown horses. Both horses and burros need at least a four-hundred-square-foot corral. Until it is gentled, though, it is not a good idea to put a wild animal in a larger area, because you can't catch it to work with it!

If your family needs guidance in horsemanship, you can seek out a 4-H horse club in your area. (4-H is a youth program offered by local county extension offices.) Young people ages nine through nineteen can learn about the care, training, and showing of horses and other animals. Different clubs specialize in different animals and breeds. It may be helpful for your child to participate in a horse club prior to owning a horse.

We wondered if a family might make the trip and come back empty-handed because other people outbid them at auction, but Kristin Schander says that's not a problem: "A lot of people want the best, biggest, tallest, or so-called prettiest horse. However, there are many to choose from."

Whether or not you adopt an animal, your family might be interested in learning more about the Wild Horse and Burro Program. Tours for the holding centers are available by appointment on Monday through Friday.

BODIES OF WATER—
AND THE CRITTERS THAT LIVE IN THEM

Bodies of water exist almost everywhere, ranging from the world's great oceans to the oceanlike Great Lakes, with their powerful surf and water stretching across the horizon, to a park "lake" that may be smaller than some farm ponds. You may be far from the oceans and Great Lakes, but thanks to the Army Corps of Engineers, almost everybody in the United States lives within easy distance of a lake.

In your travels, you might want to try out some new water-based activities. Lake activities include fishing, bird watching, hiking, boating, swimming, tubing, waterskiing, snorkeling, and scuba-diving, for starters.

Every body of water is a unique ecological system supporting a unique range of plants, fish, birds, and animals. When you are traveling, your kids will want to explore every one of them. Even a swimming pool or a puddle after a rain may hold strange surprises. With a few safety precautions, you can indulge a child's natural curiosity about water and learn more about the plant and animal life that lives there.

You can learn a lot by simply comparing the different bodies of water encountered on a vacation. How is the water different? Why? How do differences in weather and geography result in different flora and fauna at each lake or pond or ocean? Park naturalists may be able to help you with the answers to these mysteries.

Maintain a healthy respect for water. It does not take much water, and very little time, to drown. Teach your family to adhere to a buddy system, where each buddy keeps an eye on the other. Life preservers are helpful for young children engaged in water's-edge activities, and they are essential for everyone who is boating. If conditions are doubtful, do not deceive yourself that strong swimming skills mean you can ignore safety precautions. Star swim team members from a local college died in our area while canoeing in turbulent waters after heavy rain. And this happened in a small, little-known river, not the Mississippi.

Underwater Spy Glass

If your children like creepy-crawly creatures, they will love to spy on slithery under-water life.

Take an empty milk carton or a large juice, soup, or coffee can and remove the top and bottom. Stand the carton or can in the middle of a sheet of clear plastic wrap. Stretch the plastic tightly across the bottom, holding it in place with a rubber band or, more permanently, duct tape. The scope works like a snorkeling mask when you gently lower the plastic-covered end into the water and your child looks down into it.

Water Trails

A boat can help you spy on water life that is inaccessible from shore. Many campgrounds rent boats—everything from rubber rafts and kayaks to foot-powered paddleboats—for a reasonable price. We are not talking luxury yachts or speedboats here. The object is just to get out on the lake or pond and study the flora and fauna.

Dave Levingston, a Midwestern father of three, enjoys family boating trips for nature study. The Levingston family carries three kayaks and a canoe on top of the family van when they travel. "Haul them around with you," he advises, "and wherever there is water, there is instant entertainment at no additional cost." Kayaks let the Levingstons move in quietly to get up close to wildlife. That has led to some awestruck moments during trips to a state park a few hours from their home.

"We put the kayaks in the water at a boat ramp that is too shallow for most boats," Dave says. "The area is chock-full of great blue herons and cranes. I've seen as many as twenty herons at a time. I've been able to slowly paddle up to within about ten feet of a great blue heron, then watch it take off with those huge long wings flapping, its wingtips making ripples in the water. It's a wonderful sight."

Dave and his wife, Emily, usually use a canoe, but each of the kids use their own personal kayak. "The theory was that we could all trade around," Dave says ruefully, "but the kids like the kayaks so much that they don't use the canoe at all. Kayaks are much easier to paddle, and they hold only one person, so the kids get to be their own captains."

Kayaks cost less than three hundred dollars new and require absolutely no maintenance, despite hard use. The investment has paid off for Dave by banishing the cost of canoe rentals and providing a no-cost family activity when traveling. The cost is minimal compared to most watercraft, and kayaks are so lightweight they are easy to travel with, compared to towing a boat trailer. If you want a used kayak or canoe, place a "wanted to buy" ad at the end of the summer.

Aside from being more fun for the children, kayaks have some practical advantages over a canoe. They are harder to tip over, because you sit down low in them. With their large cockpit openings, they are easy to get into and out of. Occasionally a kayak does turn over (especially with brothers and sisters in the vicinity). If that happens, you just fall out as you would in a canoe.

As far as security goes, Dave does not see traveling with over a thousand dollars' worth of water vessels tied on top of his van as a big problem.

You could lock them onto the top of the car if you are a nervous type, but they aren't easily removed and hauled away. Maybe if you left your vehicle parked in a high crime area, it would be a problem. For the most part, we don't worry about it. We tie them on with rope and lots of knots. It isn't a simple task to take them off.

Whether you rent a boat or are considering purchasing one, inquire about the fees for licensing. Believe it or not, depending on where you live, even a rubber raft may require a license.

THE SKY'S THE LIMIT: LEARNING FROM LOOKING UP

In Psalm 19:1, King David sang, "The heavens declare the glory of God; the skies proclaim the work of his hands." Wonders await all of us who can find the time to look up.

The night sky is free and has fascinated philosophers and scientists for millennia. Seeing the heavens isn't as easy as it used to be, though. Our modern view is diminished, in part, because city lights create a haze. If you travel away from the light pollution, as well as air pollution, you will be in for a spectacular treat!

A full moon is good for seeing the moon itself, but a dark night is better for seeing the rest of the sky.

You do not need a telescope or binoculars, both relatively modern inventions, to enjoy the night sky. If you want a magnified view, however, start with ordinary binoculars. For beginners, it is easier to make sense out of what you are seeing with binoculars than a telescope. As you travel, binoculars also will be useful for looking around during the daytime. If you have a camera with a zoom lens, you can use it like a telescope at night to help you see more details in the stars and the moon.

The next step up is a telescope, and you can make, buy, or borrow one. There are inexpensive telescopes, but they are frustrating to use. What good is magnification if it makes everything look like fuzz? A new telescope with reasonably good optics (lens and mirrors) starts at several hundred dollars. If you belong to an organization that might be willing to buy a telescope to loan to its members, why not suggest it? Perhaps you can share ownership with your extended family or with other families in your church or neighborhood. A homeschooler support group might buy a telescope and other educational equipment to loan to members.

Your family might enjoy making a project out of building a telescope using commercially made optics. If so, get a copy of *Build Your Own*

Telescope by Richard Berry. *Astromart.com* sells used telescopes and lists "stargazers parties" and events, astronomy clubs, and observatories.

You can tell a poor-quality telescope by its advertising—it boasts about high magnification. The quality of a telescope or binoculars depends on the quality of the lens and the size of its aperture (opening) rather than on the number of times an object is magnified. For tips on selecting a good telescope or binoculars for astronomy, visit *SkyandTelescope.com* or *Telescope.com*.

"Basically, go as large-diameter as you can (a) afford and (b) transport," recommends David Chandler, author of two books for beginners, *Sky Atlas for Small Telescopes and Binoculars* and *Exploring the Night Sky with Binoculars,* which features nearly two hundred objects that can be seen with an inexpensive telescope or binoculars. (Many of the star atlases are designed with much more expensive equipment in mind.)

Telescopes are either refractors or reflectors. Refractors are telescopes that use lenses—like looking through a pair of binoculars. Reflectors use a concave mirror combined with what is essentially a microscope lens (an eyepiece) to create the enlarged image. David Chandler suggests starting with a Dobsonian-style scope, a simple-to-use type of reflector telescope.

Astronomers tend to have strong differing opinions on such matters. Astronomer Michael Mickelson suggests a small-aperture (four to six inches) refractor for under a thousand dollars, such as those made by Mead or Celestron, two reputable makers of astronomy equipment. According to Mickleson, a professor of physics and astronomy at Denison University in Granville, Ohio,

> There are now very simple-to-use motor-driven, computer-controlled telescopes for well under a thousand dollars. Once aligned on a known star, you can tell the computer what you wish to look at and the telescope will be directed to it. You would be amazed!

Changing Constellations

As the earth rotates and orbits the sun, we actually are looking out into space in different directions. Therefore, the whole sky appears to rotate, changing the way constellations look at different times and from different positions on earth. To follow the stars, start with *Peterson's Field Guide of Astronomy*, which comes with monthly star charts.

We have an inexpensive device (under ten dollars) called The Night Sky, invented by David Chandler. The device, a planisphere, is a rotating star finder that creates less distortion of the constellations than most star maps or planispheres. It has a dial with a star map on each side sandwiched between two plastic masks. It works by rotating the dial to set it for the day and time to help you identify constellations and stars. You use the map on the front when facing north and the map on the back when facing south. Chandler also makes an inexpensive red flashlight called The Night Reader for poring over star charts in the dark without affecting your night vision. You can make your own by covering a penlight with red cellophane.

The Deep Sky: An Introduction by Philip S. Harrington is for anyone with a telescope or a pair of binoculars, but who does not know where to start. It introduces double, multiple, and variable stars, nebulae, and galaxies, with sky charts and photographs, so you will know what to look for.

SEARCHING THE NIGHT SKY

Before or during your trip, get to know your way around the universe. With or without a telescope, here are some tips for finding your way:

- The mountains and craters on the moon are more tangible and concrete than the more subtle variations of the stars. For a phase-by-phase, night-by-night guide, read *Exploring the Moon Through Binoculars and Small Telescopes* by Ernest H. Cherrington Jr.
- Look over back issues of *Sky and Telescope* at the library. You can peruse the table of contents for back issues at *Sky and Telescope's* Web site. The magazine offers a discount to astronomy club members when five or more of the members subscribe. If you have a child with a passion for astronomy, consider joining or starting an astronomy club.
- Check tourist guides, such as the AAA guides, to see if you'll be passing near a science museum with a planetarium or astronomy observatory. The difference? A planetarium mimics the night sky by projecting tiny lights on a domed ceiling in a darkened room. An observatory is the real thing, complete with a huge telescope.

- Hasbro offers an astronomy edition of their popular Monopoly board game. Instead of landing on Park Place and building houses and hotels, you can learn about comets, planets, star clusters, nebulae, and galaxies as you move around the game board and build observatories.

- Although anyone can find craters on the moon, finding deep-sky objects takes practice and experience. Start by learning constellations, then use them to locate other objects. To make the most of low-pollution skies when you travel, first spend time in your backyard (or at your apartment window) learning the ropes.

- Some observatories sponsor events that are free for the public. The astronomers who run the observatory at a local university are virtually always "on duty" on a clear night, and they welcome visitors. Call to see if you can stop by on a cloudless night at an observatory near you. You'll find devoted night-sky enthusiasts who enjoy sharing their feelings of wonder and awe.

- Make up your own constellation stories, which are simply the result of seeing a pattern in the stars and making up a story about it. Steve and Ruth Bennett, in their book 365 *Outdoor Activities You Can Do with Your Child,* suggest inventing your own constellations, such as the "Meatball Minor" or "King Kong's Tricycle."

- Get a list of astronomy organizations by country and state or by province at the ABCentral Web site. Click on "societies," then on "astronomy." The site lists twenty-five clubs in Canada as well as over two hundred in the United States, and hundreds more worldwide.

- Watch for a satellite. Select one of interest and log on to the online Skywatch program from NASA that will report the next time you will be able to see it. You will have to specify what city you want to see it from (or manually add your longitude and latitude if that city is not listed) and the time zone you are in. If you cannot see it from that location, the program will tell you. It will provide a display of the sky to show stars, constellations, sun, moon, and visible planets, and it will show the track the satellite will take across the sky as observed at your location. The space shuttle and other spacecraft can be seen with the unaided eye as they pass overhead if you know when and where to look.

Find Your Way at Night Without a Compass

Here are some simple tips from the Boy Scouts of America on finding your way at night. Your family might enjoy trying them out, which could be good "just-in-case" training for an emergency.

- Use shadows from the moon. Since the moon comes up in the east and goes down in the west—just like the sun—you can use the moon to find directions. The shadow-stick method will work with the moon on nights when it is bright enough to create shadows. Push a short straight stick into the ground. Angle it toward the moon so that the stick makes no shadow. Wait until it casts a shadow at least six inches long. The shadow will be pointing east from the stick. A line at right angles across the shadow will be north-south.

- Find the North Star. Because it is located directly over the earth's North Pole, the North Star appears to be stationary in the sky. For night travel you need only look to it from time to time and adjust your route accordingly.

—Boy Scouts of America, *http://www.scouting.org*

LEARNING FROM THE DAYTIME SKY

Of course, you can look up at the sky during the day, too. Travel provides a golden opportunity to study the clouds—especially if you are flying! Learning about weather is science in a practical setting.

Weather may affect your route and your choice of destinations and activities. Predicting it is both an art and a science—science as we learn more of nature's secrets, and art because, although there are always reasons for the weather, we do not always know what they are. As logic would have it, there is a Web site called *www.weather.com,* affiliated with The Weather Channel, which has worldwide weather, searchable by city, state, and country. It links to a "one-stop weather education site" called Weatherworks. Weatherworks offers weather-related curriculum, designed for classrooms but open to all. Weatherworks provides sample science activities, weather questions, satellite images of storms, and an online store with cloud cards, posters, and weather books.

Would you like another frugal way to explore the sky, have fun, and learn about the wind and the atmosphere? Go fly a kite. By the way, contrary to popular belief, a gusty March day is difficult kite-flying weather. Kite-flying experts prefer a clear day with a gentle breeze. Want to build your own kites? Check the library for books and encyclopedia articles. There you can learn more about the aerodynamics that make kites fly. Check the children's department, since, for some silly reason, most people think of kids and kites as going together. (Actually, many adults are serious kite fliers.)

Kite flying brings people together in a common experience that transcends cultural and even language differences. Avid kite flyers—and even adults and children with a passing interest—may enjoy a kite event. There are usually spectacular stunt kites to watch at these events.

The One Sky One World International Kite Festival holds kite festivals around the world and has an online store with inexpensive kites. You can get ten 14-by-21-inch paper-bag kites for less than ten dollars, including shipping and a couple of kite string lines. Ten plastic kites with string are less than forty dollars. The organization promotes "protection of the planet, peace, friendship, and understanding between all people."

Nature is full of surprises, and scientists call surprises "discoveries." Keep in mind that you do not necessarily have to teach for your children to learn. Often the best way to facilitate your children's learning is to put your child in the right location and then sit on your hands and bite your tongue. Your trip can ignite a fire of interest in your children. When they begin to pursue knowledge on their own, allow them to make discoveries and to ferret out the connections by themselves.

Like bringing a horse to water, you can give your children travel experiences, but you cannot make them learn. Through your travels, you have brought your children to "water." Now have a great time together and let them drink.

Chapter Five

Free and Frugal
Field Trips and Day Trips

Most of us remember field trips from school. What is your recollection? Exciting? Boring? Standing in line? Squabbling in line? A family field trip need not be boring, and if it is, you can leave whenever you want. You can make your trip about something your family is interested in.

Although we are focusing on day trips in this chapter, there is not one idea we suggest that you could not use when traveling long distances. The trick is to keep your eyes open for unique and inspiring experiences, wherever you are. Make the world your university without walls.

Field Trip News

For a free sample copy of *The Frugal Family Network* newsletter, send a self-addressed, stamped envelope to: Frugal Family Network, P.O. Box 92731, Austin, TX 78709. Editor Angie Zalewski, who travels with her husband and two sons, ages six and eight, also offers a free weekly e-mailer, "Quickie Frugal Tip," at her Web site, *www.frugalfamilynetwork.com.*

WHERE TO FIND FRUGAL FIELD TRIPS

You know how you may not notice a particular model of automobile until you buy one? Suddenly, you'll see that same model at every corner. It's the same way with field trips. They are there all along, but you will not see them unless you are looking for them. Families are often surprised to find out about the scope of field trip possibilities, most of them inexpensive or free, within an hour from home.

Judith saw more of the local sights in the two weeks before she moved out of New York City than she had in the entire six years she lived there as a young adult. Suddenly she valued what had been there all along, the way a tourist would. Perhaps we take our historical buildings and local customs for granted because they are easily accessible. We do not have to expend a lot of time or money to get to them, so it's easy to overlook their value.

It is amazing how little most people know about their hometowns. When Melissa and her husband lived in Boston, they were frequently astounded that their friends and associates had never visited local historical landmarks such as the Old North Church or Plymouth Rock. (The rock, by the way, was a major disappointment. They had envisioned something much bigger. If they had not seen it, however, they would continue to have an erroneous impression of it.)

Learning about local history can help children establish a sense of community as well as bring history up close and personal. Melissa says,

We recently moved from our country home to a metropolitan area. As you can imagine, it has been a struggle for the children to get used to a whole new way of life. In an effort to put down roots, we read our local city guide and discovered a contest sponsored by the community arts council. My daughter drew a picture for the contest. Believe it or not, we were told hers was the only entry from a child. The focus of the contest was a defunct airfield, Norton Field. How remarkable to discover that years ago, where a nearby development of small homes now stands, the Great Ohio Air War (a mock air battle) helped develop the first air-to-land communications! We learned a lot about World War I, the history of air warfare, and famous early pilots.

How can you find out about inexpensive field trips in your area? Here are some low-cost sources to scan:

- The bulletin board at your public library. Most libraries also have counter space for fliers from nonprofit groups, and some libraries have newsletters about author visits, used-book sales, speakers, storytellers, and other events.
- Your local newspaper and community weeklies. Check the community calendar section. Many papers have a weekly entertainment section that lists art shows, live theater and music performances, speakers and other events at local colleges, and hobby shows and meetings.
- City and regional magazines, usually available at your library. If there is a rural electric cooperative in your area, check the event listings in its magazine, which lists unusual events you might not see elsewhere—a workshop on trimming pine trees, for example, or a solar power exposition. Cooperative members get the publication free, and others may be able to view it at the library.
- Newsletters from special interest groups, such as your local or state historical society, computer club, ham radio operator's club, Audubon Society, and so forth.
- College bulletin boards and publications. Many of the events are free and may include nationally known speakers, dancers, musicians (classical and otherwise), and top people in fields such as archaeology, marine biology, and many others. Some colleges mail free event notices to anyone who asks.
- Publications and the Web sites for your local chamber of commerce, tourist center, or city government. If you peruse the literature rack for tourists, the events and attractions in your hometown may surprise you.
- Newsletters from organizations such as Parks and Recreation departments, arboretums, the YWCA and YMCA, and state parks within an easy drive.
- The same sources just listed, only in nearby towns and the nearest metro area.

Be prepared to find some peculiar attractions. For example, Sandra Gurver, author of *The Cockroach Hall of Fame—And 101 Other Off-the-Wall*

Museums, has seen some doozies that might make unique family memories. After all, if you do not know much about cockroaches, it would be educational, right? As an added benefit, the curator at a small and unusual museum will often have more time to spend with you.

Beyond Events

Do not feel limited to "events." Most businesses—from your local one-hour photo lab to a doughnut shop—are willing to show an interested family around if you come in when they are not busy or make arrangements in advance. Don't be embarrassed—just ask. Most people are flattered and pleased to have someone interested in their work. You do not have to go out of your way. If you get in the habit of being curious, your daily errands will provide plenty of possibilities. Some options include:

- the post office
- a grocery store, bakery, or butcher shop
- flower shops or garden centers
- factories
- your local newspaper or community weekly
- electronic media, such as a cable company or television and radio stations
- print shops
- the courthouse, including courtrooms with trials in session (You can call ahead of time to find out what kinds of trials are upcoming.)
- state or local government, such as council meetings or zoning commission—where you can learn how local concerns can lead to a new law or regulation
- pet stores
- farm stores
- veterinarian (older students can volunteer)
- utility companies (water treatment plants, electric company)

Learning About the Country

Want to get out of the city? Visit a local farm during the fall harvest season, says Teri Brown, who writes "The Field Trip Lady" column for *The Link,* a free bimonthly newspaper for homeschool families. She has found that many small farms augment their incomes by attracting visitors.

Even if you live in the city, it would only take you an hour or so to find your way to the best farm-fresh produce you have ever tasted. Every October we visit four or five farms to get fresh apples, apple cider, and gourds and Indian corn for fall decorations. Each farm is unique. We have found farms with hay bale mazes, farms with country crafts for sale, with petting zoos, dried flowers, and even one with a mini-train to ride.

Call your county extension office to see if they have a listing of farms in your area that sell fresh produce, and keep an eye on your local paper for local happenings.

Let Information Soak In

"Some days you must learn a great deal. But you should also have days when you allow what is already in you to swell up and touch everything. If you never let that happen, then you just accumulate facts, and they begin to rattle around inside of you."
—E. Konigsburg, author

Charleen Skalski has created a family tradition of visiting apple orchards every fall with her five-year-old son and some out-of-state relatives. "My cousin and her family, who live in Indiana, visit every year around Halloween," says Charleen. "We visit the apple orchards and other farms in the area with the children and have a great time. By the end of the day, our traditional apple pie is baked and demolished—yum!"

Organic farmers tend to be passionate about what they do, as are herbalists. "Most people who run herb shops and farms love their profession," says Teri, "and are willing to share their knowledge with those who have a few curious questions." Ask herb farmers if they offer a newsletter or classes.

Visiting Other Neighborhoods

If your family lives in the suburbs or the country, a visit to a nearby city can be educational. You may want to visit locations that illustrate the daily activities in business and government, such as offices, courtrooms, subways, bus stations, contractor supply stores, or factories.

Even if you have lived in the city all your life, your children's knowledge may be limited to a small area. Try visiting ethnic areas, low-income areas, high-income areas—any area that's different from where you live. It is one way to learn that people are people no matter where you go. Melissa says,

> We have a home church, which we love and support. However, we feel it is important to visit our brothers and sisters in Christ. Our goal is to visit a different fellowship, on average, once a month. We've worshiped and fellowshiped with believers from dozens of denominations, cultures, and from all sides of town as well as visiting with believers when we have traveled out-of-state.
>
> One thing that we have found: We have Christ in common, and that is more important than skin color, style of music, or even language barriers. We've found out that people on "the other side of town" can be just as friendly (or friendlier!) and can enrich our lives with their insights into what's really important in life—our relationship with God and with our family.

Conferences and Conventions

Going to a conference on a topic your family loves immediately immerses you in a community of people with a shared interest. A conference serves as a temporary city that appears and reappears at intervals, like Brigadoon, complete with a village market—in this case, a vendor area with specialized products you might not find elsewhere. At some conferences, you can learn more in a specialized field in one weekend, and make more personal contacts related to your interest, than you normally would the rest of the year put together. Where else but at a clown or puppetry event can you learn to make a balloon animal or make a rabbit puppet look animated?

Conferences that welcome families offer a day or weekend jam-packed with activities, festivities, performances, and meals. If you attend a dynamic conference, your family will be talking about it for months. Judith has attended numerous conferences, either because she was interested in the topic, or because she was assisting with her husband's photography business. Their daughter, Nancy, has had the opportunity to meet people who are experts in their own niche, such as Frosty Little, a former Ringling Brothers clown. If you attend the same conference every year, you will find that arriving is like visiting your hometown—a warm welcome from friends you made in past years.

There is a convention for virtually everything. Certain conferences are family-friendly and provide a good time for all at a reasonable cost. Arrive at a La Leche League conference or a clown conference, and you will see families having a great time learning together. An annual event for adoptive families gave Nancy a chance to be "the norm" once a year and see her friends from past years.

Judith and Nancy attended their first storytelling conference together when Nancy was fourteen. Being on a tight budget, they took advantage of the option to roll out their sleeping bags on the floor of a sponsoring church, sharing their quarters with six other frugal participants. The conference pretty much takes over the tiny village of Chesterton, Ohio, one weekend a year.

"It was like a slumber party," remembers Judith.

In the morning, Nancy and I went to some of the same workshops, and then we split up and went to different ones. She hooked up with some of our new "slumber party" friends, who took her under their wings. She even got out there and performed a humorous, off-the-cuff story at a story-swap. Our getaway weekend made a big impact on our relationship, which was suffering under the strain of adolescence. The cost was well under a hundred dollars, including meals cooked by the church groups in town.

You will have to use some judgment when deciding whether to bring your children to a conference intended for adults. Teens can nearly always fit in. Having younger, school-age children with you at an event where there are few children can actually be an advantage over attending an event with a lot of children.

At a puppetry conference, for example, there are always a few children, although the programs are not designed with children in mind. The children tend to get a lot of attention from the adults, and their questions and concerns are taken seriously. The children tend to integrate into the activities rather than congregate in a pack with other children. These conferences are a mix of teaching and entertainment, as the keynote speakers and workshop presenters usually perform at the conferences.

Some of the conferences are quite specialized—the Fellowship of Christian Magicians, for example, shows people of all ages how to use magic to present the gospel. Similar ministry organizations offer conferences for clowns and puppeteers.

Music is another arena for finding an enthusiastic, welcoming community. A bluegrass event will have everybody jamming, and your children can meet and get to know the top people in the field. If bluegrass is not your style, there are scores of other musical specialties to choose from, ranging from Irish folk music to Suzuki violin.

How about an invention convention or a horseshoe tournament? A local, state, national, or international competition may provide an exciting, economical vacation destination. Lesser-known sports have followers every bit as avid as football fans, but the prices are lower, the peer pressure is less, and the high-profile participants are easier to meet and talk with.

GROUP FIELD TRIPS

Now that you know where to find your field trips, you'll need to find ways to make them affordable. When you're a tourist in your own neck of the woods, you won't have to spend extra money for lodging.

One way to save money is to harness the power of group discounts. Many large employers offer employees travel discounts. If your employer doesn't, or if you are self-employed, you may still be able to get a discount. Ask friends and family if they are allowed to obtain discount tickets for you to any educational event or location. If you are a military or government employee family, you may also be eligible for various travel discounts. Check with your travel office on base for details.

If you have participated in field trips with a club or organization, chances are you have benefited from the initiative of a volunteer. Rock clubs, for example, may arrange permission to go hunting at a quarry or private farm at little or no cost.

If you do not belong to an organization that sponsors field trips, Teri Brown suggests forming a field trip group. All it takes is three or four families to get started. "Be careful, though," Teri warns. "On one of these excursions we ended up with a puppy who is still with us today!"

You can reap other benefits from setting up a group field trip yourself: You can make it exactly the kind of trip you envision. If you do that, chances are other people will enjoy it too. Frustrated because working moms and dads never get to go on these trips? Why not set up an evening or weekend trip so other working parents can come?

For ideas, look at your family's interests. Does the moon fascinate your children? Call the astronomy professor at a local college and inquire about field trip possibilities. That astronomy professor may be willing to give a talk, show slides, and offer the use of a telescope for a group, even a small one. The professor, however, might not take time to do this for just one family.

Look at your own interests. What have you always wanted to learn about? This is your chance to pursue it and to keep the cost low by taking advantage of free events or group discounts.

For many organizations, setting up a field trip is as simple as lining up a date, announcing it at a meeting, and asking the newsletter editor to put it on the schedule. Then you wait to see if anyone registers. If your destination places a minimum or a maximum on the number of participants, registration becomes critical and a deadline may be needed. Do not be discouraged if you do not get a response from other families. That happens sometimes. You never know what will strike people's fancy at a time when they can be there at a price they can afford. Keep in mind that most people wait to register until the deadline approaches.

Want to open up registrations to the public? Send your local newspaper a news release a month or so ahead of time. Your children can learn how to write a news release from library books on publicity, and your local newspaper may be willing to provide you with guidelines. Clip out articles about other events from the newspaper and use them as a template for your own article—another good project for a child or teen. There is nothing quite like being published to encourage a young (or old!) writer.

You can also suggest a field trip day for sites that interest you and let the staff at your destination do the work. A park, historical society, or fire station might be open to suggestions for an event or open house, and they could publicize it through a member newsletter and news releases.

Chris O'Connor, a homeschool support group leader and speaker, designed a field trip information sheet for group members to submit when they set up a field trip. You can use her categories as a guideline for gathering information. Include the following:

- date and day of the week
- time and length of the program
- title of the program
- host organization
- brief description of the activity
- address and directions
- meeting point (in the lobby, for example)
- cost
- suggested age range, if any
- minimum and maximum attendance
- contact person and telephone number for registration
- registration deadline

SAVING MONEY WITH MEMBERSHIPS

Joining your local museum, science center, or zoo may be economical if you use the membership often enough. Conversely, you *will* visit more frequently if you have a membership. Judith's family joined the Center of Science and Industry (COSI) and found that they no longer spend an exhausting full day there just to get their money's worth. Instead, they stop for a few hours now and then, whenever they have a chance.

One large adoptive family we know found they saved money by buying a membership, even though they only used it once. At one zoo, the attendant instructed the family to pay the regular admission fee, then buy a membership inside the zoo and show their receipt to get the admission fee deducted from the total. The cost of admission added up to more than the cost of a family membership, so they got a refund! Instead of a one-day pass, they got a full-year membership.

A membership at your destination might make sense so that you can go back as often as you like during your vacation, perhaps for a few hours a day. For example, if you visit San Diego, you might consider a membership to the world-famous San Diego Zoo. The zoo offers a dual membership to the San Diego Wild Animal Park as well as zoo bus passes and a magazine to enjoy the rest of the year as a reminder of your vacation.

Consider alternating your memberships—one year a science center, another year a historical society, another year an arboretum or a zoo. Memberships are easy to buy and mail as gifts—something to remember when family members ask about what your family would like to receive for Christmas, birthdays, and other gift-giving occasions.

YOUR ADMISSION IS FREE: RECIPROCAL MEMBERSHIPS

When traveling, check your memberships to see if any of them offer reciprocal admission to other sites in an area to which you will be traveling. Reciprocal memberships, offered by many museums, science centers, zoos, aquariums, and historical societies, can save a family hundreds of dollars a year and offer experiences you might otherwise bypass due to the cost. Melissa says,

> Several times a year our family visits a local conservatory that sponsors events such as an annual tropical butterfly exhibit and a frog exhibit in cooperation with the local zoo. Family membership costs less than just two visits, yet it also includes free admission to arboreta, botanical gardens, and conservatories all over the United States, and a few in Canada. It also includes some gift shop discounts.

The Morgan family also bought a membership in a natural history museum about an hour's drive away. It was less expensive than other, more local memberships, and it allowed the family to attend attractions in their hometown for free, such as the zoo and a science museum. The program is affiliated with both the American Zoo and Aquarium Association and the

Association of Science and Technology Centers, so the family membership gave them free admission to a variety of museums and zoos in other states as well.

For reciprocal zoos, visit the American Zoo and Aquarium Association (AZA) at *http://www.aza.org,* which offers a search engine by state to locate a zoo or aquarium in the states you will visit. For example, with a seventy-dollar family membership to the St. Louis Zoo Friends, aside from perks such as free train rides and parking, you gain free admission to over 120 other zoos, aquariums, and wildlife parks in the United States and Canada. Member zoos that are free to begin with, offer an alternative—usually a discount in the gift shop or free parking.

Another source of reciprocal member benefits (they call it a Passport Program) is the Association of Science-Technology Centers (ASTC), whose members include more than 550 science centers, science museums, and related organizations in forty-three countries—for example, the U.S. Space and Rocket Center in Huntsville, Alabama, and the Flandrau Science Center and Planetarium in Tucson, Arizona.

A few caveats:

- Participating ASTC museums within ninety miles of each other are not required to offer free admission to each other's members. Contact the museums located within ninety miles of your museum to check on any restrictions.
- A "family membership" may mean different things to different museums. Large families should ask for details before signing up.
- Reciprocal agreements can be changed or severed at any time. In other words, be aware that your free admission to your favorite zoo could suddenly be canceled. It happened to us.

PERKS FOR VOLUNTEERS

By volunteering to help for a few hours at events or attractions you would like to visit, you may receive free admission. Most attractions offering educational programs depend on volunteers, and they reward their volunteers with free admissions or memberships, gift shop discounts, free parking, and other perks. If your visit coincides with a special event, your family might enjoy volunteering. Some likely prospects include:

- Community theater groups sometimes offer free seats to volunteer ushers. They also need help with box office, lighting, the refreshment booth, and cleaning.
- Conferences of all kinds need people to work behind the scenes. Ask if free or reduced admission is available for volunteers.
- Nonprofit festivals, living-history events, international festivals, Renaissance fairs, Revolutionary War and Civil War reenactments, and many others may offer free admission to volunteers.

Volunteering has educational benefits as well. Your family learns more about the event as a whole and what goes into putting it on. You learn people skills, and you learn the answers to a lot of visitor questions. Children and teens who feel like a part of the effort may take more interest in the event than if they were merely attending it as a visitor. Those who put in an honest effort often receive heartfelt thanks from the organizers. You may also get to know speakers and experts personally.

Special Benefits for Homeschool Families

Homeschool families sometimes qualify for special educators' discounts or benefits at a variety of noteworthy attractions. These may include:

- An educator discount (sometimes called a teacher discount) at many museums and attractions. The discount also usually applies to gift shops and bookstores.
- Most major educational attractions host a Homeschool Day. You can save money on educational travel if you plan your vacation destinations to visit an event or attraction at the right time.
- Homeschool support groups frequently host field trips that offer discounted group rates to educational sites.

Occasionally a group may set up a more ambitious travel project, sometimes arranged through a travel agency. For example, World Strides (formerly American Student Travel) has a homeschooling division that offers guided tours for students and their parents to educational destinations, such as

Washington, D.C., and New York City. Some travel agencies have tour host programs: You pick the destination and line up the people, the agency makes all the travel arrangements, and you get either a commission or free travel.

Some homeschool groups have a field-trip coordinator to plan and schedule group trips. Be sure to take your turn at arranging a field trip. If each person in the group sets up a field trip just once a year, the group can choose from a rich variety of activities. By banding together, you may receive group benefits and discounts for educational activities, just like a school. Often a parent receives free or reduced admission when they accompany their child, just as a classroom teacher would.

You might need some documentation to show that you qualify for a homeschooler rate. In Ohio, for example, the school superintendent sends a letter acknowledging the family's homeschool status; a copy of that letter can be shown as proof. In other states you may receive a letter of approval or proof of enrollment in an umbrella school that covers homeschoolers. Every now and then you may be the first person to ask if the policy on educators' discounts includes homeschool parents. Don't be shy. It costs nothing to ask.

Traveling at Home

Yuri Padowinikoff lives in British Columbia, Canada, in a custom-built 1950 Ford "house-bus" and sponsors an online discussion list on building and living in homemade "house trucks." Yuri remarked, "Putting on my sage advice hat, I must say that the best traveling experience is this: Never stop traveling once you get home. The viewpoint of a stranger in a strange land shows you more of your environment than you might otherwise notice. There's still so much to learn about our own backyards; all that is required is an adventuresome mind and eye."

Homeschoolers—and parents thinking about homeschooling—may travel to homeschool conventions to attend workshops and enjoy fellowship with like-minded families. While most of the conventions are for parents only, a few offer workshops for children and teens as well as parents, and those conventions may be worth traveling some extra miles for. Aside from workshops, the vendors' area gives parents a chance to do some comparison shopping and to see a wide range of materials before deciding what to buy. Many of the vendors offer "show specials" to encourage families to buy on the spot. You can save on shipping costs for cash-and-carry purchases. Some homeschool organizations match up out-of-towners with local families willing to host them during the convention, so the out-of-towners can avoid hotel bills.

MR. FIELD TRIP
Melissa's children know that Dad is always up for a field trip.

> My husband, Hugh, is "Mr. Field Trip" at our house. I'm more of a homebody. Hugh's been dragging me on educational field trips since before we had children—the kids have made it that much more fun for him. I may protest a bit when I'm taken out of my sanctuary and thrust into primitive camping, outdoor drama, or concerts. He loves to find something new, though, and he views it with so much joy, it's contagious! I feel like we've just barely dipped into the contents of the barrel for available field trips in our area.

Chapter Six

"Are We There Yet?"

Traveling frugally sometimes means being cooped up for long distances in cramped, uncomfortable conditions. That can be a strain for even the most mannerly, sweet-tempered family members, let alone hot, tired, and cranky ones. So why not use that time wisely and keep your captive audience busy?

Inexpensive and free educational activities can accomplish more than providing a way to pass the time, though. Learning can take place just as easily in the car as in a classroom. In a classroom, you can talk about land and rock formations and various terrains. From a car, you can actually observe them. Turning waiting time into learning opportunities can improve behavior, concentration, and attitude—and that translates into more learning and more fun.

Even if they are equipped with electronic gadgetry, every family has days when we find ourselves out of batteries—literally and figuratively. Our children need to know how to cope with such times. Take advantage of downtime to get to know your children better, develop a closer relationship, and show them how to make the best of any situation.

THE RULES OF THE ROAD

To bring home treasured memories instead of a best-forgotten nightmare, consider adopting these Rules of the ROAD:

R—Respect your child's needs

O—Offer clear consequences

A—Avoid a frenetic pace

D—"Do," don't just "see"

Respect your children's needs and be realistic in what you expect from them. Do not expect them to be quiet for extended periods of time. Instead, go prepared with activities for the trip.

Offer clear consequences at the onset of misbehavior. Have small consequences for minor misbehavior. Some of the techniques you use at home may be difficult to administer in a car or a plane. To be effective, the consequence should be easy for you to carry out—so easy that you will do so at the very first sign of misbehavior, instead of threatening, oh, say, three, four, or ten times.

For example: Stanley is teasing his brother. You call for a consequence immediately. The child puts his head down and counts to three (for a very young child) or (for an older child) writes or recites a poem or verse that illustrates the principle involved, counts by fives to fifty, backward by twos, or whatever, at his age, requires a little concentration but takes only ten to thirty seconds to do. Then he tells you what the rule is, such as, "No hassling other people." You say, "That's right!"

Before instituting any consequences, such as taking away a toy for a while, Melissa and Hugh first try reason.

> Even when the kids were small, this often worked. We would ask, "Would you like someone to do that to you?" or "What would Jesus do?" This makes kids think about the Golden Rule and how they would like to be treated. If all else fails, we use an old ploy called The Quiet Game. The first one to make a sound of any kind loses the game. Believe it or not, this works!

For a trip to Washington, D.C., with two ten-year-old boys, Judith and her husband brought a roll of nickels (two dollars' worth) for each boy. There was a five-cent fine for misbehavior. Each boy could use the money that was left as spending money when they arrived in Washington. Two dollars goes pretty far on postcards, even in Washington. Depending on the child's age and motivation, you might want a roll of dimes or quarters instead.

Avoid a frenetic pace. This comes under the "less is more" principle. Leave enough leisure time so you can go for a walk, take a nap, answer questions, and pull over if you come across a wonderful site to see on the way.

"Do," don't just "see." Appeal to all the senses. Your children will absorb

more learning and enjoy it more if they can talk, not just listen, and touch, not just look. People, especially children, learn best when in motion. Tasting and smelling are important too. Combining food with a new experience makes it more memorable to children.

Travel time is a good chance to get to know one another better and catch up on one another's lives. With time away from the hubbub of daily life, you can take time to discuss issues and debate opinions. Just make sure you listen respectfully to your children's opinions when you ask for them. Otherwise, they will quickly learn to keep their ideas to themselves.

Children can get bored in the dark, and bored children are whiny children. A reading light is handy so children can read or play games if you're traveling at night. Judith's family found a light that plugs into the cigarette lighter (twelve-volt outlet) at an auto parts store, ending the need for replacement batteries. Twelve-volt extension cords are available for the backseat. (The dog ate Judith's, but that's another story.) You can also use a rechargeable flashlight for this purpose. If you recharge at a motel or campground, leave a note on your steering wheel to remind you to retrieve it. (Don't ask how we know.) Book lights that clip onto a book are available at stationery shops and bookstores.

Kids can also use their lights to learn and practice Morse code. They can also practice Morse code during the day by making clicking noises, such as clicking two spoons together, although it appears to be more fun to send a message than to receive it, so be forewarned.

For siblings sharing the backseat, travel writer Kyle McCarthy suggests providing masking tape so siblings can stake out their territory. Now *that* sounds like the voice of experience. (See *http://www.familytravelforum.com*.)

Driving while the children are asleep is another strategy. Rather than driving late into the night, Duke and Sandra Merrion prefer to go to bed early and leave in the wee hours (usually between 2 and 4 A.M.). They then stop and set up camp at midmorning and have the rest of the day to enjoy themselves.

A GREAT TIME FOR LEARNING

If your children's brains are properly trained, they can make the best of all kinds of situations that others find boring. With an active imagination and plenty of stored information, prisoners of war have stayed sane without any outside stimulation, reading material, or anyone to talk with. In his effort to negotiate for the freedom of hostages in Lebanon, Terry Waite was taken hostage himself and kept in solitary confinement for 1,460 days. His collection of memorized Bible verses and poetry was a great comfort to him, since he had no access to a Bible or any other books for most of that time.

The whole family might work on memorizing poetry or historical works, such as a portion of Martin Luther King Jr.'s "I Have a Dream" speech or Mark Antony's ironic eulogy after Julius Caesar's assassination in Shakespeare's *Julius Caesar* ("Friends, Romans, countrymen, lend me your ears. I come to bury Caesar, not to praise him"). The meaning and cadence of the words sink in better when you become intimately familiar with them.

Most of us have used a memory trick—or mnemonic—at one time or another. For instance, how many of us learned that "Columbus sailed the ocean blue" in 1492? Mix memory tricks with real-life learning experiences to help your children remember facts and figures. While you're exploring, make directions memorable. Ned (north) Eats (east) Shredded (south) Wheat (west), in clockwise order, will give you the directions on a compass. People of a certain age may prefer: "Never Eat Slimy Worms." Make up a memory trick of your own or encourage your kids to. Create one that has special significance for your family.

You may want to begin with the world's continents. "Eat An Aspirin After A Nighttime Snack" will remind you of the seven continents: Europe, Antarctica, Asia, Africa, Australia, North America, and South America. You can reinforce it with a mental picture. Suggest that your child draw a picture of a giant (or a dinosaur, or whatever your child likes) eating the words for the continents and then eating an aspirin.

After your child knows the continents, zero in on a country and then a state or province. Finally, your child will really know what that small speck on the map—your destination—represents.

The Bear Hunt game is another fun way to develop memory skills. You may know it in a different version, but it is as old as the hills. The first person says, "I'm going on a bear hunt, and I'm bringing…" and he names an item that is either serious (like a sleeping bag) or silly (like a jump rope). Each person repeats the items already mentioned and adds one more. Kids do get better as they practice. Judith and John were stunned one day when the boys in the backseat were able to go on with an endless number of items. What gave them away were the giggles. They had written a secret list!

BIBLE MEMORY GAME

Christian families can reinforce their children's grasp of key Bible concepts and help them memorize Scripture. All you need is a Bible.

Find five (or more) favorite Bible verses. Write them down on paper for each child. Then say, "I'm thinking of a Bible verse. You can ask me three (or ten, depending on your child's skill) questions to figure out which one it is."

Your children will look at all the verses many times, trying to figure out the verse. They will also think about the meaning of the verses, looking for clues, and cementing the verses in their memories.

PLAYING "WHAT IF?"

As a young girl, Judith's daughter, Nancy, loved to play What If? during car trips. While the game was entertaining, it was also thought provoking—it highlighted things Nancy could do if there were some kind of emergency. Judith was constantly challenged to come up with new what-ifs, and she invited Nancy to come up with some of her own. Over the years, the What If? game triggered many thoughtful discussions on difficult topics. Here are a few what-ifs to get you started:

- What if we get separated (including where would we meet)?
- What if a stranger asks you for directions?
- What if we get robbed?
- What if you find a strange package?
- What if you get lost in a strange city?
- What if someone wants to take your picture?
- What if someone threatens to hurt you or your parents if you tell anyone what he or she did?
- What if we have a car accident? What would happen next?

Parents cannot anticipate every possible scenario, but we can help our kids rehearse some of the situations they might encounter and help them develop problem-solving skills.

Don't Worry if It's Not Good Enough for Anyone Else to Hear

Singing is a free and lifelong source of enjoyment. If you can hardly carry a tune in a bucket, sing anyway! The time your family spends in the car while traveling is a great time to learn how to sing in rounds or in harmony. You might try playing music tapes to carry the melody and help everyone learn the words so they can sing along.

The *Geography Songs Kit* from Audio Memory Publishing includes songs about states and capitals, mathematics, history, and the Bible. You can hear forty sample songs at *www.audiomemory.com*.

 wiseguy

Free Sing-Along Songs

The car is a great place to teach your children folk songs. Can't remember the words to the songs you learned as a child and want to pass along to your children? Go to *http:// www.dalymusic.com* and print out the music for hundreds of songs that are considered public domain. Choose from their collection of children's songs as well as hymns and classical, Christmas, folk, and ragtime songs.

Literature for the Road

"We kept a good book or two going on long or short trips," says Judith. "Often, one was a biography or historical story, and the other an action novel, like *Twenty Thousand Leagues Under the Sea.* We would alternate books." The habit dies hard. Now that the children are grown, Judith often reads aloud to her husband, because sharing the same book is a companionable way to spend time together in the car, versus listening to the radio, which tends to stifle conversation.

During travel, the book often related to the destination in some way—historical fiction, a biography, or information about the area. Books on tape are another way to share a book in the car, especially for those who cannot read in the car without getting carsick. For those times that one person is interested and the others aren't, there are headsets.

Foreign Language in the Car

Language experts recommend listening to a new language on audiotape at least ten minutes a day for one to two years before studying language books. This is easy for a family to do while traveling in the car. You won't understand the language at first, but you can still benefit from listening to it. Eventually the strange sounds will sort themselves out, and you will start to hear words and sentences instead of "blah, blah, blah." The Learnables is a good audio series to start with. It comes in a variety of languages and the lessons focus primarily on listening—which is how we all learned English. The tapes also come with a picture book that is identical for every language, a special advantage for those who want to learn more than one language in the series.

In the United States, the most common language after English is Spanish. Spanish music tapes are easy to find, and your family may enjoy them. If you live or travel near a metro area, you will probably be able to tune in to Spanish radio stations. Many stations throughout the Southwest broadcast exclusively in Spanish. In other parts of the country, stations may broadcast only a few hours a week in Spanish. Call the radio station to find out if and when foreign language programs are scheduled.

If you have a VCR in your vehicle, you can bring along foreign-language versions of English movies—*The Wizard of Oz* in Spanish, for example. Borrow these videos from the library or order them through a video store. Examples from our metro library include *Madeline* and *Babar,* appropriately in French; *101 Dalmatians* in Spanish and French; and the Spanish versions of a *Cool McCool* cartoon and Dr. Seuss's *One Fish, Two Fish, Red Fish, Blue Fish*. Multilanguage soundtracks with subtitles are available on just about every DVD on the market these days. If the movie is familiar to you and your family, you probably won't need subtitles. And you'll learn the language much better if you try to watch without them.

Busy, Busy, Busy: Frugal Arts and Crafts

Often new friends express surprise when they notice Melissa's children hauling backpacks everywhere. Since John and Lori are homeschooled, why do they need backpacks? Well, the backpacks aren't for textbooks; John and Lori carry an assortment of craft supplies, writing tools, books, and games. They never know when their parents will need to take them on an unexpected business trip or to a meeting. They've learned from experience that they can bring inexpensive fun with them wherever they go.

To encourage drawing, writing, and game playing during traveling or waiting times, you can provide lap desks or folding lap tables, available at discount stores. Some have beanbag bases for comfort, and others have storage inside for pencils, craft materials, art supplies, small toys, and books to keep children occupied. A rectangular aluminum cake pan with a sliding lid serves the same purpose. The top is smaller than a commercial lap desk, and the cavity is deeper, which can be an advantage. (This idea is from *Confessions of a Happily Organized Family* by Deniece Schofield.) Each "desk" can be labeled with the child's name.

Lap trays with sides are helpful for projects with parts, such as models or puzzles. You can use a child's lunchbox with flat sides, a cake pan, a plastic dishpan, a shoe or boot box, or a lap desk with the top removed. Bring along refrigerator magnets and let your kids play with them in the car, using a cookie sheet (nonaluminum) as a lap desk. Better yet, use a jelly-roll pan, which has a lip around it.

Pack some secret supplies to dole out on your trip. You might want to use a colorful bag or shoebox, one for each child, but keep the purchases a secret. Whenever children start to become restless, pull another surprise out of the bag. Your kids will think you're a magician!

Here are some items to include in your secret supply:

- marker pens or colored pencils (Crayons will melt in the sun.)
- dry-erase markers for drawing on car windows (Wipe away with a tissue. Just be careful about what your teenagers are writing back there!)
- card games, including some that teach facts (Available at department stores.)
- an inexpensive portable musical instrument, such as a recorder, harmonica, or jaw harp (Buy or borrow tapes or books with easy instructions.)
- some of your children's own toys that you have kept out of circulation for a while

- old Christmas cards (You can make new Christmas cards from old ones, even if you're traveling in July). Kids can cut out pictures and glue them to new paper. Add ribbons, lace, or your children's artwork. Don't forget to bring along addresses.)
- safety scissors and glue sticks
- origami paper and a book on how to make it
- binoculars or a microscope (A lighted microscope with prepared slides is fun to use in the backseat after dark.)
- supplies for making bracelets, necklaces, and other jewelry (Take apart broken jewelry or junk jewelry from yard sales.)
- puppets or supplies for making simple ones—such as small paper bags, old socks or mittens, or hollow rubber balls (Draw eyes, cut a slit for the mouth, and squeeze the ball to make the puppet "talk." Some children open up more easily when a puppet is involved. Your puppet can peek over the backseat, creating an impromptu puppet theater.)
- a map for the backseat (With a photocopier, you can enlarge the section containing your route. Use the same idea if you are flying. Try to identify the roads, cities, rivers, and other landmarks on the map. Consider copying your map onto card stock [heavy paper]. The children might enjoy marking your route with a highlighter. Then *you* can whine, "Are we there yet?" and the kids can answer!)

Sea monkeys, available by mail order and in some educational toy stores, are actually tiny brine shrimp that are acrobatic in the water. They make a good car pet, according to eleven-year-old Zephyr Goza. Even though the critters are tiny, he says, "You can see sea monkeys perfectly fine, especially the adults." He says you do not need to clean the tank, which you can hold in your hand, but you would not want to leave it in a hot car.

Games like Magna Doodle and Etch-a-Sketch work well for long trips. Ever wonder what an Etch-a-Sketch looks like inside? Pat Wesolowski, editor of the *Big Ideas, Small Budget* newsletter, tells how to find out: "Did you know that if you make a box in the center of the Etch-a-Sketch and continue out, making the box larger and larger, that eventually you will have erased all of the particles off of the screen, and then you can see the inside workings of the Etch-a-Sketch? I'm not joking. Try it!"

Some kinesthetic kids—kids who learn best from hands-on activities—can stay happy for hours with plastic interlocking building bricks such as LEGO-brand bricks. LEGOs enhance science and math lessons, especially if you have the Technic type, which feature motors, levers, pulleys, and gears. Check out Richard Wright's Web site for ideas and lesson plans using LEGOs *(http://www.WeirdRichard.com/activity.htm)*. Richard travels with a mobile LEGO and science lab for PCS eAdventures, an educational company that specializes in making science fun.

freebee

Toilet Paper Kazoo

Make a surprisingly good-sounding kazoo out of a toilet paper roll and wax paper. You can bring wax paper and an empty roll from home, although you will probably find several empties along the way. First, let your kids decorate the roll. Then tape wax paper to one end, completely covering it. Put your lips on the wax paper end and hum a song. This homemade, pocket-size instrument will give your kids memorable vibrations on their lips and plenty of giggles! Talk about sound waves, vibrations, and melody.

Your children may be inspired to build mock castles, forts, museums, Native American settlements, or models of places you visit in your travels. Use travel brochures or picture postcards to help with their designs.

Sarah Delaporte, a columnist at the 20ish Parents Web site, says that buying a roll of cellophane tape for younger children (why not buy a roll for each child?) will keep them occupied for hours. Aside from craft projects and cellophane masterpieces, they can tape their mouths shut and try to talk to one another. Note: Don't let children play with the tape if they are under three years old or if they still put unauthorized objects in their mouths.

Inexpensive, double-sided, write-and-wipe maps teach kids geography. The maps, about the size of a placemat and the price of a children's fast-food meal, come in two versions—one for the United States and one for the world. A full-color side shows and names each state or country, continent, city, and body of water. A black-and-white side has no names, only borders and dots to show the capitols on the state map and major cities on the world map. Your kids can fill in the rest and check themselves using the other side. The maps are available through teacher-supply stores and online.

Fun on the Run

"Never, never, ever go on a trip empty-handed. Always bring something to do. And why not something that's fun?" —Cole and Calmenson, *Fun on the Run*

Your children might be interested in a program called Lone Scouts offered by the Boy Scouts for youth who aren't affiliated with a scout troop or who are traveling in an area where troops aren't available. The Lone Scouts program gives children who are traveling extensively a way to earn badges and stay current with scouting activities, until they are able to participate in a local troop back home.

MILEAGE MATH AND OTHER LEARNING IDEAS FOR TRAVELERS

See if you can interest your child in the educational aspects of car travel. Here are some questions for a game of Mileage Math:

- Who can find the cheapest gas station?
- How much gas do we use per mile on the highway? in the city?
- How much gas does this car use versus our other car?
- How many miles do we have to go? Who can keep track of the odometer?
- How long will it take to get there if we travel the speed limit?
- If we stop for dinner at six o'clock, what city will we be near if we drive sixty miles per hour?
- How much money have we spent so far? How much do we have left for meals?
- What direction are we going now? Learn to read a compass and how to use the sun and stars for guidance.
- Which coupons save us the most money?

- What is our elevation, and what is the grade of descent down the mountain?
- How much hotter is it today than yesterday?

Can your kids take over some of the road maintenance? Bring a tire gauge and teach them to check the air pressure in the tires first thing in the morning before driving. Teach them to check the oil and fluid levels, fill up the gas tank, and wash the windows and headlights. Just make sure your pit crew is old enough and mature enough to handle these tasks safely. If your family becomes a crackerjack pit crew, everyone will get a little stretching, and you will get the kind of service we *used* to get at gas stations!

A window seat on an airplane gives your child a bird's-eye view, literally. Bring along a book about clouds and see if the children can identify what they are seeing. Sounds are less alarming to children if they know what they are. If children observe for a while, they can learn what the various sounds mean, such as the wheels retracting or the flaps rising. Before you fly, consider reading a book about the early days of flight. Older children enjoy learning the basics of aerodynamics.

BUSY BOOKS, PUZZLES, AND BOARD GAMES

We could write a book on the topic of keeping children occupied while traveling. In fact, other people have. You can find more great ideas for hands-on activities in books such as *Fun on the Run,* which can help put a stop to bickering siblings and grownups with migraines.

wiseguy

Keep a Straight Face

Here's a simple game called Keep a Straight Face for when your crew is tired of sitting still. Let your young comics and actors try to make each other crack a smile. Break into teams or play one-on-one. No touching or tickling is allowed. Other than that, almost anything goes! —From *A Simple Choice* by Deborah Taylor-Hough.

Check out a variety of travel game books from the library and leave them in strategic spots for your kids to find. They'll think it was their idea to read them—which, of course, is true. Melissa's son John eagerly taught himself and the other family members new games every time they fired up the family van!

We advise parents to keep custody of any library books on trips. Otherwise be prepared to replace lost or damaged items. Try to buy at least one book for each child to keep. Plan ahead—be on the lookout for small educational, quiet toys, activity books, art kits, and games at garage sales, dollar stores, and outlet stores at least a few months before your trip. Then parents can listen to the refrain, "You sank my battleship!" instead of "Daddy, he pinched me!"

You don't have to limit yourself to travel games. Read aloud popular trivia books, such as *The Guinness Book of World Records*. Then take turns thinking of a new world record that your family could tackle. *Car Smarts: Activities for Kids on the Open Road* is a page-turner full of eye-opening trivia. For instance, we were crushed to discover that tumbleweeds are not indigenous to the American West. According to *Car Smarts,* tumbleweeds "came to America from Russia around 1890." If you are traveling on a plane, you may enjoy ideas from *Just Plane Smart: Activities for Kids in the Air and on the Ground* by Ed Sobey.

The Usborne Book of Air Travel Games has instructions on how to create your own captain's log. What's to keep a car traveler from doing the same thing?

The Penny Whistle Traveling with Kids Book contains stretching exercises that can be done in a sitting position and can make a cost-cutting car trip much more pleasant.

Try duplicating a picture from a coloring book using a graph to help learn about proportion. Using a pencil and straight edge, divide a picture into equal quadrants (or more sections if needed). Create the same number of quadrants on a blank sheet of paper, proportional but not necessarily the same size. Then try to replicate the picture by sight, using the quadrants as a guide.

Bring tracing paper and coloring books along and use the coloring books for tracing, instead of coloring. Also, look for some low-cost sticker books with replaceable stickers. You can find marked-down activity books at dollar and discount stores. Coloring, sticker, and activity books based on the Bible are available at Christian bookstores.

You can find inexpensive, pocket-sized games at toy stores. Among our favorites are scaled-down versions of Monopoly, Scrabble, and Mousetrap.

Make Your Own Activities and Books

Your family might enjoy making their own activities and books. You will save money and keep everyone busy at the same time. For instance, you can make your own paper dolls by drawing them on paper first and then cutting them out. Draw clothing separately and be sure to cut them out with tabs on the ends so they'll stay on the doll. You could cut out costumed people from travel brochures, or you can cut paper dolls from figures in advertisements, magazines, and catalogs.

You or an older child could also make books or games (such as the traveling Mankala game, below) out of recycled materials.

freebee

Free Game

Mankala, an African stone count-and-capture game, has been enjoyed for at least three thousand years. You can buy Mankala at a specialty game store, but it's more fun to make your own. Bring it out when the kids ask, "Are we there yet?" You only need an egg carton, rubber bands, and forty-eight small, smooth, painted stones, pennies, seeds, buttons, or marbles. Directions for making and playing the game are in the resource guide.

Host Gifts Kids Can Make

As you travel, you may be visiting friends, relatives, or host families. Use your craft supplies to help your children create handmade host gifts, perhaps personalized with the host's name. Here are a few ideas:

- Paint a cool rock for a paperweight.
- Make a Christmas ornament or decoration.
- Send a mailbox decoration a few days before your arrival. (If your host uses it, it will be easier to find your host's house.)
- Cover and decorate a piece of cardboard and add some thumbtacks for a one-of-a-kind bulletin board.

High-Tech Versus Low-Tech

Even families who limit the use of electronic games, perhaps to an hour a day, may decide to make an exception for long hours of travel. We don't want to disparage the use of high-tech options. Some of us still can't afford them or don't feel they are worth the money. Some parents are concerned about eyestrain and addiction to the fast-moving excitement of modern electronic games; however, videos, audiotapes, CDs, and even game machines can be educational. Perhaps moderation is the key.

Most vehicles already include a tape or CD player. Many families have added conveniences such as a VCR or DVD in their minivans. You can play educational tapes on car trips or use a tape to help your children learn about your destination before the journey. You can find travel videos for practically every major destination in the world. Check audiotapes, CDs, or videotapes out of the library (if you have time to return them).

Prices for many high-tech entertainment devices are affordable if you shop wisely and buy last year's model or buy used equipment. You can purchase a portable black-and-white television and car adapter, for instance, for less than the cost of dinner and a movie.

Taking a Break

Taking a break allows kids to run off some steam and gives adults a chance to relax—if they will allow themselves those few minutes. If you are driving, you can decide when to take a break. Will delaying your arrival by five or ten minutes really matter? If you're not in the driver's seat—you may be on a bus, plane, boat, or train—take advantage of scheduled stops and transfers to exercise. Skip the restaurants and shops. You can eat in your seat when your family must sit quietly anyway.

Here are a few quick ways to unwind:

- For a quick outdoor game that keeps everyone in sight, try blind-man's bluff.
- For physical fitness on the road, bring a Frisbee, a jump rope, or a ball.
- Blow bubbles on breaks. Hands will be presoaped and ready for washing. Giant bubble makers, which have a rod for a handle and a

specially looped rope that creates bubbles, are easy to pack and use. They make a great mixer for children and adults at your destination as well as a fun break on the road. Make your own solution with nine parts water, one part Joy dishwashing liquid, and one-fourth-part glycerin, available at drug stores. The glycerin is optional, but it makes the bubbles tougher. Stir ingredients gently, trying not to create suds. If you want to use a different brand of dishwashing liquid, try a small amount, since not all brands work for this purpose.

- Plain old races or relay races are quick and fun.
- Have a Keystone Kops dress rehearsal in a safe place. When you stop the car, everyone gets out, races around the car, and gets back in. If your family members take turns being in assigned seats (next to the window, etc.), this is a good time to make the change.
- A game of Twister, which you can play during rest stops, will get everyone's kinks out—or add some, as the case may be.
- Some airports have active play areas, either free or for a small charge. Some feature a baggage-claim slide!

Need a longer break on a long trip? Do your Christmas shopping while you travel. Bring along a list of sizes and preferences. A local YMCA may have a reasonably priced indoor pool. To escape the heat and rest on a hot afternoon, stop for a movie, a library, or a public swimming pool.

You never know when you might see a pond or a park. Bring some stale crackers or dried bread to feed ducks or squirrels. Bring some chalk for sidewalks and a magnifying glass for a quick nature walk.

MAKING MEMORIES ON A BUDGET

Sometimes kids remember playing tag with Dad at the airport, but they don't remember anything about the expensive theme park. We're often amazed at the memories our children have of our family trips. It doesn't cost extra money to make special memories, but it can take some extra effort.

MEMORABLE SOUVENIRS
Souvenirs will keep memories of your shared adventures fresh for years to come. Why collect expensive T-shirts that say "All I Got Is This Lousy

T-shirt," a plastic paperweight with "Niagara Falls" stamped on the side, and similar tourist memorabilia? Starting a collection that has special meaning to your family will be a better investment. We can get plenty of T-shirts and tourist paperweights from other people's vacations—for twenty-five cents at their yard sales. Here are some lower-cost, higher-value souvenirs to consider:

- inexpensive postcards (Your child might want to add a note about experiences connected with the places on each postcard.)
- rocks or fossils
- leaves or flowers to press
- books
- an object for a charm bracelet from each trip
- magnets from each place for your fridge
- Christmas ornaments (or items you can use as Christmas ornaments) to create a memory tree over the years
- friends!

Pat Wesolowski found a good use for low-cost souvenir items: "Buy your children (when they aren't looking) a small gift such as a deck of cards or a Christmas ornament that is memorable to the place you are visiting." These items later appear in her children's Christmas stockings and trigger memories and discussion of happy travel memories.

Along the way to and from your destination, your family can add information to scrapbooks or collections. On the way home, kids and adults can spend hours organizing treasures and writing captions in memory books. Another keepsake is a photo album for the trip. How about letting your car-weary children put your memory album together on the ride home? Your children might enjoy labeling family photos, perhaps adding humorous captions. You can add postcards, photo captions, stickers, stamps, coins, brochures, paper restaurant napkins, and other flat mementos. At home, you can leaf through the pages of your memory book or photograph album. Touching tangible objects will help keep the lessons from your trip in sharp focus for many years. You can discuss what you liked best and what you might do differently on your next trip.

Your children might also enjoy sharing with others what they have learned and experienced during their travels. One way to do this might be for them to create a display of items they collected along the way, including photographs, brochures, and other interesting objects, and then offer to present the display at a library, their school, a local museum, a historical society, or a club meeting.

Make a Scrapbook

A scrapbook can be one person's project or a family effort. It can be an assortment of photos and keepsakes, and you can make it a hybrid journal-scrapbook with the best of both. At the very least, be sure to date and label photographs with the names of family and friends in the pictures. Labeling is easy to do right away and sometimes impossible later, when memories have faded.

On a nature trip, a few pressed flowers or leaves help capture your experience. Brochures and programs bring back the memories. You might want to cut pictures out of the brochures rather than using the whole brochure, and watch for a few interesting items to clip out of newspapers from the places you have stayed. Maps make a colorful background for the pages.

LETDOWN PHENOMENA

We have found that we can mitigate some behavior problems if we're ready for them. We know that we'll be tired after a trip and that we shouldn't take it out on one another. After a long-awaited event, the Allees have often noticed that the whole family is grumpy and out of sorts. That's when behavior problems are most likely to surface. Judith says,

> We finally noticed the pattern, and my husband gave it a name: Letdown Phenomena. We found it helps to warn the kids ahead of time: "You know, we are planning for a fun-packed vacation. Let's beware of Letdown Phenomena and not let it make us miserable when our trip is over." Somehow, just acknowledging the problem seems to help.
>
> Now we try to have something to look forward to after a trip or event. We try to stay in touch with our new friends (e-mail has helped there), and the pretty seashell becomes a soap dish that we can enjoy every day. Maybe it would help if we were more organized and got everything unpacked right away and back to normal. We never do. Maybe that's our way of hanging on to our trip a little longer.

Chapter Seven

Family Volunteering

"My older kids worked very hard from sunup to sundown," Alice Read says, describing her travels with her husband and five children to build houses with Habitat for Humanity in Papua New Guinea. "No one complained. 'If the villagers live this way every day, we can for nine days,' was their feeling."

The family slept in a hut on the floor "packed like sardines, which the little boys loved," recalls Alice. That was two years ago. The children, who were ages six, eight, eleven, fifteen, and sixteen at the time, still collect books and soccer uniforms to send to the village school, knowing how much those items will mean to the children there. "The villagers owned the clothes on their backs and a pot to cook in. Period."

Be Surprising

"Always do right. This will gratify some people and astonish the rest." —Mark Twain, 1835–1910

Supporting a good cause feels good. A vacation helping others helps children understand the proverb, "It is better to give than to receive," and to appreciate their blessings.

Another plus—you meet the nicest people on a volunteer trip! You make friends quickly, but without the superficiality that often pervades casual encounters back home. It is one of the reasons volunteering on vacation makes such an impact on the people who have done it.

LEARNING WHILE VOLUNTEERING

When you take a volunteer vacation, you can try something poles apart from your normal routine. If you normally sit at a desk, you can build trails. If you live in a city, you can experience the countryside, or vice versa. If you usually teach, you can learn along with your children and teenagers.

Family members can travel and try out a new field or career. What job, in a perfect world, would your child love to have? What job would you like to have if there were no barriers? Even though you may not have the qualifications to be hired for that job, you can look for volunteer opportunities that provide on-the-job training. Judith, for example, has a job today presenting workshops for parents, facilitating support groups, and writing press releases for a mental health association. She learned those skills by volunteering for causes she was passionate about. Children and teens can learn new skills too. As a traveler, your menu of opportunities is unlimited.

Most teens who go looking for work have a blah résumé and perfunctory reference letters. A young volunteer can build a dynamite résumé with glowing reference letters about intriguing experiences. Keep a record of the number of hours spent volunteering and ask for reference letters as you go.

Traveling with a college-bound teen? Cafi Cohen's two teens, now grown, turned their volunteer experiences into advance college credit plus impressive portfolios for college entrance. Whether or not you home-school, you might want to read Cohen's book *And What About College?: How Homeschooling Can Lead to Admissions to the Best Universities and Colleges* for ideas on custom-designed volunteer jobs for teens and how to document the experiences for résumés, college applications, and advance credit.

Your volunteer trip may have hidden benefits. For instance, rubbing shoulders with prominent evangelists or renowned archaeologists can motivate a young person toward a career. Some organizations provide more tangible benefits, such as training, academic credit for volunteer activities, a small stipend for living expenses, or even health insurance.

COUNTING THE COSTS OF VOLUNTEERING

Volunteering, even on a shoestring, requires self-sacrifice. Is it worth it? You'll want to consider the benefits and the costs before you commit time and money to your expedition.

Volunteering isn't necessarily cheap. In some cases, you must pay all of your own expenses. In fact, a few volunteer vacations are more expensive than a carefree holiday. Certain volunteer programs depend on fees from volunteers to support the project—a fund-raiser of sorts to carry on their work.

Dorothy Nielsen is a single mother who volunteered her time to work in orphanages in India through Global Volunteers and in Romania on her own. She raised the money for her trips with local fund-raising efforts. "You pay a fee to Global Volunteers," says Dorothy, "and people always wonder, 'Where does all this money go?' But when you volunteer, you can see where the money goes. Every minute of the day, you are watching this money work.

"There were fifty-four children in this primal living situation. It was awful," she observes about working in an orphanage in India. "I went with a team that put in indoor plumbing and electricity, and we painted and completely refurbished this whole building. Now they have a refrigerator, a washing machine, and a clean cooking area."

In Romania, Dorothy spent her one-month vacation in a mountainous village in two orphanages, playing with the children and holding the babies. She brought crib toys and mobiles—because children spent almost all their time in their cribs—and medical supplies, such as antibiotic creams and vitamins. "You can't go into these places as a snobby American with an 'I know best' attitude. Yes, the conditions were horrifying and miserable and awful. But that doesn't make the people horrifying and miserable and awful. They are just trying their best to survive. The people were wonderful. I want to go again."

WORKING ON YOUR *VACATION?*

"You mean you really work? On your vacation?" That is a typical reaction Bill McMillon gets from reviewers about his book *Volunteer Vacations: Short-Term Adventures That Will Benefit You and Others.* The next question he gets is: "Who would want to do that?" Thousands of people, according to McMillon. And some of them are parents traveling with children.

In some cases, a nonprofit organization may offer a stipend, housing, and even transportation, usually for volunteers with specific skills. (Some of those organizations are discussed later in this chapter.) More commonly, though, volunteers pay their own way and expenses. Fees vary—a lot. As of this writing, sixty dollars per person gets you a one-week backpacking trip in Kentucky to construct trails, and that includes food. Other programs cost the volunteer nothing but transportation expenses. It may be expensive to travel to a Native American reservation or to a South American orphanage; however, once there, the cheapest (and perhaps the best) way to see a place and get to know its people is by volunteering.

Will your vacation be a tax write-off and offset some of your expenses? Perhaps, if you volunteer through a tax-exempt, nonprofit organization registered with the federal government—and you itemize your taxes. Make no assumptions. Check with the organization and an accountant about any tax advantages, and get in the habit of keeping all relevant receipts.

FINDING THE RIGHT OPPORTUNITY

If you are exploring the possibility of a volunteer vacation, how can you find which one is right for you? Hope Sykes is a seasoned RVer with over two hundred thousand miles under her belt in the United States and Canada. She suggests you start by finding out what issues your family is passionate about.

> Did a newspaper story catch someone's attention? Did you spot a homeless person during your travels? Did you see litter scattered about in an otherwise beautiful state park? Once you've identified a subject and area where you would like to volunteer, research the topic so that you will be better informed and so that you can educate others.

For example, find out how many homeless people there are in your country, or find out how much food is wasted in your country every year. These are big problems—not ones that a single family can solve. Yet one family can make a difference to someone, and that gives you and your children some mental binoculars, helping you to bring national and world problems into focus. It makes these problems more personal and approachable. It also makes research easier and more interesting at the library, on the Internet, or through nonprofit organizations or government agencies.

To introduce children to volunteering and to the needs of less fortunate people, you might want to look for some children's books on the topic. Teens can find books in the young adult (YA) section, and many teens can handle adult-level books. Don't overlook fiction that relates to your topic. Your librarian can help you find books and magazines at the right reading level. For ages four to eight, *The Lady in the Box*, written by Ann McGovern and illustrated by Marni Backer, is about a homeless woman and how a family is able to help her. *Uncle Willie and the Soup Kitchen* by Dyanne DiSalvo-Ryan and Mira Reisberg, intended for ages six to eight, tells the story of a little boy who helps his uncle gather food around the neighborhood and prepare it for homeless people at a soup kitchen.

What would you like to learn about as a family? Think about people who are already involved in that field and how you can help them through a volunteer project, a job shadow, an internship, or an apprenticeship.

The difference? Interns and apprentices usually participate in a more formal learning process. An apprenticeship is long-term commitment that culminates in becoming qualified to perform certain work. The understanding is that an intern or apprentice will perform hands-on work in the field in exchange for training, and in some cases there is minimal pay or benefits as well. A job shadow literally walks around with a person in the workplace, usually for a half-day or a full day, to observe what the workplace is like, either in a business or a nonprofit organization. Some job shadows have a chance to help as well. A "one-day apprentice" is a job shadow with the implication that the shadow wants to perform some work. A volunteer can mean any unpaid work—skilled or unskilled, long-term or short-term, with or without a commitment to train the volunteer.

Although we usually think of nonprofit organizations when we think of volunteer work, you can also volunteer for a business. One preteen girl volunteered with a struggling T-shirt business to design storefront displays and come up with ways to bring in customers. This gave her valuable experience in sales and marketing and showed her how a business is run. If you want to learn something, think about where you could go to learn it. Do you have a self-employed friend or relative you might want to visit? Perhaps they would be open to an unpaid, short-term internship.

INVENTING YOUR OWN VOLUNTEER JOB

Although utilizing an existing program has its advantages, you do not need a program to help someone. In your travels you can find someone who needs a helping hand and make your family available to lend it for a few hours or days at a time.

"Volunteering can be as simple or as complex as you want to make it," says Hope Sykes. For the simple part, she recommends the Random Acts of Kindness Foundation *(http://www.actsofkindness.org)* that suggests ways for people of all ages to perform small kindnesses.

"Little things can mean a lot," says Hope. Not every activity has to be so involved or take weeks of travel time. You're having a mobile adventure, remember? Maybe you'll only be in a new town for a few hours." The foundation's Web site suggests a wide variety of activities for school-age children and teens, families, faith groups, service clubs, and businesses. In addition, you can become a kindness coordinator. The foundation wants to add your family's experiences to their kindness "idea database."

A pastor, an organization for the elderly, or a school in a low-income area may have ideas for finding a worthy project at your destination. You can also check with relatives and service clubs to find a project that interests you.

Adoptive Families of America (AFA) maintains a list of orphanages and their needs, ranging from formula and baby bottles to clothing and medical supplies. Families are encouraged to collect supplies and deliver them personally to an orphanage. You can also adopt an orphanage and send items on a regular basis, perhaps setting up a collection at your church or school or watching for needed clothing and other items at yard sales. Doctors will sometimes donate medication samples. There is nothing like seeing someone in greater need to inspire you and your family to count your blessings and give to others. Visit AFA's Web site *www.AdoptiveFamiliesMagazine.com* or go to *www.orphanage.org,* which has links to orphanages worldwide.

If you would like to volunteer for a particular cause, Hope suggests checking phone books under social service organizations to see if an organization already exists. If you call an organization close to home, the staff may be able to help you contact a similar organization in the area you plan to visit. You may want to volunteer with a local organization for a while before leaving home. That experience may help you to know what you are looking for and to be a more valuable volunteer at your destination. You can also check phone books as you travel and call organizations on the spot, even if you are only in town for a few hours or days. To contact organizations in advance, check with your librarian or search the Internet.

"Don't hesitate to ask for references on the organization," says Hope. "A really good program will greet you with open arms and may even have a waiting list."

Sometimes you can design your own volunteer program and propose it to a sponsoring organization. Nonprofit organizations often don't have programs in place, but they would still love to have some help. Farar Elliott, director of the Ethan Allen Homestead, is intrigued by the idea:

> The Homestead is a small museum and historic site. At a museum like ours, we would be happy to have a family volunteer for us for a week. In the summer there's lots to do here, and it would be great to have independent, capable families to help on the historic farm.
>
> You could easily combine your volunteer work with other educational experiences. For example, we are on a bike path that goes all around Lake Champlain—Vermont to Quebec to New York. It would be fun and cheap to visit museums and historic sites around the lake, traveling on bikes and camping at the many state parks. Lake Champlain is incredibly rich in history, since it was here that the French and Indian War, the Revolution, and the War of 1812 all had major events, not to mention the Native American, French, and English settlements. Plus, Canada is so cheap to visit, and the government does such a good job with museums and campsites!

You can also do your part from home. After Angie Peltzer volunteered in two orphanages in Thailand during college, she started an organization called Go M.A.D. (Go Make A Difference). Go M.A.D. is currently looking for volunteers to help from home or from a dorm room by developing Web sites, creating brochures, drafting letters, applying for funding and grants, researching organizations that need volunteers, and creating a volunteer database.

You Don't Have to Be Formal

"Don't limit yourself to formal internship programs. One of the best ways to find the internship you want is to propose it yourself to the employer or organization you're most interested in working for." —Hope Dlugozima, James Scott, and David Sharp, *Six Months Off: How to Plan, Negotiate, and Take the Break You Need Without Burning Bridges or Going Broke*.

VOLUNTEERING AS A FAMILY

The idea of volunteering on vacation is not new. When we started this book, we were excited to find hundreds of educational volunteer opportunities. But when you want to volunteer along with your children or teenager, finding a place and appropriate volunteer work is not always easy. We contacted numerous volunteer organizations about how families can fit into their programs. Some will tell you that, officially, they do not permit children, although there may be exceptions. Others were open to parents volunteering with their children, but many of those agencies had little or no experience in working with families.

Then we found Family Matters, which has trained about five hundred volunteer centers in the United States to include whole families as volunteers. As a program of the Points of Light Foundation, Family Matters wants family volunteering to become the norm so that families will feel welcomed and needed when they approach nonprofit organizations. In the meantime, we asked executive director Eileen Cackowski how families should approach an organization that has concerns about having children on site.

"You break down the jobs so parents can do adult kinds of things, and kids can do kid kinds of things. And you make it clear that you will supervise your own children." If the organization does not know how to break down the tasks into child-friendly chunks, you can break them down yourself.

For example, Eileen once visited a food pantry where three-, four-, and five-year-old cousins had climbed into a huge bin full of canned goods for the poor. Surrounding the bin were barrels for sorting the cans. One child was in charge of peas, another was in charge of SpaghettiOs, and so on, and they sorted all the cans from the bin into the barrels. "You've never heard so much giggling," Eileen says. "They were able to empty a couple of bins of food in about three hours. The kids were loving every minute of it."

In this case, having small volunteers was a clear asset. (They fit into the bin!) Sometimes it is hard for agencies to see the bright side of families volunteering together. They worry about children running wild through their offices and about kids getting injured or hurting someone else. Part of Eileen's work is showing agencies how to use families effectively.

"Even with agencies like Habitat for Humanity, who will tell you, 'No small children,' there are ways for families to work together," says Eileen. "There is a Habitat project in Utah where the adults are working on the house, and off to the side the kids are making birdhouses. When the family drives past the house later, the adults can say, 'I helped build that,' and the kids can say, 'I helped make that.'"

Children planted flowers at another Habitat site in Michigan while their parents did landscaping. Our local Habitat sometimes provides childcare on-site for volunteers. If the children are busy helping, the Habitat organization might call it childcare, but we call it volunteering.

One innovative food pantry has a table with notepaper and crayons for children to use while their parents are volunteering. When a struggling family gets a basket of food, they also get a handwritten note, a picture, or a set of placemats made by a child who cares.

Families who need food often must bring their small children with them to the pantry. One food pantry had a play area for the children of both clients and volunteers. The volunteer children played with the younger ones and were responsible for modeling positive social skills. A volunteer watched all of the children while the adults and teens worked in the pantry.

Aside from traditional family groups of parents and their minor children, other combinations of families can get involved. Grandparents volunteer with their grandchildren, uncles volunteer with their nephews, adults volunteer with their parents, and Big Brothers and Big Sisters volunteer with their "Littles." In Florida a group of noncustodial dads and their children used to meet on weekends to play miniature golf or see a movie. Now they meet on Saturday mornings to do a service project together. Afterward, the fathers talk while the children play, providing an informal support group.

Meals on Wheels, which delivers lunches to homebound seniors, loves to have families volunteer together on a regular basis. Children make good "runners," allowing the driver to stay in the car while the runner takes the lunch to the door. At age ten, Judith's daughter served as a substitute on days when a scheduled volunteer could not make it. Seniors love meeting the children, and children and teens get to do "real work" even as they help to close the gap between generations.

Sources for Volunteer Opportunities

Here is an overview of some programs and books that can help you match up your family's skills and interests with service learning opportunities.

- Family Matters, (800) VOLUNTEER. Enter your ZIP code or the ZIP code of your destination, and you will be connected with the nearest local volunteer center. Participating volunteer centers are approved Family Matters sites, meaning that they will already be up to speed on the idea of families volunteering together. (Don't know your destination's ZIP code? Check the directory at your library or post office, or go to *http://www.usps.gov/ncsc.*)
- Volunteer Match, an Internet-based service that matches volunteers with nonprofits. You can search by ZIP code or city and by field of interest and time frame.
- The Idealist Web site *(http://www.idealist.org)* is a free, intriguing resource for people who want to explore internships, jobs, or volunteer opportunities with nonprofit organizations worldwide. It is a service of Action Without Borders, a nonprofit organization that "promotes the sharing of ideas, information, and resources to help build a world where all people can live free, dignified, and productive lives." With Idealist's searchable database, you can search by your age, the countries that interest you, the dates you are available, and keywords related to your field of interest (archaeology, health, gardening, or education, for example).

- *Volunteer America: A Comprehensive National Guide to Opportunities for Service, Training, and Work Experience,* edited by Harriet Clyde Kipps, lists almost 1,500 organizations. Look for it in the reference section of your library.
- The book *Volunteer: The Comprehensive Guide to Voluntary Service in the United States and Abroad* is available from the Council on International Educational Exchange.
- Global Volunteers offers volunteer projects worldwide to families, including children of all ages. You can contact them at 375 Little Canada Road, St. Paul, MN 55117; (800) 487-1074; *http://www.globalvolunteers.org.*
- America's Second Harvest *(http://www.secondharvest.org)* is the largest domestic hunger relief organization in the United States. Second Harvest distributes food to twenty-six million hungry Americans each year, eight million of whom are children. Their Web site can link you to volunteer opportunities with nearly two hundred food banks or food-rescue programs.
- Mennonite Central Committee *(http://www.mcc.org)* is the relief and development arm of the North American Mennonite and Brethren in Christ churches. Founded in 1920, MCC has over seven hundred volunteers in around fifty developing countries involved in food relief, agriculture, health, education, and social services.
- Habitat for Humanity creates affordable, decent housing for people worldwide. Homeowners and volunteers build the houses under trained supervision. Houses are sold at no profit, with no interest charged on the mortgage. Since 1976 Habitat has built more than one hundred thousand houses in more than sixty countries, including some thirty thousand houses across the United States. Chapters have varying age requirements, with a minimum age ranging from fourteen to eighteen years old.
- The National Registration Center for Study Abroad *(http://www.nrcsa.com)* has a "Traveling Abroad with Children" information page at their Web site that includes programs that provide childcare or include older children and teens along with parents.

RVing Volunteers

So many RVers volunteer that some special services have sprung up to connect them with volunteer opportunities. For example, RVers can work on Habitat for Humanity projects through the Care-A-Vanner program. A caravan of RVers travels to the next Habitat project that needs help. Your team, which soon becomes friends, can move in for a few days or a few weeks and plunge into a Habitat project.

Volunteers on Wheels (VOW) promotes mobile volunteering among RVers. VOW was founded by four women writers and full-time RVers who developed a friendship over the Internet. The women decided to promote volunteering jointly through VOW and singly through their individual publishing and Internet presence. Shelley Zoellick edits a print newsletter called *Families on the Road* (and offers a free online discussion list by the same name), and Jaimie Hall coedits *The RV Lifestyle* newsletter and writes regularly for RVing publications. She's also at work on a book about working while traveling. Stephanie Bernhagen is author of *Take Back Your Life! Travel Full-Time in an RV.* Hope Sykes's Web site, *www.Maxpages.com/EnabledRVer,* has resources for RVers with disabilities, including resources for those who want to volunteer.

Hope Sykes points out these advantages of RVers volunteering:
- You can go where help is most needed.
- You can bring your family with you.
- You'll have familiar housing and cooking facilities.
- You'll have access to a mobile office, should you require it.
- Depending on the volunteer organization, you will probably be able to work and camp on site, saving on local transportation costs and housing. If the organization knows ahead of time about your needs, they may be able to provide a spot for your RV or a campsite with hookups.

"RVers—especially young families—are unlike other volunteers in that they may only be in a city for a few days or even hours," says Hope, "so better preparation is a major factor. The real secret to successful volunteer travel opportunities is in planning as much as possible so that you can focus on the task at hand and have some fun at the same time."

International Volunteers: Paying Your Way

International organizations place volunteers around the world with minimum commitments ranging from a few days to a year or two. Some programs have no requirements, while others are quite specific in terms of age, education, physical conditioning, work experience, language capabilities, or professional skills.

In some programs the volunteer pays a fee, living costs, and transportation, essentially providing financial support for the program. Occasionally, the organization pays all costs and a stipend for living expenses, usually (although not always) for volunteers with professional skills needed in the designated country. This is especially common for healthcare professionals of all kinds, lawyers, architects, and so on. Do not assume, however, that you do not have the necessary skills. You might be just what someone is looking for. Many positions require no special skills at all, although some are more physically demanding than others.

The Value of Digging a Ditch

Volunteers are servants, not all-knowing experts and problem solvers, according to an organization called Global Volunteers (GV), which sends teams of volunteers on projects worldwide. This is how GV explains its philosophy:

> One of our teams in Guatemala was asked to help dig a ditch for a clean water system. Now you might ask, "Why encourage people to travel all the way to Guatemala to dig a ditch? Certainly even the poorest of people can do that." That question might even be more poignant given this particular team of volunteers, because among them there were several teachers, a school superintendent, a couple of lawyers, a journalist, a nurse, and a couple of business people…. Some might argue that these volunteers could have made a more substantive contribution if they had used their particular skills and expertise rather than digging a hole in the ground.
>
> To fully understand the value of the servant, you must realize that in a subsistence society, where people live off the land and do not survive if they don't work the land, it is extremely difficult to organize a

group of community people to dig a ditch, even for a life-saving potable water system. However, there was now an unexpected resource available. So there they were, fourteen Global Volunteers and forty villagers strung out in a long line digging a ditch that would hold pipe through which clean, potable water would flow....

But as in many stories of development, the water did not solve all the community's problems. The villagers soon discovered that running water needs to drain...but they soon figured out a solution. With the help of other volunteer teams, they installed a community sewer system. The results were clean, potable water and a sewer system that will grow to serve the health of the village children as well as to serve the mutuality of understanding that Global Volunteers strives to accomplish.

Global Volunteers welcomes families with children of all ages to participate in one- to three-week projects worldwide. Each year GV coordinates more than 150 teams of volunteers who participate on short-term human and economic development projects in the hope of establishing mutual understanding among people of diverse cultures. GV has projects in Africa, Asia, the Caribbean, Europe, the Pacific, and the United States. Children twelve years old and older can work on projects alongside a parent or guardian. For younger children, the parents can choose a project in a location where day care is available, or one parent can supervise the children while the other is working on the project. Program fees for children under twelve cover food and lodging costs only, which vary depending on whether you stay with a host family or in a hotel or dorm.

GV qualifies as a tax-deductible organization in the United States, which may help you to do local fund-raising to cover your fees. For an adult or a child twelve years old or older, fees range from under five hundred dollars in the United States to several thousand dollars overseas, plus airfare. The program fees help to support GV's projects.

The Idealist organization serves to connect volunteers through their Web site with organizations seeking helpers. While the greatest number of Idealist openings is in the United States, recent postings also include volunteering at a family television network in New Zealand and nursing injured wild animals in Thailand. The Idealist site lists about fifty international organizations under "Organizations Promoting Global Volunteering." The listings are not usually clear about whether you can bring family members. Some of the opportunities are designed for college students as internships. They may be for individuals only—not your spouse, let alone your children. Inquire about policies for those projects that interest you.

VIRTUAL VOLUNTEERING

Virtual volunteers work via computer, but that does not necessarily mean they work entirely online. Volunteers may spend some of their time in person and some time online. Jobs range from designing Web sites to corresponding with a shut-in via e-mail. You can volunteer while traveling if you have computer access, and school-age children can get involved.

For information on how to get started in virtual volunteering, search the Internet with the keywords "virtual volunteer" and check the resource guide.

wiseguy

Standing By?

"Everyone agrees that something is wrong with present times; but nobody really believes that he is contributing to the present wrongness, and each looks upon himself as a more or less innocent bystander of the times." —Anonymous

MISSION TRIPS

Many families desire to share their faith close to home or around the world. In the past, missionaries were seldom accompanied by their families because conditions were primitive and missionaries needed lengthy training. Some opportunities will still be out of reach for many families; however, we've discovered that families can find a way.

Deep South is a ministry that utilizes families to carry out their work. The Ianni family recently traveled south as part of a Deep South mission trip, repairing houses in Appalachia. Sam and Pam Ianni feel that service to others is an important component to education.

Their three homeschooled children (Sam, eleven; Ruth, ten; and Tim, eight) learn in the car as well as at their destination and at home. In the car, they read aloud from the Felicity books—part of the American Girl series—about the Civil War era. The family researched and mapped out their itinerary ahead of time on the Internet. On the way, they visited Civil War sites. The Ianni kids mainly helped the project through fund-raising efforts and running a lemonade stand while their parents worked on houses. Adults and children worked together to make life better for several Mississippi families.

Information on Missions

If you can't go yourself, you can become a part of missionary work through your prayers and financial support. In addition to the organizations that we've already mentioned, which will send information on request, here are some free offers from missionary groups:

Christian Freedom International (CFI) will send you free prayer alerts, a one-year subscription to their monthly magazine, and an eighteen-minute video on Christian persecution in Burma. CFI is "dedicated to helping persecuted Christians in some of the most dangerous places on earth; you can make a major difference in the lives of suffering believers."

Melissa's Web site, www.eaglesnesthome.com, lists many more free offers and opportunities to learn more about missionary efforts.

Other cultures can give us fresh insight into our values. In Haiti on a mission trip, Sandra Merrion noted how generously people shared what little they had. If one of the children received a doll from a missionary, the doll itself was divided: "Someone gets a leg, someone gets an arm, but everyone gets a piece." Despite the poverty, the children were happy playing games with whatever they had, using a round fruit as a ball. What Sandy remembers most about the children in the village was their happy eyes. "It wasn't until the children got older that they realized the poverty they live in," she says.

A Journey to Bible School

Bruce and his wife, Laura, travel extensively across the United States with their son, sixteen-year-old Christian, and two daughters, eighteen-year-old Rachel and twenty-two-year-old Alyssa. They recently journeyed from their Colorado home to a Bible school in Pennsylvania. Although the focus of the trip was spiritual growth and ministry, family members also visited historic sites, such as President James Buchanan's home. Bruce says,

> Our family helped out at the Bible school a couple of days by serving meals and setting up chairs. When we stayed at a relative's or a friend's house, we cooked some of the meals and purchased some of the food, so we didn't put a big burden on our host. We also helped with cleanup.
>
> Every evening after Bible school there was a church service. We were able to grow spiritually, and we received challenges to evangelize. We were also challenged to let go of the material things of the world in favor of the riches of God's kingdom.
>
> As in any trip, you sit in the car for a long period of time. It was unseasonably warm, and our air conditioning went out on the trip. It was uncomfortable. All people have a tendency to get a little testy, listless, and worn out. However, any time you move closer to God and seek to serve him, relationships within the family are strengthened. Christ's commandment to us is to be a servant to all. When everyone in a group or a family has that attitude, then it is really easy to get along, because each person is seeking to be a servant to someone else.

Sharing Your Faith

If you are a Christian interested in ministry opportunities, here are some resources to guide you:

- Intercristo can help you find your ministry niche. Intercristo helps match interests and abilities with ministry jobs around the world. Find Intercristo online at *http://jobleads.org*.
- The World Vision Web site offers useful information about how to raise financial support. It also includes links to other mission organizations.

- Mercy Ships, a division of Youth with a Mission, encourages involvement of whole families, offering ministry opportunities for teens and leadership opportunities for adults. Children ages twelve and below must be accompanied by a parent, who then serves as a staff member of the team. The organization encourages young people to "do cool things for God." They refer to Paul's letter to Timothy, which reminded him not to let anyone look down on him because he was young. Instead Paul encouraged him to be an example in life, in love, in faith, and in purity. You can apply with Mercy Ships online.

Living a Life of Simplicity

"I'm calling on believers everywhere to join me in a radical, far-out life of simplicity that will seem crazy to many of your family and friends. You can live a greedy, self-indulgent life. Or you can choose the way of the cross, living for others as Jesus did and still calls us to imitate today." —K. P. Yohannan, *The Road to Reality: Coming Home to Jesus from the Unreal World*

MISSIONARY SHIP

We can be inspired and encouraged when we read about families who have found ways to fulfill their missionary dreams. Here's a letter from Marianne Lako, who shared her family's missionary story with us:

Our family has been with Mercy Ships for twenty years, and we raised our three children on board the *Anastasis,* while serving the ministry. Our kids were two and three-and-a-half when we joined the mission. A few years later our son made his arrival. Our kids are now twenty-four, twenty-two, and eighteen years old—we have two girls and a boy.

One of the great experiences for us as parents was that our family was involved with missions, and we did not need to send our children to boarding school as there was (and is) a school, from preschool through twelfth grade, on the ship. Both our girls graduated from the ship's high school.

In 1986 we heard about King's Kids and joined as a family for a summer outreach in British Columbia, Canada. It was a six-week program and a wonderful experience to be involved with together.

In the summer we would arrange for longer outreaches away from the ship. For these outreaches, staff, families, children, and teenagers could apply and join us. These outreaches would take place in different parts of the world. We have been involved with outreaches in Jamaica, Mexico, Nicaragua, the United States, and Western and Eastern Europe.

Ministry work overseas can be expensive, uncomfortable, and exhausting. However, Lako believes it is worth it. "Love for the poor and needy is something that is life changing and definitely worth the price." She said the most important reason for family travel is "to show the world, where families are more and more falling apart, that a family can be a strong unity. If you believe this is something your family wants to do, you can get really creative in getting finances together to make it happen. In most cases, we were the tour organizers. We would try to cut costs by way of transportation, our housing situation, etc."

A Strong Missionary Family

Travel with an eternal purpose can strengthen family ties. Jeannette Lukasse, from Holland, travels on mission trips with her husband and five children. The family has spent fifteen years in Brazil, taking ten or more trips with King's Kids in Brazil and a two-month trip to India. They have been back to Holland five times for three months each time. "Our kids are now nineteen, eighteen, seventeen, fourteen, and thirteen. We have traveled since the oldest was four months old." Two of the children have disabilities. Dilma, eighteen, is deaf, and the youngest, Davi, is paraplegic and uses a wheelchair. Those challenges have not kept them from traveling with the rest of the family.

Jeannette says that her family travels and ministers this way "to be together, and to teach our children to be happy in all kinds of circumstances—sleeping on floors, in buses, in airports. Of course, they will look at our attitude and copy. Also, our travels gave them a tremendous opportunity to grow in knowing God. Seeing him provide, they experienced miracles instead of just reading about them."

Jeannette believes a family can cut costs when traveling with children by getting the children "used to sober but healthy meals" when not traveling. If they, for example, are used to lots of expensive snacks, chocolate, chips, and other such foods, they will want them when they travel as well, where it might be much more expensive to buy them. She networks with other ministry workers and friends who live in the country where she will minister. She talks to others who have been in certain cities before and can give tips on how to save money.

> In India we traveled by train for three days and three nights instead of going by airplane from Bombay to Calcutta. It was a fun way to get to know India and the culture better. We saved by eating the food of the country instead of always looking for the well-known McDonald's. We ask local friends where to do our shopping.

If a family says they can't afford a learning journey, she would ask them what their priorities are—such as a nice car and televisions in various rooms. "It's normally a financial sacrifice to travel with a family, but seeing what we have learned together, I believe it's worth it," says Jeannette.

The teen years have brought a few changes. "With teens, we ask them to pray about the trip, whether they are supposed to go with us," says Jeannette. "For example, on our trip to India, our oldest was sixteen and didn't want to go. We had prayed about it and sensed that we were to go with the whole family, so we asked him to pray about it and trust God to tell him. So our son came some days later to tell us that he would go, not because he wanted to, but because God told him to go. It was a wonderful trip, and he enjoyed it very much. Our last holiday, two of our teens felt they were to go with different King's Kids teams and not with us. One felt he had to stay home, and two came with us. We all had a good time."

Independent Adventures for Teens

Often families that participate in volunteer and missionary trips together find that their children mature quickly. Your teen may be ready to experiment with flying from the nest by traveling to conferences, becoming an exchange student, participating in mission trips or volunteer projects, or joining other youth organizations, such as Boy Scouts or Girl Scouts and 4-H, which sponsor national and international events. Internships for teens offer hands-on learning opportunities.

Teens can use travel to gain life experience. They can even plan volunteer opportunities and internships for college credit, saving thousands of tuition dollars. Travel can help young people achieve confidence to successfully navigate into responsible adulthood. Ministry to others can put life into perspective and help youth appreciate their own home and family. If we see that most of the world's people have fewer worldly goods, we can be frugal ourselves without feeling deprived.

How Far Can You Go?

"How far you go in life depends on your being tender with the young, compassionate with the aged, sympathetic with the striving and tolerant of the weak and the strong. Because someday in life you will have been all of these." —George Washington Carver, scientist, 1864–1943

Tamara Cohen and her brother, Jeff, traveled more than the average teen, taking advantage of the flexibility of their homeschool schedule. Their mother, Cafi, author of *And What About College: How Homeschooling Can Lead to Admissions to the Best Colleges and Universities*, says,

> When we lived in New Mexico, both our kids—at ages thirteen and fourteen—took several two-week trips to fix houses in an impoverished Pittsburgh neighborhood. Our son, Jeff, traveled to the Alabama Space Camp facility for seven-day sessions three times. In addition, from the age of thirteen to seventeen he attended four or five Civil Air Patrol encampments all over the nation. Tamara, having completed what we defined as high school by age sixteen and not ready for college, spent nine months in Australia on a student-exchange program. Both kids traveled alone frequently to see out-of-state extended family.

My daughter earned all the money for her trip to Australia by working for two years at a dry cleaning establishment, from age thirteen to fifteen. Not only did the trip cost our family nothing, we also saved money on clothes, housing, utilities, and meals while she was gone!

For teens who want an independent adventure and like the idea of hard work in the outdoors, the Student Conservation Association has high-school Conservation Work Crews (CWCs). Students live in tents and work as teams on conservation projects for one month. The program is tuition free, and financial aid for transportation expenses is available for students who qualify. Another source is the Touch America Project (TAP), a volunteer program of the U.S. Department of Agriculture. TAP gives youth, ages fourteen to seventeen, work experience and helps to develop their awareness of the environment while working on public lands.

TEENS IN MINISTRY

Each year ministries involve thousands of young people in short-term outreaches at home and around the world. Often missionary children will follow their parents into ministry, as travel seems natural to them. Ministry may seem more intimidating, both financially and emotionally, if it is outside of a teen's experience.

If your teen is interested in ministry work, you can find service opportunities close to home, or in a nearby city. Young people can contribute to short-term missions efforts, which will give them a taste of missionary life without a permanent commitment.

The following organizations help Christian students find service opportunities:

- Intercristo *(http://www.jobleads.org)* helps match interests and abilities with ministry jobs around the world.
- The Christian Connector offers free information on Christian colleges and universities, Bible colleges, short-term missions, ministry opportunities, Christian music, Christian teen publications, and Christian teen events and conferences. You can access their Web site at *http://www.christianconnector.com.*

Resources for Teen Travelers

For many teens, attending a conference or church-sponsored event or participating in an intern program provides some travel independence while offering adult guidance and supervision. Here are some programs for teens who want to do ministry work that involves travel:

- Acquire the Fire is a series of conventions in twenty-six cities across North America with intense gatherings of thousands of young people and youth pastors. Sponsored by Teen Mania, the convention uses modern technology in audio, lighting, video, drama, and pyrotechnics for a powerful presentation.
- Honor Academy, also sponsored by Teen Mania, offers a one-year ministry internship for teens. Teens need to do their own fund-raising to defray the cost.
- *Studyabroad.com* is an online resource listing thousands of study-abroad programs in more than one hundred countries throughout the world.
- The Council on International Educational Exchange (CIEE) sponsors study, work, travel, and volunteer programs in Europe, Asia, Africa, and Latin America. It offers budget charter flights and travel services. A nonprofit organization, CIEE offers financial assistance for U.S. students and professionals for educational programs abroad.

Being a full-time student has its perks, such as discounts and special travel programs. Here are some travel resources for high-school and college students:

- CIEE's student identity card provides student discounts, insurance, special airfares, and emergency assistance services for students in a degree program.
- *The High-School Student's Guide to Study, Travel, and Adventure Abroad* is published by CIEE. Other CIEE books include *Work, Study, Travel Abroad; Going Places;* and *Smart Vacations: The Traveler's Guide to Learning Adventures Abroad.*
- *Teenagers' Guide to Study, Travel, and Adventure Abroad* by Marjorie Adoff Coeh, Del Franz, and Adrienne Downey.

Chapter Eight

Budgeting and Lifestyle Changes

Imagine yourself meditating on a rustic wooden swing in a garden fragrant with flowering vines and multicolored flowers. As the swing gently rocks, can you picture in your mind a dream trip with your family? Or do the practical concerns of transportation, food, and lodging make educational travel look like an impossible fantasy?

Educational travel starts with a dream. You can learn how to turn your dream trip into reality. With the right information, you will probably only need to spend half or even one-third the cost that other families spend. Travel experts do not pay full price for transportation, lodging, or other travel expenses. You do not have to pay full price either.

We offer our experiences, not because we are financial geniuses, but because we both have a passion for family travel and field trips. We don't have a choice between traveling frugally and traveling in luxury. Our choice is to travel frugally or not at all.

We can attest, however, that when you travel frugally, your children can learn along with you. Learning about frugal and debt-free travel is an educational journey in itself. Without even realizing it, your children acquire a proficiency in the subjects of consumer math and home (and away-from-home) economics. This experience translates into proficiency in the classroom. Few schools teach about avoiding high-interest travel debt, saving for a trip, starting a travel business, or feeding a family on the road. Teachers don't test a child's knowledge of the trade secrets of discount airfare, finding the best deal on a car rental, and hotel-rate bargaining. This is not an exaggeration: The economics of educational travel can make a tangible difference in a child's future success or failure.

In addition to academic gains, counting pennies can spur families to learn how to exercise creativity. With some creativity, a trip can be educational and unique without blowing the budget. For instance, the typical Florida vacation includes a mandatory mouse in an expensive theme park. The creative vacation may include visiting the manatees at closer range in a public park. True, we may need to scale down everyone's expectations and take a shorter trip— or a longer trip closer to home. Whether a family dream vacation is long or short, we need to take practical steps to turn it into a reality.

THE FIRST STEP: BUDGETING

The longest journey begins with a single step: budgeting! There are two ways to budget for travel. One way involves figuring out how much money you need to make your travel dreams a reality. You then find a way to come up with that money and calculate how long it will take. The other way is to figure out how much money you can budget, then find out where you can travel within that budget—like the runaway who asks the bus ticket agent how far he can go with fifty dollars.

Whichever method you choose, you will need to honestly assess your available funds. You may want to spend some time learning about simple bookkeeping with your children. Buy or make an inexpensive ledger, or simply use a notebook with pages divided in half. Track your income on one side and your expenses on the other. Buy a small notebook for each family member who spends money. Record every penny spent for several months. Transfer the information to the family ledger on the expenses side.

Children can save their spending money for a trip and contribute to saving money on household expenses. If your children are small, help them keep their own records, even if it is only keeping track of pennies. Older elementary-age children can start learning about the family finances and can help keep a record of your travel funds. If you let them know you sincerely want their opinions, they may even come up with some creative ideas for saving money instead of spending it. Our children do what we do, not just what we say. If we want them to learn sound lessons about debt and savings, we need to teach them by example.

Your checkbook is a good starting point for tracking expenses. Some families even turn over their bills to their teenager. The teen writes checks (the parent signs them) and keeps the checkbook balanced. Aside from learning to handle a checkbook, kids can learn what it costs to pay for electricity, phone service, water, and a mortgage, and how little money is left over at the end of the month.

Budget Planner

You can send for a free copy of the "Consumers Take Charge Budget Worksheet," a two-page budget guide in an easy-to-use format from Consumer Alert, a nonprofit membership organization that encourages a free market. The worksheet includes hints about keeping track of your money to get started on the path to financial fitness. Send a self-addressed, stamped business-size envelope to Consumer Alert, 1001 Connecticut Avenue, NW, Suite 1128, Washington, DC 20036; or download it from their Web site at *http://www.consumeralert.org.*

PROJECTING YOUR TRAVEL EXPENSES

The average family vacation in the United States in 1998 cost $1,060, according to the Travel Industry Association of America. Assuming that some families spend much more than that, we must be helping to keep that average down. Whatever you spend, you will want to squeeze out every ounce of value. If you lower costs, you can travel more frequently, take a longer trip, or come home debt free.

Now that you have tracked your funds, how much money is left after expenses? Perhaps not much—but it's a start. Before you start saving, you'll need a target figure for your trip's expenses. Otherwise, you won't know when you have met your goal.

To start, figure the actual cost of whatever activities you'll be doing on your trip—that is, visiting museums, going to a theme park, or taking a class. In addition, count the cost for your basic needs while traveling, such as food and shelter. Of course, you also need transportation, and transportation expenses vary widely. (Because saving on transportation can make or break your budget, we have devoted an entire chapter to the subject.)

Be as specific as possible when you list your travel needs. Include three meals a day, plus snacks. How many days will you need to pay for lodging? Will you need to purchase new clothes or pay for laundry services? Plan for some guilt-free spending money for each family member. If you do not plan for it, everyone's spending may get out of hand.

After adding up all of your projected travel expenses, add an arbitrary 10 percent (or more) for unforeseen expenses. Have a backup plan in case you need more money. The best bet is to make that extra money accessible in an emergency but hard to get at otherwise. It is easy to splurge on luxury expenses when you are on vacation. (Know how we know?)

After adding together all the items on your list, you have created a travel budget. It is your blueprint to make your educational travel dreams a reality. Post a copy of the plan on your refrigerator, on top of the coffee table under glass, on the dashboard of your car. Post sticky notes on your wallet to remind you to save.

GROWING YOUR TRAVEL SAVINGS

Clink, clink, rattle—coins hit the bottom of an empty pickle jar marked "Travel." *Plunk, plunk, slide*—as the jar fills up with spare change, the coins make a different sound. On the wall, your vacation funds chart (formerly a mild-mannered yardstick) looks like the sign the United Way posts at the beginning of their annual fund-raising campaign. The bottom inch and a quarter are colored in red to show how much has been saved so far. That leaves 3¾ inches to go! It is definitely going to take more than spare change to make this trip possible.

The 21 Percent Solution

Although nearly all adults have a dream vacation in mind, only one in five families (21 percent) currently saves for it. —Travel Industry Association of America

When Melissa asked her silver-tongued son John to describe how slowly their travel fund was growing, he came up with this: "As slowly as a dead turtle on the back of a sloth with arthritis, wallowing in quicksand." Now that's slow!

But just as the red line creeps up on the United Way chart and eventually hits the top, so can our travel funds. By spending less now, we can add more to our savings and avoid the traps that credit card companies have laid for us.

Maybe you don't need to make a major sacrifice to finance your next trip. You may be able to find savings by cutting back on "invisible expenses," those small but unnecessary luxuries that occur even in the most frugal families. Minor luxuries may seem insignificant, but they can add up to a vacation if saved over the course of a year.

Over the years, Melissa's family has found small economies that have made educational travel possible for them:

> We don't use cable television. We borrow most of our newspapers and magazines. We carefully save for presents. Christmas expenses can keep a family from realizing their dreams. It is so easy to overspend, so now we have a separate savings account for Christmas expenses. Our children know ahead of time that we can spend forty to fifty dollars per person, and that's it. They don't have unreasonable expectations, and they carefully consider their wish lists. I think that we all enjoy our presents more because we choose them so carefully. We know we didn't go out on a financial limb to get them. Our limit for birthday presents is twenty-five dollars.
>
> If you earmark the money, you can enjoy guilt-free spending. I think that if you don't save, your temptations are greater. The thinking goes, If I'm already in debt anyway, why not spend a little more? Frugality in many different areas, large and small, has helped us allot the "extra" money for travel.

One family found that if the adults cut out their morning takeout gourmet coffee and pastries at work, they could save about four dollars a day. That's twenty dollars a week, or a thousand dollars a year! Even if you make such a change, the money tends to evaporate in the daily money flow. That is where having a concrete goal helps. Go ahead and send for brochures, read guidebooks, search the Internet, and get excited about your trip. Then when you have to make a financial choice, your travel will seem as real as that doodad or takeout dinner that cries, "Buy me." This new focus can help your family move away from feeling deprived by penny pinching and move toward getting excited about your travel.

Found: Twenty Dollars a Month (or More) Toward Your Travel Fund!

The Internet may be headed the way of commercial television—a free service paid for by advertising. You can find free Internet service providers (ISPs), saving about twenty dollars a month, if you are willing to put up with ad banners—and if you use the Internet, it's unlikely you can avoid those for very long anyway. The drawback with free ISPs is that customer service may lag behind compared to a subscription service. For those who depend on Internet for a livelihood, reliability is worth paying for. Otherwise, an occasional delay in fixing problems won't hurt, and you can plunk between two hundred and three hundred dollars a year into your travel account.

The Marousis family, whose journals made up their book *Road School,* saved every penny they could toward "Plan Z," which represented their dream of traveling for nine months. Come up with a catchy family code word for your trip—maybe the name of your destination—to remind yourselves not to spend money frivolously. For instance, when relatives ask you to join them at a pricey restaurant, you say the code word, then casually mention that perhaps fast food would be more fun for the kids anyway. Whenever possible, make a tangible connection between the money you saved and your trip—put aside real cash, place it in designated envelopes, and take it to the bank with your kids.

Children can get on the money-saving team as well. Perhaps they can make their own Popsicles instead of buying them, or make their own popcorn instead of buying packaged snacks.

Some cuts are easier to live with if you know they are temporary. Maybe you can cancel your newspaper subscription for a few months and read your neighbor's paper a few days later. Read magazines at the library instead of buying them. See what it is like to live without cable television for a while. During your campaign to save trip money, write letters or use a free e-mail account instead of making long-distance calls.

One word of warning: Examine "free" computer deals closely. They come with conditions, such as requiring you to commit to a high-priced Internet provider for several years. In today's market, twenty dollars a month for three years is a lot of money.

Another action you can take to grow your travel savings is categorizing your checkbook expenses as well as miscellaneous cash expenses. You may be surprised by some of the totals. Small expenses like renting videos and going to movies may add up to a big figure under "entertainment." You might want to decide on a limit for each category to eke out more money from your budget.

Saving for a vacation can be hard work, but we tend to appreciate things more when we wait for them. Spend your waiting time researching and preparing for the trip. As you plan your trip, you may find ways to save even more money. Then when your bank account is fully grown, you will be ready to take advantage of special travel deals or offers.

The Scrooge Syndrome

If we're not careful, penny-pinching can lead to the modern version of the Scrooge syndrome: drudgery, stress, and endless peanut-butter sandwiches. How can we avoid the Scrooge syndrome? Spend money where it counts and scrimp mercilessly and without regard to convention where it doesn't count. We can save more for our dream trip, but we can still share with others and enjoy life.

The Credit Trap

Life is full of choices. We can't travel without making some sacrifices. If we save for travel instead of borrow, we can help our children learn about self-control. Yes, we can wait for something that we want. No, we don't need to indulge ourselves today.

Using a credit card for travel expenses does have some compelling advantages: (1) Your credit card company can go to bat for you if you get ripped off, (2) you have proof positive of your purchases, and (3) you can avoid the risks and hassles that go with carrying large sums of money or traveler's checks. One family we know intentionally pays for all purchases by credit card to earn frequent-flier miles and then pays the card off every month.

Most credit cards cost nothing (except for cash advances) if you pay them off each month. But that is a mighty big "if." If you are one of the self-disciplined few, you probably have credit under control. If you aren't, your vacation may end up costing you much more in the long run.

If you are one of the many who are strapped by consumer debt, think about making some major life changes to turn your situation around. Most of us drive home from our jobs in a vehicle that is owned by the bank, to a house that is owned by the bank, get a drink out of the refrigerator owned by the bank, sit down in an easy chair…flip on the television…and watch news reports on the enormity of the public debt.

Slaves to Debt

The rich rule over the poor, and the borrower is servant to the lender.
—Proverbs 22:7

Credit-card interest can keep you perpetually in debt. You wind up so busy trying to keep up with last year's expenses, for items that are long gone, that you do not have enough cash to meet current expenses.

Some will wonder, How could we possibly afford to travel—unless we borrow for it? The answer is simple, but it is not necessarily easy. We can save and plan for the good things in life—and pledge to take no more credit-card vacations. We can plan our vacation budget to teach our children wise stewardship. We can refuse to use our credit cards to purchase consumables such as food and clothing. We can save thousands in interest by paying extra principal on the debt we already owe, instead of staying trapped in the never-never land of minimum payments.

Low-Cost Debt Counseling

If you can't meet your goals, travel or otherwise, because you're mired in debt, get help. Credit counselors can help families with budgeting, getting out of debt, and rebuilding their credit rating. These services can sometimes help you consolidate your debt or negotiate with your debtors to reduce interest or waive late and over-limit fees. (Contact information for these services is in the resource guide.) Some financial counseling services you may want to contact include:

- Consumer Credit Counseling Service
- Cornerstone Christian Counseling
- Larry Burkett's Christian Financial Concepts

Finally, local ministers can help you find financial help and counseling from local services or from within their congregations.

Taking Extended Time for Travel

Do you dream of travel but cannot get away from work long enough or often enough? A big part of planning for educational travel is finding time for it. Time is democratic—we all get the same amount every day. But for many families, time is at least as great a barrier to travel as money.

You might have better luck negotiating for more time off than for a raise in salary. If that does not work, maybe you can extend your vacation time with unpaid leave.

As an alternative, take time off between jobs. Maybe you can find a new job, but negotiate for time off before starting to work. That takes the pressure off of job hunting when you get back. In an economy in which good workers are in short supply, your new manager may be very flexible.

You might consider a job that fits better with your travel plans. Dana Nibby is a world traveler who finds ways to get time away from the rat race. His article "Take This Job and Love It: Leisure-Friendly Workplaces" suggests these leisure-friendly jobs:

- University jobs. Some universities offer nine-month positions ranging from food service to secretary to professor. Even year-round positions often come with generous vacation and holiday time.

- Jobs in the high-tech field. Computer programmers and engineers may be able to get assignments to work in Europe and other areas where the general population cannot get work permits.
- Ask to be temporarily reassigned to someplace you would like to visit. Work for a European company that has branches in your home country (or a U.S. or Canadian company with branches around the world), and request a temporary transfer.
- Get a job in the travel industry. Travel perks go to office staff and customer service reps, not just pilots and flight attendants.

Peter Plumb and his wife, Pam, took six months off with their eighteen-year-old son, David, and their twenty-year-old daughter, Jessica, to explore India and French Polynesia. Peter does not regret a minute or a dollar spent. The family's journey, a long-held dream, took advantage of a specific window of time: David was between high school and college, and Jessica was a junior in college. It was perhaps their last chance to spend such extended time together before the kids permanently flew from their parents' nest.

Monty Johnston worked as a shop manager for a stainless-steel fabrication shop in South Carolina, and his wife, Cindy, worked from home as a medical transcriptionist. They spent less money and more time (seven months) traveling with their two children, Monica, then thirteen, and Jake, then eleven. "We were not and are not anywhere close to wealthy," says Cindy. "As a matter of fact, we never had much spending money left over after obligations were met."

So how did the family pull off traveling for seven months? Cindy calls it her "throw caution to the wind" method.

> Basically, we sold our home and another house that we had a half interest in, quit our jobs, and took off. We planned and planned for more than a year before it all came together, but in a nutshell, that's what it boiled down to. We kept back an amount to use for a down payment on a home and to get reestablished after we were finished with the trip, and we stayed on the road until the rest of the money was almost gone. Then it was time to stop. It's the best thing we've ever done.

The Johnston family learned about the desert, mountains, prairies, and cityscapes by visiting twenty states from Florida to California (which Monica loved and Cindy hated) as they meandered around the country. Monica and Jake were already homeschooled. As they traveled, family members took turns reading aloud about whatever they were seeing or doing.

Both the Johnstons and the Plumbs were physically close for a long period of time—the Plumbs in a sailboat and on a hiking expedition, and the Johnstons in a travel trailer, a thirty-foot bunkhouse model, pulled by their elderly 1976 Jeep Wagoneer. Both families feel that spending such a long stretch together in such close quarters created a bond they would have missed out on if they had not made time for it.

Cindy Johnston has a certain sense of loss now that she is back in her hometown.

> We had something so special, and I truly do not believe that it can be recaptured while living a traditional lifestyle. When living on the road, the "rest of the world" was just a small sector existing as a part of our lives, while our family was the "big picture." Living traditionally, the world is the "big picture," and the Johnstons are the small part. Living on the road, sharing a travel trailer, constantly surrounded by new places and new people—it all fostered feelings of trust and confidence and interdependence that I have difficulty finding words to express.

Both families feel that their experience changed them. "Anyone who goes on a sabbatical for six months doesn't come back the same person," Peter Plumb says. "You've done some things that are completely different and are way out from the ordinary course of your life," he explains, "so you look at your previous life, when you come back into it, with a different set of eyes."

Cindy's family had changed so much that, when they returned home, they changed their plan of buying a house. Their experience empowered them to switch gears.

> When the fun was over and it was time to get back to the grind,
> my husband had tasted freedom for too long to go back into a

forty-plus-hour-a-week job working for someone else. So instead of buying a house, we used the money we still had to start a business. Now, a year later, we're 50 percent owners in a stainless-steel fabrication business, a real dream come true for my husband.

We don't have much money, and we're renting a house, but we don't feel any worse off financially than we were before we left. We may not own a home, but we own a business. For the price of a house that was too small in a neighborhood that we hated, I got the chance to travel and live my dream, and now my husband has the opportunity to fulfill *his* dream. It seemed like a pretty good trade-off to us. And anyway, what we shared as a family was worth much more than every single penny we spent. Our only regret is that we didn't have enough money to travel longer.

HELP FOR PLANNING YOUR TIME OFF

Overwhelmed by choices? Not sure where to start? A few fee-based organizations can help you find what you would like to achieve in your time off with your family—whether it is a time off between jobs or a sabbatical during key times in your adult life.

The Plumb family planned their six-month trip with the help of a sabbatical specialist. Programs like the Center for Interim Programs and Time Out help people turn a vague fantasy into a detailed plan of action. (A sabbatical can be a formal leave connected with your job or simply time you have set aside in your life.)

Why use a sabbatical specialist?

"Contacts!" says Peter Plumb. "While you could do it yourself, it would be hit or miss." The Center for Interim Programs connected the Plumbs to a boat broker, so they could sail a forty-three-foot boat in French Polynesia, and to an organization that provides host families in Nepal. Working with Interim helped the family decide what was important to them and make a plan.

Interim founder Neil Bull says his program works with anyone who desires to take time out—often students, but also families "of any configuration," retirees, couples, downsized employees, and others between jobs. Fees currently run about two thousand dollars, although Neil says Interim considers fee reductions on a case-by-case basis.

Chapter Nine

Working Vacations, Portable Businesses, and Fund-Raisers

You can transform your travel dreams into reality without waiting until "someday." If you are prepared to work, you can find additional income for a trip in three ways:

1. Host a fund-raiser or find sponsors.
2. Earn extra money before the journey.
3. Earn money during the trip, on the road.

Whichever method you choose, children who help their family with a fund-raiser or a home business discover that academic subjects have real-world applications. While your children are learning important business skills, they can grow in maturity and wisdom. See if you can find an idea in this chapter that fits the need of your family.

FUND-RAISERS FOR FAMILIES

Fund-raising works best if your family will be building houses for the homeless, planning a mission trip, taking children's books to Appalachia, or volunteering for other worthwhile endeavors. You can use the same fund-raisers that work for youth groups, schools, and other charitable organizations. Donations might be tax deductible. Check with the organization. You may need to have donations and proceeds from fund-raisers sent directly to the organization and earmarked for your expenses.

Dorothy Nielsen, a single working mom living from hand to mouth, dreamed of traveling to India and Romania to visit and volunteer at their orphanages. Thanks to fund-raising, her dream came true. "One of my girl-friends hosted dinner and appetizers," she says. "Everybody who came drew an envelope out of a basket for a door prize. Restaurants gave us gift certificates for lunch or dinner; hotels gave us a certificate for one night's stay." Dorothy used those incentives to inspire people to financially support her trip. In the end, she raised more than five thousand dollars.

Dorothy started out with a small crowd of people she knew, and then she expanded her contacts.

You just have to start talking about it and just do it—you just have to do it. I've gotten money from my doctor, my vet, my dentist. There's a coffee shop in town and a workout gym, and they both let me put out jars for donations. I wrote a little bit about what I was doing, labeled the jars, and left them there. I live in a small enough town that everybody pretty much knows what everybody else is doing anyway, so it's not like I'm a stranger. The first couple of times, it's kind of difficult, but then it just gets easier.

Some organizations have suggestions for getting donations or sponsoring fund-raising events. Set up a sales table at a fair, festival, church event, or white elephant sale, or ask for permission to set up outside a grocery store or other high-traffic area. Arrange information about your trip on the table to inform buyers of how their purchases will help promote education and service. You can decorate the table with maps, photos, travel brochures, pictures, or objects of interest. Want to make sure people will stop? Invite them to sample ethnic dishes from your destination.

Jules Michaels, a volunteer coordinator for Global Volunteers, says that many companies and organizations are willing to sponsor volunteers, but you must show them how they can also benefit in some way. This may be as simple as offering to come back and speak about what you saw and learned. "Fund-raising is a great way to focus your commitment to volunteer and involve others in your community with your experience," says Jules. He suggests starting with your personal contacts:

- friends and family
- Kiwanis, American Legion, Rotary, and civic or other organizations
- your church or religious affiliation
- local businesses (look for matching grant programs)
- your employer or your spouse's or parents' employers
- organizations with which you, your spouse, or family members are affiliated, such as 4-H, local community theater, fraternities or sororities

Next Jules suggests brainstorming to identify organizations that have a heartfelt connection to your cause. If you will do mission work for people with disabilities, you might want to contact a wheelchair manufacturer or medical supply company. If you want to teach English in Mexico, contact teacher associations.

Colleges can be good sources for fund-raising information, and you may be able to arrange college credit for your experiences. Contact financial aid offices, foreign study offices, and independent study offices.

Large sports arenas, like the Metrodome in Minneapolis, usually have an auxiliary booth, which raises money by selling hot dogs or other refreshments. Maybe you can get a group of friends together to work at the booth, or perhaps a service club would be willing to do it to raise money for your trip.

What can you sell at a fund-raiser? Here are some small-scale ideas to get you started:

- Sell prepaid tickets to a car wash. Pat Wesolowski, a frugal at-home mom, tells of a team of kids who raised big bucks to travel to a competition by preselling three-dollar tickets, in advance for a car wash. "They sold fifteen hundred dollars in tickets, and only a handful of folks showed up to get their cars washed on the appointed date," she said. Presumably, because the price of the ticket was small, many people were glad to contribute by buying a ticket, even if they did not get around to having their car washed.
- Prepaid tickets have also been used successfully for fund-raisers such as a pancake breakfast and a class for learning ballroom dancing.

- Make homemade Easter candy, such as chocolate eggs decorated with the name of the child, or personalized Christmas cookies. You could also sell sugar-cookie dough to busy parents, ready for the fun part (rolling, baking, and decorating).
- Collect donations for a white elephant sale.
- Have a silent auction with items and services donated by friends, family, and merchants. The trick is to get enough people to come to the auction, so you might want to have it in conjunction with another event. You may hesitate to ask for donations, and you may get some noes. If it is for a good cause, though, you will have plenty of donations. Many merchants use such donations as a form of publicity, and sometimes they are actually moneymakers for the merchant. Judith's husband, for example, donates gift certificates for photography to schools, churches, an educational television station, and other nonprofit groups. People frequently spend much more than the value of the donation. The more gift certificates he gives away, the more he earns.
- Many churches and charities find cookbook sales successful. You may be able to collect recipes from people who live in your destination area, members of a club or church, or friends and family. Shop around for the best deal with local printers, letting them know about your service project. Compare local printing prices with prices from a company that specializes in fund-raising through cookbook sales. One example is Fundcraft, which offers a free "Get Cooking" computer software CD-ROM. The software lets you enter recipes, spell-check them, and print copies.
- Have a phantom tea—"phantom" because there is no actual event. Let your kids help create fancy invitations, either on a computer or by hand, inviting neighbors, friends, or family to your invisible tea. Enclose a tea bag for them to enjoy, and state that the donor can pick the date of their own convenience and the location of their choice. No need to leave home or spend money for a new outfit, or purchase fund-raiser items they do not want! Be sure to include a self-addressed, stamped envelope for donations.

Finding a Commercial Sponsor

Some clever travelers have found a commercial sponsor to foot all or part of their travel expenses.

The Romp family of Shoreham, Vermont, found commercial sponsors to help pay for their dream trip. It helped that their mode of travel was newsworthy: The family of five rode a four-person bicycle, pulling a trailer caboose for the smallest child. They traveled from New England to Alaska that way—a six-month, forty-five-hundred-mile odyssey.

Forty-six-year-old Billy Romp had a twenty-year career in bicycle retail and touring. His wife, Patti, and twelve-year-old daughter Ellie race mountain bikes. Eight-year-old Henry favors bicycle tricks and jumps, but he has the stamina to ride all day on tour. Three-year-old Timmy rides the caboose. Billy says the "sheer audacity" of the expedition attracted news media ranging from *People Weekly* and the *New York Times* to The Discovery Channel and bicycling magazines.

"In all, more than fifty newspapers and thirty television stations interviewed us as we pedaled from town to town," he says, which made it easier to attract sponsors, who love being part of a media frenzy.

Although the Romps paid the basic expenses for their six-month trip, they received support from a variety of commercial sponsors—not huge corporations, just companies, organizations, and individuals who took a personal interest in the family's adventure.

In looking for sponsors, think about your "sphere of influence," the people and organizations with whom you have personal contact. Your equipment suppliers are a likely prospect. Ortlieb USA, in Auburn, Washington, agreed to sponsor the Romps' trip by providing waterproof outdoor equipment, such as panniers and bags. Some companies offered helpful discounts. Billy contacted the custom builder of their unique four-person bicycle, Santana Cycles in LaVerne, California, who extended employee pricing on parts and accessories, saving the Romps hundreds of dollars. A company called Specialized provided the family with helmets, shoes, and tires. Several companies offered "pro pricing." The Romps could buy their products directly from the manufacturer, usually below wholesale price and with free shipping. The family even received free chiropractic services along their route through the sponsorship of Preferred Chiropractic Doctor, an organization that offers members a discount with participating chiropractors.

The moral is, ask. A sponsorship can be a win-win proposition for all parties. However, it pays to know *how* to ask. Billy adds this advice to anyone thinking about pursuing sponsors:

> The main item you have to offer in exchange for their support is exposure. Describe your plan to generate exposure for the company, one that emphasizes a positive image and real knowledge of the methods of media publicity. This knowledge is easy to come by—it's the nuts and bolts of press releases, media events, contact management, phone calls, faxes, and e-mails to the three main media types: print, radio, and television.
>
> The keyword is *persistence,* both in seeking sponsorship and in garnering publicity. Be prepared for extended phone tag and follow-up. "Free" sponsorship, support, and equipment can cost much in terms of time and energy expended.

The Romp family plans to publish a book tentatively titled *Wind in Your Face.* Let's hope their book will help pay for their next trip!

Recycling for Dollars

If your trip is not for a ministry or charity or for a high-profile odyssey like the Romp family's, you can look at other ways to earn travel money.

Dianna, a single mother, and her son Jason turned to recycling.

> To finance trips to Washington, D.C., and Disney World, we collected aluminum cans. We looked at it this way: One, we were picking up trash along the road, which was a community thing. Two, we were recycling, which was a worldwide thing. And, three, we were walking, bending down, picking up—we were getting exercise. Plus, we were earning cash!
>
> Recycling became an unbelievable learning experience. One summer we kept count of how many different types of cans we found, and Jason made a chart to see which cans we found the most of. We found more beer cans than pop cans. That involved graphing and counting.

You will get more money for recyclables if your state requires cash deposits for cans and bottles, although in those states, fewer people litter the roadways with containers. (And that, of course, is the main idea behind requiring the deposit!) In other states, you can earn a little money for aluminum, but recycling tin cans and glass will probably be a labor of love.

"Will Work for Travel"

What skills do you have? Do they translate into a home business or sideline business? Do not overlook your homemaking skills. They are valued by people with more money than time.

Perhaps you can exercise a neglected skill, something very different from those you currently use. You can trade your services in exchange for needed funds. We're not talking about just "kid stuff" here. Many projects have been turned into genuine moneymakers and even full-time careers.

A homeschool dad wanted to go on a short-term mission trip with his family, but the money just was not in the family budget. When he heard that friends needed their house painted, he jumped at the chance. He had painting experience (although at the time, he was working at a different occupation) and offered to do the job for the price of the trip.

Here are some tried and true ways for kids or adults (or a family working as a team) to earn a sideline income with the proceeds earmarked for travel. If your children is involved in 4-H, a youth program sponsored by the county extension office, they can use some of these endeavors as 4-H projects. Among other things, 4-H encourages kids nine to nineteen years of age to keep financial records and make a profit in a home business:

- Have a yard sale extraordinaire. Get rid of the clutter and encourage your kids to do the same. Months in advance, invite friends and family to box up the goods cluttering up their attics, garages, or basements, which you could sell on consignment (keeping a percentage). Or you could offer to clean out the items yourself in exchange for the goods.
- Mow lawns, garden, or landscape. People will pay dearly to get their flowers or vegetables planted in the spring.
- Raise a small crop, such as a pumpkin patch, pretty Indian corn, a berry patch, or a few beef cattle or sheep, and designate the profits for travel.

- Sew curtains for homes or RVs. RVers are a good market, since they often need custom sizes.
- Offer cooking or catering services. Offer something people would enjoy but rarely take time for, such as homemade bread, cakes, cookies, or pasta noodles. There is a market for freshly baked whole-grain products. Try posting a notice at a local food co-op, in grocery stores, or on the bulletin board at church. You can also offer to cater a few small-scale events.
- Cleaning—one of today's best-paid sideline professions! You can work for a cleaning service or start your own for even more profit.
- Crafts. Create a stockpile of inventory to sell at craft shows (especially at Christmas) or set up a booth at school festivals. One mother set up an annual Christmas craft show in her home with a friend, usually in October. For customized or time-consuming items, she showed samples and took orders.
- Painting house numbers on the curb or on mailboxes, using stencils, is a low-tech way kids can make money. One young man found that he made more money by accepting donations than he did by charging a set fee.
- Caring for younger children. Teenage homeschoolers, with their flexible schedules, are much in demand, both for families and organizations such as La Leche League or church groups.
- Design Web pages. This skill can be a profitable sideline, and some teens earn a hefty wage per hour, compared to fast-food jobs.
- Entertain at birthday parties. Be a clown or a storyteller or organize games. Your children may enjoy helping, especially if they get a share for travel spending money.

Homeowners in upscale neighborhoods will compete to pay for these services. To succeed, you need reliability, punctuality, persistence, and the right price—low enough to attract customers, high enough to make a fair profit. Be aware that most people undercharge for their time when starting out. Find out what the going rate is. Then calculate all your expenses, add in a reasonable wage and profit, and let the learning begin!

Adults may be willing to moonlight temporarily as a way to raise travel funds. You can apply to work as a temp, and not just as receptionists or factory workers either. Some agencies, like Manpower, have special divisions that fill highly skilled or technical jobs in construction, computers, engineering, and accounting. Look under "Employment Contractors—Temporary Help" in the telephone directory. Some enterprising travelers may be able to find work on the road this way.

EARN MONEY AS YOU TRAVEL

Some families earn money while they travel, often with an existing business. One family makes handmade dulcimers during the winter and then sells them at craft shows. Others have "real jobs" during the year. When they travel, they bring along craft items to sell, work at a campground, or find other ways to earn a sideline income to finance their journeys.

Jaimie Hall, coeditor of the *RV Lifestyle* newsletter, and her husband, Bill, started traveling full time in 1993. They work on the road for at least six months of the year, usually as seasonal workers for the National Park Service. In between, they have sold Christmas trees and worked for temporary agencies.

There is other seasonal or temporary work—like driving for UPS at Christmas, or tax season work, but in those cases you need to have housing. An RV is one of the cheaper ways to stay in an area for a short period of time. I do know folks, though, who go from seasonal job to seasonal job and have no house, no furniture, few possessions, and make it work. I think talking to others and determination can make something work!

If you know your stuff, you can buy antiques and collectibles and sell them. This can be a profitable sideline business. One collector we know specializes in Heisey glassware, which is plentiful where she lives (where the original factory stood), but less available in other parts of the country. She takes a load down to an antique mall several states away and sells her finds at a premium price, which pays for her travel expenses. Others buy as they travel, then sell their items back home or through Internet auctions.

Duke and Sandra Merrion of Indiana have a sideline business selling specialty farm equipment for an importer from Europe. They have attended organic farming conferences in various states displaying a spading machine and a compost turner. Taking the equipment to demonstrations and occasionally delivering a spader has given them a working vacation to twelve states. They have taken advantage of those trips to make educational side trips and to sightsee along the way.

Wondering what might be a good sideline for you? The more you know about your market, the better. What are you involved in? What do you know a lot about? What "communities" are you a part of?

Browse the vendor tables at a homeschool conference, and you will find many homeschool families sitting behind the tables, selling products from their home businesses. Lynn, a homeschool mother of four, sold T-shirts promoting homeschooling. Her children drew the designs, and Lynn bought the T-shirts wholesale and had them silk-screened professionally. Some homeschool support groups encourage family industries. Often the families sell learning aids originally created for their own families. Many specialize in Christian products that minister to spiritual as well as educational needs.

Mary Carney, author of *Cooking Ahead,* gives workshops at homeschool conventions in exchange for booth space for her books and baking products and a booth for her teenage daughter. Her daughter has a package babysitting service for tired parents shopping in the vendor hall. (Yes, she watches over attendees' packages while they tour the hall!) She wasn't sure what to charge, so she decided to accept donations—and found out that she earned much more than she would ever have charged. Their convention trips give mother and daughter time away together, and their sideline businesses pay for the trips.

A Family Photography Business on the Road

The Allees sometimes take their home-based photography business on the road. They seek jobs photographing reunions, conferences, and other events, then plan their educational forays around their work.

That's one way. Do you have a successful service or product? You can translate that into a traveling business by developing contacts in other states or areas. You might need to change your service or product slightly, however. Try out your ideas on a small scale close to home. For instance, Judith's family found that their original photography business—photography of families and children—is not portable. It requires too much long-term marketing and reputation building in an individual community. Photographing events, however, requires a different kind of marketing, primarily through referrals. By letting people know they were interested in jobs that involve travel, they got a chance to submit a bid for several conferences. Because they travel only occasionally, they do not have to worry about filling their schedule with out-of-town jobs.

Going to Sea as a Sailor

"Again, I always go to sea as a sailor, because they make a point of paying me for my trouble, whereas they never pay passengers a single penny that I ever heard of. On the contrary, passengers themselves must pay; and there is all the difference in the world between paying and being paid." —Herman Melville, *Moby Dick*

Travel Businesses Equal Travel Discounts

Perhaps you would like to be a home-based travel agent, earning commissions as well as travel discounts for your own family. Jennifer Dugan, mother of two preschoolers, started a home-based travel business after her children were born. She specializes in family travel and offers others (often at-home mothers) a chance to do the same thing by working through her agency (Dugan's Travel). By doing this, she is able to combine family and business.

Jennifer's e-book (electronic book), *Bizy Guide to Operating a Home-Based Travel Agency*, is available at the Bizy Mom's Web site, along with a variety of e-books on home-based businesses, including some that may fit well with your travel plans.

Want a free trip? By putting together and guiding a tour, you can travel for free. Travel agencies like Trans World Travel (TWT), a worldwide Christian travel agency founded in 1947, will help you put together a tour for thirty-five to forty-two people. You line up the people and accompany them on the trip, and TWT lines up the travel. For smaller groups, they will help arrange cohosting. In most cases, you receive one complimentary trip for every six or seven passengers you line up. You also have the option of earning a commission in lieu of complimentary trips or a combination of cash benefits and complimentary trips.

TWT primarily works with pastors, priests, and church-affiliated groups. It also works with alumni groups, teachers, and leaders who put together a tour for people with an affinity toward a special interest such as art history, archaeology, or agriculture. TWT provides brochures, travel presentations, films, and guidance throughout the planning stages.

Policies vary about bringing children. Teens are most likely to be able to come on tours with you, but some tours are intended for whole families, so you may be able to bring younger children as well.

BE A CARETAKER

If you are open to unusual surroundings, responsibilities, and situations, you may consider caretaking as a way to make your travel dreams a reality.

> We are looking for somebody who will live in our home and care for our dog and birds. The period is from January 1–March 30. We live in a large house in a quiet street. Garden. Our small town is half an hour south of Rotterdam. Please call...

This ad for a house sitter in the Netherlands is representative of what you might find in *The Caretaker Gazette*. A bimonthly publication, the *Gazette* features positions ranging from unpaid temporary house sitters to highly paid caretakers for wealthy estate owners. Caretakers may or may not get private quarters. At the very least, you secure a free place to stay, possibly in a setting that would far exceed what you could afford. If you intend to bring children, make sure the owner is aware of this before your trip so you can avoid any misunderstandings.

TELECOMMUTING AND TELEWORKING

Telecommuters work off-site for one full-time employer. Most telecommuters work from their homes.

"Telework" is a broader term that includes people who work anywhere from a client's office to the beach, according to the International Telework Association and Council, which has affiliates in the United States, Canada,

Europe, and Asia. An increasing number work from wherever they like, thanks to cellular phones, pagers, e-mail, and increasingly powerful and lighter laptop and pocket-size computers. The flexibility regarding office location could be used by someone who longs to travel but needs to earn a living. (Most telecommuters, however, are required to spend some time in the corporate office each month, which occasionally may complicate travel plans.)

Current and former employers are the best places to look for teleworking opportunities. Many such jobs start out as everyday nine-to-five office jobs and evolve into teleworking because the company values and trusts that particular worker—and managers are willing to be flexible in order to keep that employee.

The benefits are not all one-sided, though. Some companies have embraced teleworking because it reduces the need for office space and lowers overhead costs. Employers also benefit from having a happier and, presumably, more productive employee.

COMMISSION SALES

Some commission salespeople may have flexibility to take time off to travel, especially during their slow seasons. Northern RV salespeople can often get away in the winter, when sales are typically low. One mother, a sales representative for World Book, was able to travel out-of-state to visit her daughter and her family for weeks or months at a time. She would bring her samples along and make contacts in her daughter's neighborhood and through church friends, loaning out sample volumes and offering to demonstrate how the company's encyclopedias and other educational products could benefit their families.

SEASONAL AND TEMPORARY WORK

Some family members travel part or full time and find jobs whenever they need extra money. You may have experience in a skill, such as computer programming or Web design, which will be in demand at your destination or along your route. If so, you may be able to take along your laptop and hire yourself out via the Internet. Check local computer papers—available at local computer stores and at many area libraries—for available jobs.

Union members, especially those in construction and related fields, can find work through union halls as they travel. Local members get first priority, but union halls provide an information pipeline about available work. Travelers are free to go wherever the work is.

Companies that operate concessions, steamboat and river barge tour companies, guest ranches, and the like offer seasonal jobs. College students, who tend to have the flexibility to work on-site for a few months, fill most of the positions. Some locations, however, such as the Grand Canyon National Park Lodges, accept families, and some employers provide trailer sites for their employees' motor homes or travel trailers. Several Web sites allow you to search for jobs by location or type of work.

If you work in a tourist area, ask about passes and discounts for employees, and find out if passes are available for other attractions in the area. Some companies want you to visit so you will be able to recommend their sites too. They may include your children.

The Romp family, mentioned earlier in this chapter, lives in Vermont, but has spent every Christmas season since 1988 selling Christmas trees in New York City at the corner of Eighth Avenue and Jane Street. The family stays in a camper parked on the corner. Billy Romp says, "We meet everybody, we know their names, we have watched their kids grow, and, many times, we have been in their apartments. The neighbors seem to be in a competition to see who can be the nicest to us, to do the most for us."

If you have a professional license, such as hairdressing, counseling, or real estate, check into requirements for working in a different state or province.

BUSINESS TRAVEL AND KIDS—DON'T LEAVE HOME WITHOUT THEM

Have you turned down jobs or promotions because they involved travel away from home, and you wanted to be with your children more? If so, you are not alone. Parents, especially those who wait to have children, see their babies grow up at lightning speed and do not want to miss out on their childhood.

You may now be able to climb the ladder to success and bring your family along for an educational travel ride. In 1999 one in five American adults traveled for business at least once, according to the Travel Industry Association of America. Business travelers brought their children along on more than thirty-two million of those business trips. Trips with children accounted for 16 percent of all business trips in 1998. That's almost two million trips that combined business and kids.

Melissa and Judith have been able to include their children in a variety of business settings, including meetings and conferences. That probably works best with few children, or older children, and it naturally depends on the personality and behavior of the child.

Bringing your family along to a business meeting will work in some settings, but it may be considered unprofessional behavior in others. If so, how can kids fit into business travel? Some hotels provide childcare services or programs. Or one parent may watch the kids while the other attends meetings.

Many business travelers are left with lonely evening hours or other times when it is impossible to meet with clients. That's time that parents and kids could spend together. Busy parents who yearn for a closer family relationship may take the family and extend the stay, perhaps over a weekend. The extra time gives them a chance to be together outside the routine of activities, telephone calls, and television schedules.

Judith's sister-in-law, Betty, is a partner in a CPA firm in Cincinnati. She wanted to take spring break off to be with her family. A client had an important meeting in another city. So the client "made me an offer I couldn't refuse," says Betty. He offered to pay airfare for the whole family of five. They worked in trips to the beach around Betty's schedule. The family got a vacation they could not otherwise afford, either financially or timewise.

When only the employee gets expenses paid, it still can make an inexpensive mini-vacation possible. Frequent-flier miles can allow parents to take their children for free. Melissa's husband, a Defense Department employee, travels occasionally for work-related training. The family also occasionally travels for their home business. She comments:

> Our children have been with us on business to Virginia and even sat in
> on business meetings. I realize that may not be possible for everyone,
> but it may be more possible than you think. If you are self-employed,
> it's up to you how you do business. If you are employed, you may find
> out that your employer is willing to give it a try.

We don't find that our children are a handicap. If anything, they have often helped to break the ice in the business setting. Of course, they have been trained since babyhood, so they know how to behave in a variety of social situations, with both adults and children of all ages. Actually, people tend to trust you more when you're with youngsters. I feel this trust is justified because of the transparent nature of children.

Our children don't always enjoy the business world as much as their parents, and they admit to being bored at times. However, they understand the necessity of earning a living, which we feel is a key to success in adulthood. They each carry a backpack filled with paper and colored pencils and pens for writing and art projects.

Your Children: A Well-Behaved Traveling Workforce

Aside from overt education in the form of museums and field trips, business trips can provide your children with "covert" learning—a better understanding of what you do for a living and how business works. Judith shares some memories of taking her daughter, Nancy, to photograph reunions and conferences:

Nancy was helpful in carrying and setting up equipment, especially as she got older. Even at age four, as the camera fired for a group photo, Nancy was the one who shouted "One, two, t-h-r-e-e!" That got everyone's attention. For the second shot she counted in Spanish, *"Uno, dos, t-r-e-s!"* and everyone laughed. For the third (and usually last shot), she switched to French or German, which, by the way, was all the French and German she knew.

Working as a family made us stand out as a business with a human side. Our daughter loved the positive attention. By the time Nancy was nine or ten, she could single-handedly run our order table at a reunion with her dad and me working close by. She passed out order forms, made change, and answered customer questions. Her work was an important learning experience for her, and we appreciated her help.

Can your children be an asset for your traveling business? That depends. Children can charm your clients. Or not. As we all know, kids do not always put on "company" behavior on request. For a child, there is a sense of power in realizing he can thwart you at the very moment you cannot do much about it.

Judith says,

> Our children started accompanying us to photography jobs when our foster boys were about ten years old. Taking one child at a time was definitely more manageable than multiple children, but if the job was flexible and the customer was understanding, we sometimes brought two or three children. Although John preferred to have my assistance, he could carry on alone for a while, if necessary, if I needed to remove a child to handle a behavior problem. It's tempting to give in just to keep the peace, but that sets you up for problems later on.
>
> We paid the children an hourly salary, but the children knew their earnings were dependent on their cooperative behavior and not creating a disturbance while we were working. At a young age, a quarter was a big incentive. We also brought books, crayons, and a lunchbox filled with small toys. When Nancy was little, she brought along her My Little Ponies dolls, which gave her an immediate "in" with other children around her age who might happen to be at the same event.
>
> Our teens earned about minimum wage, plus a bonus of five to thirty dollars if we had good sales, so the teen was able to share in rewards of a job well done. Those earnings were especially useful when we traveled, since it gave them a way to pick up some extra spending money.

MINDING YOUR TRAVELING BUSINESS: PUBLICATIONS

One way to glean ideas for a traveling home business is to read about what works for others. *Workers on Wheels* is a free e-mail publication for people with traveling businesses. This publication features a variety of mobile entre-preneurs: craftspeople, consultants, accountants, sales reps, sign makers, writers, and photographers. Some of these people are hobbyists earning a sideline, while others earn a full-time livelihood. The publication also covers topics such as using a computer aboard an RV and handling taxes along with articles on making hobbies pay and the personal stories of people who have developed profit-making ventures. Subscribe at *www.WorkersonWheels.com*.

Another publication for people who want to work while traveling is *Workamper News,* which lists help-wanted ads for employers ranging from campgrounds and national parks to circuses and ski resorts. The jobs offer parking for your RV, or they may offer housing. Some positions offer a swap—a few hours' work for a free campsite—while others are full-time salaried positions, although they may be temporary.

Free Sample Issue

A free miniedition of *Workamper News* is available by calling (800) 446-5627. The Workamper's Web site, *http://www.workamper.com,* contains thousands of job openings ranging from part-time volunteer positions to full-time careers in campgrounds, theme parks, motor sports, resorts, and so on. If you subscribe to the magazine, you may also place a free situation-wanted ad both in the magazine and on the Web site. About half of Workampers who have used the service have received job offers within a week of placing their ads.

Some working campers are professional entertainers, such as singers, magicians, and storytellers. Entertainers commonly approach a campground about providing a free site in exchange for entertainment on the weekend at the clubhouse.

David Helflick travels to perform music programs in schools. His book, *How to Make Money Performing in Schools: Definitive Guide to Developing, Marketing, and Presenting School Assembly Programs,* covers arts programs of all kinds, from puppeteers to mimes as well as educational programs such as drug abuse prevention and disability awareness.

THE TAXMAN AND OTHER BUGABOOS

Doing business on the road may make it more important to have access to telephone, voice mail, and possibly the Internet. (We discuss communications in a later chapter.) It is also important to keep adequate financial records for the day when we "give to Caesar what is Caesar's" (Mark 12:17).

See your accountant to find out what records you should keep and how to separate personal expenses from deductible business expenses—including the wages you pay your children or your spouse for legitimate work. Your accountant knows the specific details of your situation and can give you individual advice.

If you can establish yourself as a legitimate travel writer, you may be able to deduct some of your travel expenses. The expenses must be related to a bona fide story or article. Consult your accountant or tax professional for details.

Networks, Recordkeeping, Taxes, and Kids—Oh My!

Let's face it: It takes a stout heart to start your own business if you don't have experience or role models to learn from. You need to understand—quickly— about marketing. Add thoughts of educational travel with kids, recordkeeping, and taxes, and you may start to feel overwhelmed. Fear can make you fail or not even try.

Don't give up on your dreams of educational travel and a business to finance it. Help is available. You can find comfort, information, and advice, both financial and otherwise. Find a compatible mentor (perhaps the owner of a similar business in another city) who will help you fill your niche. Network with your trade association or the local Small Business Administration. Contact S.C.O.R.E., the Service Core of Retired Executives. They're there to help keep your business afloat, instead of sinking your financial boat.

wiseguy

Changing Your Life

"The man who wants to lead the orchestra must turn his back on the crowd."
—James Crook

If you look at what entrepreneurs have in common, you see that most of them had a parent who was self-employed. Maybe you didn't have that advantage. Your children can, though, if you start even a tiny sideline business. Another trait entrepreneurs tend to have in common is that they experiment with several business ideas before finding the one that works for them. If you keep your investment low, you can't lose much, and what you learn in the process may lay the groundwork for future success for you or someone in your family. It's a win-win proposition, whether you make money or not.

Chapter Ten

Frugal Food for the Road

Ah, there is nothing quite like pulling out of your driveway to create immediate hunger and thirst in children. Although we may forget to plan for
them, hunger, thirst, and, to some extent, children are predictable. Keeping
everyone fed regularly reduces general crabbiness. Here are low-cost ideas for
eating out, picnicking from the grocery store, cooking on the road, packing
food, and bringing your own snacks to an event or attraction.

How can vacation food be educational? Include your children in planning
menus, budgeting, and preparing food for your trip, and watch them learn.
Young people can experience the challenge of cost comparisons, handling
coupons, and list making, and their help can be valuable to busy parents.

Although some children will only eat familiar food, gradually exposing
them to different cuisines can be an important part of their education.
Ethnic restaurants can give your family experiences with new tastes, neighborhoods, languages, and customs. Some children have more interest in
sampling your food if you announce that it is "for adults" than if you entreat
them to try something different. On the other hand, tired and frazzled travelers often feel less stressed by familiar comfort food, whether home-cooked
or from McDonald's golden arches. Vacations, like weddings, can provide
"something old, something new."

Take time to enjoy your meals together. "The way to a man's heart is
through his stomach" applies to women and children, too. Sharing a good
meal creates important family memories. If you celebrate family church, you
may even want to share a spiritual meal together as a family, complete with
communion bread and juice or wine, according to your custom.

PORTABLE, PACKABLE, PALATABLE FOOD

Eating out three times a day plus snacks is a money sieve. It robs your travel time and gets old pretty fast, especially if your food budget is slim and the meals are nothing special. By packing some of your meals, maybe you will be able to afford some unique, more memorable restaurant meals.

Melissa's family likes to get a quick start in the morning with a simple breakfast.

> Our family plans for breakfast in our room, cabin, or tent. Instead of dragging the kids to an expensive restaurant, we get to eat in comfort. We bring cereal and canned milk, or buy milk at a grocery store the night before. I use a small plug-in hot pot to make tea at campgrounds that have electric connections. I'm not the campfire type—especially early in the morning! Some hotel rooms provide a small coffeepot. If you omit the coffee, the pot can be used to make hot water for tea, hot cereal, or instant soup for lunch. Think safety first. We're also careful to clean up all traces of food so that we don't attract bugs or make more work for the staff.

The Allees are more likely to eat a leisurely, big breakfast in an inexpensive area restaurant, which is the cheapest way to have a nice meal out—and John gets his coffee in a real cup rather than Styrofoam. They often split two meals between three people, and then they have a quick packed lunch in the car or at a roadside park.

If they are rushed or plan on having dinner in a restaurant that day, they nibble on fresh fruit for breakfast, eating as they drive. Based on suggestions from *Fit for Life* by Harvey and Marilyn Diamond, the idea is to eat one piece of fruit, and when you get hungry have another piece, and so on until lunchtime. Judith, who sometimes experiences low blood sugar, finds that fresh fruit for breakfast keeps her blood sugar on an even keel, and it is quick, enjoyable, uncomplicated, and easy to buy when traveling. It helps the whole family increase their intake of fruit and vegetables, which is sometimes hard to do when traveling. The downside is that you are not "finished" with breakfast until lunchtime, and sometimes it is not convenient to keep eating another piece of fruit.

Hotel breakfasts served in the dining room are expensive compared to the actual cost of the food served. You may find, however, that many hotels offer a free continental breakfast. "All you can eat" breakfast buffets can be especially frugal for large families or families with hungry teens.

If your children don't mind, you can eat sandwiches for breakfast, lunch, or dinner. Packed frozen in the morning, sandwiches are thawed but still fresh by lunchtime. Pack lettuce and tomato separately. Look through over one hundred sandwich ideas in *The Book of Sandwiches* by Louise Steele for original ideas if you want to avoid boredom and a family food strike.

Frozen packages of meal-size portions or individual servings provide home-cooked meals on the road. Freeze dishes that are good cold, or prepare them for times when you will be doing some cooking on the road. We have found that home-frozen foods make an ideal contribution to meals with any host families or relatives you plan to visit who live within a three-day range of home.

If you buy the makings of s'mores (graham crackers, marshmallows, and chocolate bars) at the camp store, you will pay a premium price. You might want to pack them or pick them up at a grocery store close to your campground.

For a quick picnic, a can of tuna and a salad from a fast-food restaurant make the basis of a good dinner for two (and three cans and three salads for six). Add crackers and fruit, and you are on your way.

The Penny Whistle Traveling with Kids Book by Meredith Brokaw and Annie Gilbar contains helpful hints for eating in the car as well as adventurous food combinations. Imagine eating hummus with tahini in the backseat. Or maybe you'd prefer crackers and cheese, which is a favorite among small children.

Hygiene can be a challenge when you are traveling, which is also the least convenient time for illnesses. It is not a good time to let down your guard on simple hand washing, especially before eating and after toileting. Baby wipes and those finger-cleaning packets from some fast-food restaurants (you can also buy them in stores) are welcome in lieu of a sink and hot water. An old dishwashing liquid bottle filled with water and a little detergent makes a good container for squirting dirty hands. Bacteria-killing gel that does not have to be rinsed off is another option.

COOLER 101

An insulated ice chest can go along on many trips, including short ones. A cooler can keep hot foods hot as well as keep covered dishes from spilling and creating a mess on the way to an event. Having a cooler extends the time we can be out, allowing us to combine field trips and errands and cut down on mileage. We have assorted coolers, large and small. They travel with us on all out-of-town trips. We also bring them to the grocery store on hot days or when we want to lengthen our time away from home so that the frozen foods are still frozen when we get home.

Keeping ice packs in the freezer makes it easy to throw a few perishable items into a cooler at a moment's notice. For longer trips, however, and when both space and weight are at a premium, try freezing much of the food and drink you plan to bring. Leave room in each container for expansion so that your containers do not break during freezing. They will slowly thaw as you use up the food, eliminating the need for ice. Then when the food is partly used, there will be room for ice, if you still need it. Buy ice at a gas station, grocery store, or campground.

The Morgan children enjoy packing their own small individual coolers with snacks and drinks. Mom keeps a separate container to dole out special snacks at opportune moments—such as when a distraction is needed. The Morgans depend on packs of chemical ice, which stays cold longer than ice made from water, to store refrigerated medicine. Nontoxic chemical ice is inexpensive and lasts for years. Some packs are designed to remain flexible, so you can fit them in odd places or use one to wrap around a wounded elbow or wrist. While ice can reduce swelling, it can also damage skin tissues if overdone. Consult your doctor and learn some basic first aid for emergencies.

If your cooler is not full, it will stay cold longer if you stuff the empty spaces with plastic bags filled with ice cubes, crumpled newspaper balls, or other insulating material. Try to park with the cooler in the shade and cover it with insulating material—newspapers, clothing, bedding, towels, or whatever you have with you. The muffler and drive train cause a hot strip down the middle of most cars. Feel underneath the cooler with your hand after you have been on the road for a while to make sure it's not resting on a hot spot. (On the other hand, if you are using the cooler to keep hot food hot, look for the hot spot.)

For frequent travelers, a twelve-volt refrigerated cooler may be a good investment. The cooler plugs into your car via the cigarette lighter, which is actually a twelve-volt outlet. The one we saw also worked on household current. You could use it at your campsite or in your motel room. It can be used as a food warmer as well as a cooler.

A thermos is not only for hot food. A wide-mouth thermos is good for keeping items like cottage cheese, yogurt, and potato salad at a safe temperature.

WATER, WATER EVERYWHERE

Water is available (almost) everywhere, and refills are free. If it spills in the car, no one gets sticky, and the container is ever so easy to wash. If found under the seat next summer, it will not be revolting beyond belief. It is easy enough to tell the kids they can drink only water. Oh, they will complain, but most of us can handle that. Where many parents (well, at least the authors) fall down is in wanting the other drinks themselves.

A hard and fast rule: Have water for everyone. Do not wait until you go on vacation to institute this rule, though. Start several months ahead, if possible, to condition the ranks. Maybe you can put the soft drink money in a jar designated for spending money on the trip, so the children will reap a reward from their efforts.

Guess what product at fast-food restaurants provides the most profit? It is not the triple burgers with special sauces—it is the drinks. Ask for courtesy cups, fast-food lingo for free paper cups for water, or bring your own. Try reserving soft drinks for an occasional treat.

Keep water accessible in the car. It is easy to neglect drinking enough water when you are traveling. Since drinking increases the potty stops, it is tempting to skip it, but this can be unhealthy and dangerous, especially in hot weather. You can, however, schedule drinks within a half-hour of stops and be realistic about allowing time for more frequent stops.

Ask around to collect some of those little plastic syrup jugs with pop-up lids and handles to use as canteens. A glass or plastic bottle with a screw-on lid for each person also works well. Use a larger thermos with water and ice cubes for refilling the bottles. Some families have individual canteens or thermos bottles, which can have great appeal to younger children. Mark or color-code each person's container.

If your family tends to develop flu and diarrhea when traveling, try practicing the same recommendations for an out-of-town trip that you would use when traveling in a foreign country. Most people have heard of Montezuma's revenge, and the conventional wisdom of "Don't drink the water" can help you avoid gastric distress. The Morgans figured this out after several bouts with travel sickness. It may be safer to bring your own water from home even on short trips, and use bottled, boiled, or distilled water on longer trips. (Tap water can develop unhealthy bacteria counts if stored unrefrigerated for several days.)

Beyond Water

If you do buy drinks, try dividing one large drink into smaller portions. (Don't take free refills if you do this. They are intended for only one person's consumption.) Do you want a third of a cup, a half a cup, or a cup and a half? Fractions! You can mark your cups if you like. Some drinking glasses are conveniently marked as measuring cups.

Instant powdered drinks travel well and are an inexpensive alternative to carbonated soft drinks. (We are talking convenience here, not nutrition.) Families with small children may want to avoid caffeine—a long journey is not the time to rev up a child's engine!

Individual juice cartons are expensive, although they are far cheaper than buying drinks at restaurants. We sometimes buy quantities of them on sale and store them until we need them for a trip. We have found that they tend to "evaporate" before the trip if we keep them in the house within easy access. (Melissa stashes them in the basement.) As an alternative, purchase fruit juice in a large, economical size (either on the road or before you leave) and then divide it into individual servings. Store individual servings in bottles, thermoses, or canteens.

CONTAINERS FOR SNACKS

Containers for packing food need not be expensive. Plastic bags with zipper closures are handy for the car. Cottage cheese and yogurt containers serve as disposable, single-serving containers. Divide canned fruit, pudding, cake, or raw vegetable sticks and pack one serving for each family member. If you do not accumulate single-serving containers, ask around. Lightweight disposable containers are helpful when you want to carry snacks with you at a festival or other event.

We also use a large, round Tupperware container that is thirteen inches in diameter and about one and a half inches high. (A variety of other brands sell similar plastic containers.) It has dividers shaped like pie wedges and is handy for carrying an assortment of relishes and snacks, such as carrot, celery, and green pepper strips; pickles; deviled eggs; and cheese sticks. Before buying one, check to make sure it will fit in your cooler.

DRINKS AND SNACKS AT AN EVENT

On-site food vendors are convenient but expensive. Sometimes unique food is an integral part of the experience. "Elephant ears" may be what your child remembers most about the fair. At international festivals, you may be able to sample food from dozens of cultures. A trip to a zoo, a festival, or other large attraction, however, can be unnecessarily arduous and expensive if you do not carry some drinks and snacks.

Paper cups weigh practically nothing and are handy for water stops. Without them, adults may have a hard time quenching their thirst at a water fountain. Small children will find it nearly impossible.

Nuts, crackers, and fresh or dried fruit make handy snacks to carry. An insulated lunch bag is useful for sandwiches. If you are wavering about whether to bring a stroller, remember that it can carry your snacks and various parcels. It may also offer a welcome resting place when your little one gets tired. (Even younger school-age children may be willing to hitch a ride on a stroller toward the end of a long outing.)

A backpack with various pockets makes a good food carrier and is a good place to stuff on-site purchases, should you succumb to any. Backpacks can carry garbage bags (to use as impromptu raincoats, to carry purchases—or to actually haul garbage), a washcloth, sunscreen, a collapsible umbrella, paper towels, and tissues. (We bring the multipurpose perforated tissues that come on a handy roll, also known as toilet paper.)

Family members can take turns carrying the backpack, and at some events it makes sense for each person to have his or her own backpack.

Some attractions forbid visitors to carry in food or drinks. In that case, you can leave your food in the car and go back out to the parking lot to eat. If possible, find out before the trip. Most attractions have Web sites that spell out such policies.

BUYING GROCERIES ON THE ROAD

Whither thou goest, a grocery store will be somewhere along the way. No need to lug fifty pounds of groceries hundreds or thousands of miles when you can buy them as you need them, giving you more space and fresher groceries.

A quick meal can be purchased at a grocery store more cheaply than eating out, and that goes double for snacks. You can buy cheese and meat by the slice, instead of by the pound. Just ask for five slices, or enough for the number of sandwiches you intend to make. If the store has a bakery, you may be able to buy individual, freshly baked rolls rather than a whole package. The same goes for cookies. Pick out just the number of apples or bananas you need, and they will be at their best.

Yogurt in individual containers is a handy, inexpensive travel snack. Yogurt aids digestion and helps your body to get back in balance if your intestinal tract gets cranky while traveling. Read the label and be sure to buy yogurt that contains "live culture" (acidophilus)—preferably plain yogurt or the kind with preserves on the bottom—rather than the premixed kind made with gelatin, which tends to be low on acidophilus and high on sugar and other fillers.

Discount clubs and many grocery stores offer food samples one or more days a week on a regular basis. One mobile family we know schedules their shopping stops for "sample day." Of course, they also buy groceries, including some of the sample items. When traveling, samples allow a taste before buying, a privilege that is considered a basic right in many cultures. Some supermarkets and bakeries give out free samples of their wares. This can make shopping more fun and may tide over a hungry child until lunch is ready. Can a whole family each try a small piece? Usually the answer is yes, but if you are unsure of "sample etiquette," just ask.

Patricia Payne is a grandmother who enjoys taking her grandchildren on RVing excursions. She shares some of the ways she keeps food costs in line:

> To get plenty of good and healthy snacks at a reasonable price, I go to stores such as MacFrugals, Family Dollar, and General Dollar. I have found that these stores have a large variety of cereals for two dollars and under, including the brands that are the kids' favorites.
>
> I buy peanuts, crackers, cookies, fruit juices, powdered drinks, pickles, and candy for a special treat, all good quality and at only one-quarter of the price at the supermarket chains. The Price Chopper Supermarket has all kinds of drinks sold by the case that save lots of money. If you have an RV, you can store the case of drinks in your basement storage, under the sofa, or under the bed until you are ready to put it into the ice chest or refrigerator. There are also some supermarkets (Aldi's is one) where you bag your own groceries and save half or more on your grocery bill. Take the grandchildren with you to these and have them help bag the groceries. They love it!

Farmers' markets and roadside fruit and vegetable stands are great places to stop for a quick break and snack. Some offer deals such as "All-you-can-drink fresh apple cider." They give you a chance to chat with local people and buy apple butter or maple syrup to take home or to give as a gift to someone you intend to visit.

Arrange to spend some time at a U-pick produce place. In many states, you'll see the signs along the highway, such as "Pick Your Own Strawberries." The cost may be less than supermarket produce, and the produce itself will probably be fresher. Kids can gain firsthand knowledge about growing and harvesting a crop.

FINDING YOUR GROCERIES IN THE WILD

According to Euell Gibbons, author of *Stalking the Wild Asparagus*, if you are a friend of nature, you need not go hungry. As a teenager in the Great

Depression, Gibbons was able to keep his family from malnutrition by foraging for wild foods to supplement their diet of mostly pinto beans. Your family can learn to identify and gather wild foods in an environmentally friendly way, including such delicacies as cattail roots, dandelion leaves, nettles, chickweed, nuts, berries, and wild mushrooms—maybe even maple syrup and possum, if you are adventurous. More important, you can learn how not to poison yourself by eating the wrong plant or the wrong part of the plant or by gathering it at the wrong time.

Eating Out

Even the thriftiest families will want to eat out occasionally when traveling. Eating in a restaurant can offer a refreshing break from the road. It has the added advantage of air conditioning or central heating, and someone else cleans up.

Eating lunch out is usually cheaper than dinner, and breakfast is cheaper than lunch. Dinner portions may be larger, however.

To keep the check reasonable, enjoy the "free" bread and crackers; order soup, salad, and appetizers instead of a meal (they are often substantial portions); and do not be shy about asking to share a meal. Just say, "Can you please bring an extra plate?" Your server probably will not blink an eye. Of course, it would be unfair to share a buffet-style meal, where you can go back for seconds. Only rarely do nonbuffet restaurants have a policy against sharing, although some have an extra charge. (If you do not care to split meals at the restaurant, you can get your food "to go.") Pat Wesolowski, mother of six and editor of the newsletter *Big Ideas, Small Budget*, says,

> Do a little investigating to discover which restaurants let children eat
> for free. If the special is one free child's meal per adult meal ordered,
> then it may be economical to order half the number of total meals you
> need as adult meals (even if the children are going to eat them), getting
> the other half for free. And, if you have an odd number of family
> members, go ahead and order an additional (the least expensive) adult
> meal and receive another free child's meal.

While you are waiting to pay for your meal, you can play Guess the Check. You may want to provide an incentive—perhaps an extra after-dinner mint or cookie—for the person who comes the closest to guessing the amount of your final bill. It is not cheating to use math skills here. After your meal, maybe your children can figure out the tip. Teach them to be generous by not skimping on the tip.

Kate Redd, in *52 Ways to Make Family Travel More Enjoyable,* suggests compiling a list of your family's best restaurant meals. You can have a family rating system: A five-star restaurant for your family might be a low-cost taco bar. How about having rating cards on a scale of one to ten for each family member to hold up (after you leave), similar to the Olympics? Ham it up.

SHRINKING YOUR DINNER CHECK

If you want food coupons, stop at the welcome center as you enter a new state. Along with maps and brochures, you will find free publications featuring coupons to use on your route. Some companies post coupons at their Web sites.

In general, there's no need to list Web sites or use a search engine to find coupons on the Internet. Just go to *www.whatever.com* (fill in the name of any national chain restaurant you want to look up). Some chains provide a listing by state or country of their restaurants. A noted pizza site gives you the nearest store that will deliver to you, wherever you are, when you enter the city or ZIP code, a catered meal at your campsite or motel room!

Coupon Corner **Newsletter**

Send for a free back issue of the *Freebie Coupon Corner* newsletter, which contains information on where to find fast-food coupons you can use when you travel as well as occasional good deals on airfare and attractions. Send a No. 10 (long) self-addressed, stamped envelope to Freebie Coupon Corner, P.O. Box 542, Oregon, IL 61061. Be sure to mention this book, since this offer is available exclusively for our readers. You also can visit the *Freebie Coupon Corner* online at *http://www.couponcorner.net*.

An online trip planning service such as *www.exitsource.com* will direct you to all your favorite chain restaurants on your route. (Forewarned is forearmed.) RVers and truckers can use *Exitsource.com* to find restaurants with truck-friendly parking areas. The "Autopilot" feature lists restaurants on your route as well as attractions, points of interest, and hotels and motels in various price ranges.

Watch for discounts and entertainment guides. Camping clubs, the American Automobile Association (AAA), and other organizations sometimes have agreements with certain merchants to offer discounts to members. If you work for a national company, check with your employer to see if employees get any special discounts. You do not have to be a grandparent to qualify for membership in AARP. When Judith's husband turned fifty-five, he qualified for a Golden Buckeye Card (an Ohio card offering discounts to "seniors"). Their daughter joked about his "old guy" card. Turns out, the discount applies to the whole family when he uses it at checkout, including restaurant meals. For that, he will put up with a little teasing.

Coupon books and coupons, by the way, may be honored by stores and restaurants nationwide, even if they were only intended for local use. Just smile and ask the manager. Often the answer is "Yes, we'll honor it." Melissa has even used a competitor's coupon, and it was happily honored.

Eating-Out Behavior

Children historically—perhaps genetically—tend to act up in public. The cause ranges from boredom to lack of training to unrealistic expectations. (Some children literally could not sit still for a half-hour if you held a gun to their heads.) This is not a frivolous concern. Some families will not travel with children because of a fear of misbehavior. If you're in one of these families, take heart. You can find economical, child-friendly travel food.

If you must eat on a plane, ship, train, or bus, try to find a location away from the childless crowd. The reaction of people without children can range from being very tolerant to being incredibly intolerant of young people's mistakes. If possible, eat in your seat or during stops (if on a bus or train), or sit with other families (there is strength in numbers) in the dining area.

Some child-friendly restaurants provide crackers, crayons, a place mat with pictures to color and games, and small toys. For a prepared parent, those items are easy enough to duplicate. Pack a private store for just such occasions. To avoid a tense atmosphere at meals, work on manners before the trip so that your children know what is expected of them in restaurants and in the company of others.

One family plays Restaurant during meals at home. The children create menus and take orders, just like real waiters and waitresses do. Parents Fred and Donna Pierce use this game as a fun way to teach their children how to behave when eating out. Incidentally, writing, reading, and math are involved.

Judith was impressed by an adoptive family with nine boys and two girls who were notably polite and well-behaved at a restaurant. The family had a policy that poor behavior in a restaurant meant you left the restaurant and waited in the car for the rest of the family. The parents took turns minding the errant child. The policy rarely had to be enforced because the children knew the parents meant what they said. (The child's meal was taken "to go," and the child ate later in the car.) Prevention might help. One mother looks for a park to let her children play in for a while before stopping for dinner. The children get "the antsies" out of their system and build healthy appetites.

If all else fails, we just eat in the car. Our car may be sticky, but at least poor restaurant behavior is no longer a problem.

FAST-FOOD RESTAURANTS

National chain fast-food restaurants are usually consistent from one location to the next, so you know what you are getting. You will not know whether you are in Los Angeles or Toronto, but the food will be delivered fast, and it will be relatively cheap. If you do not go to fast-food restaurants often when you're at home, a visit can be a real treat when you are traveling. If you do go often, it will be drudgery for most adults—but it will never be enough for most children.

Most of the food is high in fat and salt or sugar—unhealthy if it were a steady diet, but the very reason children love it. You can reduce your fat, salt, and sugar intake if you know what to order. Most restaurants post (or provide on request) nutritional information about their menu items. Nutrition information is also available at most of the chains' Web sites. Use this information to discuss nutrition with your family to make more informed choices.

For example, fat grams for Burger King sandwiches range from sixteen to sixty-five, depending on which sandwich you pick and whether or not you say, "Hold the mayo."

Remember that the add-ons are what turn two-dollar sandwiches into twenty-dollar checks. If everyone sticks to water and basic sandwiches, the meals are inexpensive, and you are rarely kept waiting very long.

Large portions of French fries cost proportionately less than small portions. If you have fries, try splitting one or more large servings rather than getting individual servings for everyone.

You can supplement your restaurant meal with raw vegetable sticks, popcorn, cookies, and other snack items from home. Take your food to a park and add in your contributions from home. You could also pass out the carrot sticks and crackers before you get to the restaurant to help hungry travelers keep their equilibrium. We tend to order less when we aren't so hungry.

Many small children can only eat half a sandwich or less at a sitting. The restaurant will cut sandwiches in half or quarters for you on request, making it easier for you to divvy up the food. (Special requests may slow down your order, though.) Sometimes "kids' meals" can actually be economical, even though you pay for the toy. They usually contain more food than a small child can eat. The trick is for an adult to buy a small sandwich and then eat the children's leftovers.

Some parents object to the kid's meal toy, especially if it is supporting entertainment or a holiday contrary to the family's values. If this is a concern, ask if a replacement is available before you order.

Although it may seem wasteful to throw away leftovers, fast food does not usually pack well and is susceptible to spoilage. Forcing your child to finish unwanted food causes him or her to learn to ignore the body's signals of hunger and satiation, one cause of obesity and eating disorders. A better and cheaper alternative is to order small quantities at first, then go back to order seconds when you see how much is needed.

CAFETERIAS

You might plan on breakfast at a museum before starting your tour, or plan for a midday lunch break or snack. Museum cafeterias, however, vary considerably in price and menu. To avoid surprises, ask for advance information.

You may find a menu on their Web site—or at least an e-mail address you can use for inquiries.

Some museums incorporate exhibit themes into their cafeteria. A local science museum, for instance, has vending machines with clear sides, allowing you to see the inner workings of the machine as it measures out your drink or snack.

Hospital cafeterias are another option. Hospitals are well marked and easy to find in any city, and we find the food in their cafeterias to be far tastier than that served to the patients. The cafeterias generally have a good selection, including vegetables and salads, which we tend to miss out on when we eat too much fast food. In a metro area, though, parking can be a problem.

ETHNIC FOOD

Children learn with all their senses, including their taste buds. Ethnic food provides a glimpse into daily life in another culture. Many homeschool families plan their traveling menu around a unit study on the culture they are visiting.

Trying new foods is half the attraction of events that feature other cultures, such as international festivals and ethnic events. Your whole family can sample exotic foods inexpensively, from spanakopita to gefilte fish. To sample a greater variety and keep costs down, create your own smorgasbord. Buy single servings of a variety of items and give everyone in the family a taste of each item.

Some vendors will give you a tiny taste before buying to aid you in selecting unfamiliar foods. Unless swamped with business, nearly all of them will gladly describe each food and perhaps its history if you ask. The vendors at ethnic events are often passionate about their heritage. Try opening a conversation, and you will quickly find out whether the person responds warmly or if it is time to move on.

Small markets provide a way to sample local ethnic or specialty foods. Large cities have specialty stores that cater to Asian, Hispanic, Polish, and Kosher customers as well as other ethnic populations. Even in your hometown, the grocery across town may carry ethnic food that is different from what is available in your area. Sometimes an open-stall marketplace provides an assortment of ethnic and specialty booths.

To find ethnic restaurants, scan the yellow pages and travel guidebooks, or contact the chamber of commerce. Most large cities have ethnic areas with specialty restaurants.

If you want to try your own hand at ethnic meals, perhaps as part of your travel research, read the La Leche League International's *Whole Foods from the Whole World.* League families from all over the world contributed their favorite recipes for you to try.

INEXPENSIVE FAMILY-OWNED RESTAURANTS

In nearly every town there is at least one reasonably priced restaurant, diner, or café that is not part of a chain. In small towns these restaurants are relatively easy to find on the main street near the center of town. In metro areas they may be tucked away on a side street next to a laundry or in the college district.

We like to "collect" such little restaurants, where you may find homemade pie and real mashed potatoes, and where the five-dollar lunch special may be meat loaf, two side dishes, and a roll with butter. Prices are competitive with fast-food restaurants, especially if you do some sharing. Service may (or may not) be slower than a fast-food restaurant, but if you are vacationing, what's the big rush? If you have diet restrictions, you have a better chance of ordering specially prepared dishes here.

From the outside, such a restaurant may not look like much, so get a recommendation from the gas station attendant, a librarian, or someone walking down the street. A host family is a great source of inside information. The resource guide for this chapter has Web sites for locating little-known restaurants and viewing their menus, including a guide to old-fashioned classic diners.

It may be a good sign if there is a line of people waiting for a table at lunchtime. That usually means the locals know the food is worth the wait. If you notice a restaurant you want to try, perhaps you can come back after the rush hour or before the next one.

"NICE" RESTAURANTS

We may need to eat inexpensively most of the time. We find, however, that when we do splurge and visit a "nice" restaurant, we savor the experience.

Eating at some more expensive restaurants may be a highlight of your trip. Expensive means more than you might normally spend but not necessarily a king's ransom. For you a "nice" restaurant might mean a restaurant with real glasses instead of Styrofoam cups—or a whole lot more.

We find that an appetizer at a better restaurant is usually not only good food, but it is often the size of an ordinary meal. Breakfast or lunch at a swanky restaurant may be downright reasonable. Or it might be just the place to go for dessert, when you can get the upscale experience with a relatively small tab.

ROOM SERVICE

Room service is not cheap, but at times it is a blessed luxury. If you order from room service, check to see if a gratuity is included in your tab rather than double-tipping. For "poor man's room service," ask at the front desk about local restaurants that deliver. Often they keep menus on file to share with their guests. Or save on the gratuity by picking up the food yourself and have a relaxed meal back at your room.

SUPPORT A CHARITY

For local flavor, try eating at a community fund-raising breakfast, lunch, or dinner. These meals usually mean huge homemade portions and are economical. They may be sponsored by a church, school, or civic organization. When you take part, you can help a charity, rub shoulders with local people, and learn about the community. Sometimes you will be able to try ethnic dishes that are more authentic than those served at local restaurants.

Find out about charity events by reading community newspapers (often available for free or for a quarter at libraries or convenience stores), looking for announcements on post office or grocery store bulletin boards, or getting information through the local chamber of commerce or a radio station.

COOKING SCHOOLS

Some frugal travelers spice up their trip with a visit to a cooking school. A cooking school may offer a memorable meal at a relatively low cost, at least compared to a gourmet restaurant. For example, L'Ecole, the restaurant of the French Culinary Institute, offers very fancy meals cooked and served by students at one low, fixed price. The Mardi Gras School of Cooking offers lunch classes taught by Creole and Cajun experts. Students learn to prepare New Orleans specialties such as gumbo, jambalaya, and pralines. In addition, students savor history, trivia, and tall tales. You get a two-hour class plus the meal you prepare during class, all for about twenty dollars a person.

Shadow a Chef

Do you have a teenager interested in cooking? Before you travel, see if you can arrange for your teen to be a job shadow for a few hours with a professional chef. Try a cooking school or restaurant, perhaps one with a specialty that interests your teenager. It might help to offer a letter of reference from a teacher or guidance counselor to show serious intentions. If your student is involved with a culinary program in a vocational school, the chef may be more open to an inquiry from your student's instructor.

The School of the Ozarks, near Branson, Missouri, has a small student-run restaurant to provide job experience for students majoring in the hospitality industry. It is more like a family restaurant with good, inexpensive food.

To add a cooking school visit to your itinerary, search the Internet under "cooking school restaurants" and include your destination (or cities along your route).

SPECIAL DIET RESOURCES

Some families may have special dietary needs or wants, such as vegetarian meals or religious restrictions. You can still meet those needs on the road, and it does not have to cost a lot. Often your best source for a special diet on the road is a grocery store or natural foods outlet.

You do not have to be a vegetarian to enjoy vegetarian meals. Vegetarians come in two main categories: Lacto-ovo vegetarians include eggs and dairy products in their diets; vegans do not consume anything derived from animals. You can find vegetarian restaurants and restaurants that have "vegetarian-friendly" menu items by checking the *Vegetarian Journal's Guide to Natural Food Restaurants in the U.S. and Canada,* edited by the Vegetarian Resource Group, or by searching the Internet under "vegetarian restaurant guide." We found sites like *www.veg.org* and *www.HappyCow.net,* which list restaurants and health-food stores by state and country. Aside from a restaurant guide, VegDining *(www.VegDining.com)* offers the Veg Dining Card, a discount card good at participating restaurants.

Rules of the Road for Cooking

One of these days an automobile manufacturer is bound to come up with a microwave as an option, mark our words. In the meantime, you can cook on the road without spending your whole trip doing it. Campgrounds usually provide a fire ring for cooking, toasting marshmallows, or just communing. Maybe you can bring some firewood from home to enjoy a campfire without having to buy high-priced cords of firewood.

Whether you plan to cook or not, you will want to bring some paper plates, eating utensils, and cups. Don't forget the can opener and tools for cutting your food. A travel toothbrush holder makes a good container for a sharp knife.

You may want to involve your children in brainstorming different methods of cooking on the road. (But try them out before you leave home.) Using an alternative method of cooking while traveling saves money. It can also be educational, exposing your children to various chemical processes and alternative technologies.

Here are a few options:

- Outdoor grills are available at many rest stops, parks, and campgrounds. A little hibachi is handy for roadside picnics. Do not carry self-starting charcoal on a long trip—it contains combustible chemicals that are, well, self-starting. You can, however, buy a small bag for your campsite and use it up or give it away.
- Sterno cookers come with little cans of relatively safe fuel. They use up very little space in your trunk and take only a minute to set up.
- Electric pans and other small appliances from home can travel with you for use at your campsite when you have electrical hookups.

- Cook with the heat of your engine block as you drive down the road, and you will amaze friends and strangers when you arrive at your destination with dinner hot and ready. *Manifold Destiny,* a flippant book about under-the-hood cookery, recommends wrapping the food in aluminum foil with several inches of overlap, which you fold over several times. Then wrap it in a second layer, with the seam going in the opposite direction of the first seam. The book has real recipes, with directions like "Cook for six hours at 55 miles per hour." Save this for a long trip—this method takes a long time. It may also take some experimentation to find the hottest spot on your manifold. Judith once tried to bake potatoes using this method, but they were probably too thick and never quite got cooked. (Thin packets are recommended.) On her second try, she forgot all about the food until days later. At least it was cooked that time!

- Camp stoves come in a wide variety, ranging from cheaper but bulkier cook stoves made by Coleman and others to featherweight but more expensive backpacking models. One model is the MSR DragonFly Multifuel Stove, made by Mountain Safety Research, a one-burner stove that weighs seventeen ounces (without fuel). It uses white gas, unleaded auto fuel, or kerosene, has a wide range of heating intensity, and lights easily.

We heard about the DragonFly from Amirah, whom we met online at the Families on the Road discussion list (RovinUSA@aol.com). Amirah says that less than a dollar of unleaded gas cooked about six or seven meals and did not leave her food tainted with a gas smell. She preferred the DragonFly to a cheaper propane stove that used more fuel and, more important, took up precious space in the car.

freebee

Free from the Catfish Institute

Call the Catfish Institute at (662) 247-4913 for a free copy of *Catfish: An All-American Restaurant & Recipe Guide,* which includes recipes for cooking the catfish you catch, along with a listing of restaurants that serve catfish.

Cooking Creatively

Amirah and her husband are RVing wannabes. In the meantime, they do car camping, using their trunk as a kitchen, for four to six weeks at a time. Here are some of the unusual on-the-road cooking methods they have discovered:

- Add boiling water to a thermos bottle to make oatmeal, rice, or soup, letting it "cook" all day or overnight without additional fuel or steaming up your living quarters (a special concern for RVers).
- Pack a dehydrator. Amirah says,

> I use a dehydrator, since we are traveling during the peak season, for many veggies and fruits. I use a solar model because we travel to warm, dry climates. It takes about forty-eight hours to dehydrate tomatoes. We love sun-dried tomatoes in many different dishes, so they're one of our staples in the summertime. We put the dehydration trays across the back dash when driving, and they dry faster that way!
>
> I found a book at the library for preparing complete dehydrated meals. I made a few of them for our car camping trips, and it saved us a bundle. Dehydrated meals are four to seven bucks at backpacking stores, but less than two dollars on average when you make your own. So when we went far, far out, away from the nearest fast-food restaurant, we still ate well and didn't have any food waste from spoilage.

- Amirah's cookware includes a pressure cooker, a cast-iron skillet, a solar oven made with a shallow ceramic-on-metal pot, and a couple of canning jars. She says that covers all the bases. "To save fuel and speed things up a bit, I put a couple of one-gallon water jugs that I painted black in the back dash of the car. By lunch or dinnertime the next day, the water is preheated and cooking time is quicker."
- Solar cooking is a good way to teach your children about harnessing solar energy. Amirah uses her solar oven for baking. "Marty and I usually baked brownies partly just because we enjoyed meeting people during our travels," she says. "The solar oven was a 'people magnet,' and the brownies were fun to share. We got adopted by

locals, and then we would go all out to solar cook them a meal—just because we could. That left them with a fun story to tell their friends for years to come!" For information on solar cooking, check the library or visit *http://www.solarcooking.org*, which has information on solar water distilling as well.

COOKING IN AN RV

If you travel in a modern RV (a recreational vehicle, such as a travel trailer or motor home), meals cooked in your RV need not cost more than they do at home. You can pull over anywhere that appeals to you—a shopping center, a parking lot, an unused church lot, or a rest area—and have a home-cooked meal. Just because you have a kitchen, though, does not mean you want to spend a lot of time cooking and cleaning up, so pretrip preparations can ease the work load. Magazines such as *Trailer Life* and *MotorHome* are good resources for information.

Jim Foreman wrote *Armadillo Pie: Don Coyote's RV Cookbook,* and, yes, it really does have recipes for armadillo meat—but you can substitute chicken. Here are Jim's three simple rules for cooking on the road:

1. Never cook anything that takes longer to prepare than it does to eat.
2. The fewer pots you use, the fewer you have to wash.
3. *No cocine toda la vaca por un taco.* (Don't cook the whole cow for one taco.)

We agree with the rules but have never mastered them—especially when it comes to number one when we are cooking for children.

Whether you pack your food in an automobile, RV, bicycle, bus, train, or on your back, food can be a big part of the fun, the good memories, and the educational value of your trip.

Chapter Eleven

Camping and RVing

Turtles, snails, and clams carry their homes with them, and so can you! You don't have to settle for a shell, however. If your travel home is a tent or vehicle, you're camping. But *camping* can be a misleading word. Many modern RVs have more amenities than some pretty fancy hotel rooms, with luxuries ranging from microwaves and air conditioners to ice crushers. Some also include self-sufficient features such as roof-mounted solar panels for a low-cost, renewable form of energy.

So why not just stay in a hotel? For many—including us—camping is not just an economical option, it is also more fun. We find it easier to meet other families at a campground, and our kids find it easier to connect with playmates. At a campground or park, we can get to know travelers from a variety of backgrounds and from many different areas and cultures. Your experience at a motel in San Francisco may be pretty much the same as one in Miami. At campgrounds, you tend to have a more personal experience.

Although the Goza family (the professional traveling storytellers we mentioned in an earlier chapter) occasionally stay at a motel or hotel due to Internet accessibility, they most often stay at campgrounds for their son Zephyr's sake. Zephyr prefers campgrounds to motels. He says, "At motels, I sit around reading—don't get me wrong, I like reading a lot!—or waiting for a television show to come on. At campgrounds, I'm out from dawn to dusk biking, rollerblading, or playing with my friends. Campgrounds have many more fun things to do."

Mom Kimberly adds,

We avoid eating out, so our ice chest, stove, and coffee-making supplies come with us everywhere—in addition to clothes, computers, a printer, books, and other stuff that follow us everywhere we go. Loading and unloading things is much easier to do at a campground than at most motel or hotels—no elevators, stairs, or lobbies to traipse through.

The Family That Camps Together Learns Together

If your family chooses to camp, you will find ample opportunities to learn about nature as well as knot tying, wilderness safety, and building emergency shelters. Your children may become more confident and self-reliant as they learn that they can cope well in relatively primitive surroundings.

Children can also learn about making wise economic choices. For instance, much of the expense of modern-day living arises from a perceived need for conveniences such as electricity, indoor plumbing, natural gas, telephone service, trash pick up, etc. Camping allows you to pick and choose your conveniences—adapting and saving as you go. Camping prices range from free (at some public lands that allow primitive camping but provide no services) to about the same cost as budget motels, if you go to a deluxe campground. Decide which kind of camping experience suits your family.

Use campground directories to plot out your route or pick a destination for a vacation stay. You might want to look over various directories at your library and buy your favorite one in print or on CD-ROM. You can also plot out a route online and search the Internet for campgrounds, RV parks, and RV service centers in the United States, Canada, and Mexico. Try the Web sites for the Woodall directories and the *Trailer Life* directory.

When possible, Hope Sykes prefers to preview her campsite online:

Something as simple as seeing what your campsite may look like before you arrive really helps relieve some of the travel tension you might otherwise face after a long day on the road. Because kids get tired easily, nerves get frazzled, and there is always the unexpected—like road construction or a missed exit—it is best to be as prepared as possible.

I've traveled over two hundred thousand miles by RV, and each campsite really is different. The pull-through site that you were promised may also involve maneuvering around Dumpsters, trees, or tight turns. Sometimes you will face back-ins. If you are pulling a forty-foot trailer, it will take some added concentration and practice.

CAMPING ON PUBLIC LANDS

Public lands cover a lot of territory and offer a wide range of services. In general, a national park has designated camping areas, with facilities such as showers, toilets, water and electricity, and dump stations for motor homes. Some national forests have low-cost campgrounds, usually equipped with fewer amenities; however, you can camp *anywhere* in a national forest without charge. Displays and programs offered by the forest service are oriented toward using the natural resources responsibly and in a renewable manner. The atmosphere at a national forest is more natural and less like an amusement park than many of the Park Service facilities, according to one outdoor-loving parent.

To explore the national park system, go online to *http://www.nps.gov*. The Web site includes details about sporting opportunities, campsites, and reservation procedures. Some parks accept reservations, while others operate on a first-come, first-served basis.

State parks typically offer more facilities and tend to be cleaner than federal camping areas. Prices for state park camping and cabins vary throughout the country, even within the same state, so shop around. Campgrounds in remote locations usually cost less. You have to pay more in gas to get there, but you will find more privacy. If a state permit is required, factor in that cost as well.

Kimberly Goza prefers state and national parks to commercial parks, because of Junior Ranger programs for Zephyr, great scenery, and lower prices. Commercial campgrounds, however, are usually more convenient to the highway. Melissa's family "discovered" a state park only an hour and a half away from the city that usually has cabin openings and unoccupied beach areas even in the summer. Her family has also enjoyed free primitive camping at an Ohio state nature preserve, where they are usually the only campers.

Consider purchasing an annual pass if you plan to visit several national parks in one year, available in person, by mail, or online. Whether or not a pass will save you money depends on how much traveling you do during the next year. In would take three visits to one of the higher-cost destinations (say, the Grand Canyon) to break even with a pass. While passes give unlimited admission for a year to all national parks, some parks charge extra for such activities as camping and swimming. A special pass is available for people sixty-two years old and older, and for people who have a qualifying disability.

The parks also offer short-term passes, good for a limited time, for come-and-go admission at the park where you purchase the pass and at other nearby national parks. If you plan well, you may be able to use the pass at several parks before it expires.

The Army Corps of Engineers provides over 30 percent of the recreational opportunities on federal lands and is the largest provider of water-based recreation in the United States, with 4,300 recreation areas at 463 lakes. For great sites across the country, browse the Corps guide to recreation areas at its Web site or inquire by mail. In the West, you can camp for free at campgrounds sponsored by the Bureau of Land Management (BLM). They publish a directory of their campgrounds, which you can request by mail or view online.

Be an Early Bird

The early bird gets the...campsite. Due to demand, reserve your campground or cabin months or even a year in advance at popular national and state parks.

The Bureau of Land Management manages over 264 million acres of public land, most of it in eleven western states and Alaska, with smaller parcels in eastern states. BLM has programs to protect rangelands, wilderness, and watershed areas and has an extensive volunteer program. In Alaska, for example, BLM uses volunteers in archaeology, trail maintenance, wildlife inventory, land surveying, office work, and campground hospitality. Volunteer applications list twenty fields of interest—including tour guide and interpretation, fish and wildlife, botany, and historic preservation—and are available online or by mail. At many locations minors can volunteer if accompanied by an adult.

City and regional campgrounds are often good places to enjoy free camping. Patty France is a single parent who travels in an RV with her fifteen-year-old son, her twelve-year-old daughter, and the family's friendly 125-pound Labrador.

> We camped at a free campground at Lock 51 on the Chesapeake and Ohio Canal in Maryland. The campground sits right on the river. A map of all the campsites and points of attraction is available from the Chesapeake and Ohio Canal information desk and most rest areas in Maryland. From there, we borrowed books from the local library and began to explore. We've seen a quarter-mile-long tunnel that was dug by hand in the nineteenth century. We have visited old lock houses, explored caves, seen owls, and heard ghost stories. And it was all 100 percent free. I sound like I work for the Park Service, I know, but it has been one of the best experiences we've ever had.

Dave Levingston, a father of three, has found that west of the Mississippi almost every small town has a city park where camping is permitted, usually at no charge.

> Facilities vary greatly, but almost always you are right in town, which means you can easily walk to the local restaurant, stores, movie theater, and more. If kids are getting tired of being out in the wild, this can give them a break. You could see a movie for what you would have paid for a campsite in some of the commercial campgrounds.

Not all the free campgrounds are in town, though. Dave stayed at a free campground a few years ago on a beautiful mountaintop in Kentucky, and he had the entire campground to himself on weekdays. "The only drawback—and there is usually some drawback to a free campground in a park or forest setting—was that there was no source of water," he says. "That just meant a couple trips down to the nearest town during the week to fill up the water bottles."

CAMPING HERE AND THERE

Aside from public lands, you have many choices for finding an economical spot to camp and to find some adventurous activities. Here are just a few of the possibilities.

PRIVATE CAMPGROUNDS

Some private campgrounds resemble a resort, with weekend events such as hayrides, pancake breakfasts, and square dances, as well as activities like miniature or full-grown golf, basketball or tennis, table tennis, and the like. Many have a "take a book, leave a book" bookshelf, and you may be able to get a jam session going if you pull out your guitar and post a sign. Stay a few days, and you will probably get to know the owners and their families. Private campgrounds are likely to be smaller and have a playground and pool within an easy walk from your campsite, and possibly within view. A visit to a Jellystone Park may feature a visit from cartoon characters Yogi Bear and Boo Boo.

Private campgrounds are generally more expensive than public campgrounds, but prices also are more negotiable, since the owners are usually on site. Ask about weekly rates and other discounts. They are usually handy to the highway and may offer discounts with membership cards, such as Good Sam Club (an RV club) or AAA. Usually the brand-name campgrounds, like KOA or Jellystone, are privately owned with an affiliation to a particular chain or organization. Some of the chains have their own discount card. Because Judith's family was traveling with some medical equipment that needed electricity, and it rained most days on their trip through Pennsylvania, they decided to stay in KOA cabins instead of using their tent. They purchased a discount card from KOA, which paid for itself within two nights.

Campgrounds in tourist areas may offer guided tours by reservation. A personal tour guide arrived at the Philadelphia KOA in a ten-passenger van and took three camping families on a six-hour tour of the city. The guide dropped the campers off at each attraction, such as Constitution Hall and Ben Franklin's printing shop, and designated a time and place to meet after each stop. She offered a running dialogue about the history of the area and the peculiarities of the people involved. It was a good overview of the city—with no parking hassles!

CAMPING AT A SUMMER CAMP OR CONFERENCE CENTER

If you went off to summer camp as a kid, you are aware of some of the camps tucked away on forested side roads, usually with an unobtrusive sign to mark the camp entrance. These facilities fit into two general categories

Campgrounds are usually intended for youth programs, while conference centers more often serve groups and families and are more likely to be open year-round. Some of the larger facilities have both at the same site. Many of these facilities are affiliated with a church or a youth organization, like 4-H, Boy Scouts or Girl Scouts, Pioneer Clubs, or Awana.

Exchange Your Time for a Free Campsite

Some campgrounds will exchange a campsite for help with chores, such as routine maintenance, bathroom cleaning, or weeding the flower beds. You can offer to entertain the weekend guests with music, a magic show, or a special-interest workshop. Workshop topics are endless—what do you know that others may be interested in? Making crafts, taking photographs, Asian cooking, cake decorating, and RV maintenance are just a few ideas. The *Workamper News* allows subscribers to place ads seeking such opportunities. Most of the opportunities on public lands have a minimum-stay requirement, but at private campgrounds, anything goes.

Some summer youth camps and conference centers offer cabins, guesthouses, dormitories, or camping spots to rent, especially during the off-season. Some families with teens have been able to work at the same camp during the summer. You also may be able to find a job at a summer camp that your child can attend as a camper. A few facilities have retreats that the whole family can participate in. (Do you have a Scout in your family? If so, some Scout camps will allow your family to camp there for a small fee, as long as there is room.)

To locate campgrounds and conference centers, contact the American Camping Association, which lists two thousand ACA-accredited camps at its Web site. For Christian facilities and programs, ask your pastor about facilities affiliated with your denomination, and check telephone books in the area you want to visit. Contact Christian Camping International (CCI) to locate member organizations by state or country. To find smaller facilities not affiliated with CCI, do an Internet search under "Christian campgrounds" plus the name of the state or province you will be visiting.

BOONDOCKING—FREE SPOTS TO PARK YOUR CAMPER OVERNIGHT

If you know where to look, you can find free parking for your camper—or possibly even your tent or tepee. Among RVers, *boondocking* refers to camping without any hookups (water, electricity, or sewer) and using only the self-contained features of the RV. Although the term comes from camping out in the "boondocks" away from civilization, boondocking has come to include any free parking spot without hookups.

Judith's family has stayed in parking lots at hospitals, truck stops, and restaurants as well as in friends' driveways. "The only time we stayed in campgrounds," she says, "is when we wanted to take advantage of the campground facilities and stay for a day or two. When we pull in at night and leave early the next morning, we simply look for a safe place to park, ask permission, and turn in for the night."

Kay Peterson, in her book *Home Is Where You Park It,* tells how her family—Kay, three teenagers, and her husband, Joe, an electrician—traveled wherever union work was waiting. The Petersons sometimes stayed at campgrounds or mobile home parks. Some of their more memorable parking spots were on private farms and ranches, sometimes in exchange for helping out with chores. Consider advertising in the area you want to visit or networking with your affinity circles—contacting people from your denomination, your service club, or your profession—to find a place. You can also simply drive around and ask at a likely looking farm or ranch.

For quick overnight stops, Kay's family often stayed at gas stations, where they asked permission after filling their tank. Kay's family also camped for long periods in remote areas, like a quarry or out in the desert, while Joe was working at a construction site. Kay found ways to stretch their holding tanks, batteries, and water supplies. It is amazing how little water you can bathe in when you have to.

A lot of business owners are open to the idea of your parking in their lots overnight as long as you make it clear that it's only for one night. You may run into more resistance if you look as if you're setting up camp. The Petersons generally pick up all the trash in the vicinity as a gesture of goodwill. Be sure you are not blocking any delivery trucks, and leave before the business opens (unless it is a restaurant with space for RVs, in which case having breakfast there before you leave would be a nice gesture). If you provide a service that will attract customers to the business (such as a hot dog stand, balloon animal booth, or period photography), your host may welcome you to stay awhile.

Churches are another host option. Just make sure you are not in the way during worship services and other church functions. If you attend church and are looking for a place to camp, the pastor may know of a good place.

wiseguy

What Shall We Bring from Home?

Before making reservations at a campground or cabin, be sure you know what will be provided for you and what you will need to bring from home. Will you need bedding, towels, dishes, dishwashing liquid, or soap? You will pay premium prices for many items if you have to buy them in a camp store. Also, do not be shy about asking if a crib or high-chair is available to borrow, if you need one. Some campgrounds will loan them for free and set them up for you.

Some stores and shopping centers allow RVers to stay overnight. Wal-Mart, in particular, has been welcoming to RVers. You may find a cluster of RVs in a Wal-Mart parking lot on a popular route, which provides a sense of security.

CAMPING CABINS

Do you desire some of the comforts of home, but you don't travel frequently enough to justify the cost of an RV? A cabin may be just the thing for you. With a cabin, you can enjoy the benefits of a natural setting and campground activities such as nature walks, water sports, fishing, and whatever else is available in the location you choose.

KOA Directory

Go to *http://www.koakampgrounds.com,* where you can enter your starting point and your destination to view a list of all the KOA campgrounds on your route, including their costs and amenities.

Deborah Taylor-Hough, author of *A Simple Choice: A Practical Guide for Saving Your Time, Money, and Sanity,* shared her "luxury camping" experience with her family of five:

We went to the Oregon coast and stayed in a KOA "Kamping Kabin" in Astoria. Great fun, and lots of educational "Lewis and Clark Trail" activities. We learned so much, had a ton of fun, and didn't spend much at all.

The KOA Kamping Kabins are the best frugal-family traveling accommodation we've discovered in the past few years. Our family of five was able to stay in the Kabin for about thirty-five dollars (the price varies from one KOA to another) per night. We needed to bring our own sleeping bags and cooking supplies, but they provided nice bunks to sleep on and a space heater to keep us warm. We usually have gone tent camping in the past (which we enjoy tremendously), but the hassles of setting up and tearing down the tent every day if you're traveling can get really old. Just tossing sleeping bags onto beds (and being able to stay warm at night during off-season travel!) is great.

According to Pat Wesolowski, author of the *Big Ideas, Small Budget* newsletter, "Most KOAs are really clean and include pools, playgrounds, and sometimes extras such as water slides and lakes for fishing and paddle boat-ing. It's funny. KOAs charge per person when you go in with a trailer or motor home, but that isn't always the case with the cabins." A mother of nine, Pat has found some two-room cabins for twenty to twenty-five dollars.

When their children were small, the Morgans spent some of their best and most memorable vacations at state park cabins. Melissa says,

> The excitement of living in a house in the woods, with a big screened-in porch on stilts, always captures the little ones' imagination. At the end of a day of hiking and swimming in the lake, the kids dropped off to an exhausted sleep. Hugh and I enjoyed some adult time, sitting on the porch.
>
> We've also rented several cabins with extended family and shared the expenses. It was a fun and convenient way to have a family reunion, whether you stick with cabins, use tents, or combine the two.

Some families save money by sharing a campsite. Call the campground first, however. They may have restrictions on the number of tents or RVs per site.

The forest service rents primitive cabins and lookout towers that forest rangers no longer use. Because the towers are in remote locations, the service suggests children using the tower be at least twelve years old and that renters be in good physical condition.

CAMPING CLUBS

Membership in one or more auto or camping clubs, such as the Good Sam Club or AAA, can pay for itself in member discounts for directories and other publications and reduced fees for campgrounds and attractions. Good Sam, one of the older clubs, sponsors rallies with family activities and a mag-azine for members. The club provides a directory of Standby Sams, more than fifteen hundred members in the United States and Canada who volun-teer to provide emergency advice and referrals to members traveling through their area. Good Sam sponsors a variety of volunteer opportunities, ranging from campground hosting to adopt-a-park beautification projects.

Good Sam's roadside service covers towing your travel trailer or motor home to an RV service center. You can earn an insurance discount by participating in the National Safety Council's Defensive Driving course at specially designated Samborees (Good Sam RV rallies). Taught by certified instructors, this eight-hour course teaches you how to react to adverse road, weather, and traffic conditions when driving a motor home or towing a travel trailer.

Tent Camping

Good old tent camping is an inexpensive standby for families. It may seem intimidating if you have never tried it, but you can learn right along with your kids. Maybe it will ease your mind to know that many campgrounds today have little or nothing to do with "roughing it." You need not start out with a wilderness trip.

Some camps offer Rent-a-Tent facilities. The tent will be set up when you arrive, and the cost is usually comparable to an inexpensive motel room. For a beginner, it is an easy camping experience, and you'll find out if you would like your own tent. As a cost-cutting alternative, you could borrow or trade for a tent, as well as other camping equipment, from a friend or relative.

Get Hooked

Campgrounds often have electric hookups. Instead of fussing over a campfire, you may find it relaxing to plug in an electric skillet or a hot pot for a quick meal or some soup after a long nature hike.

Ask around or advertise for a good used tent, RV, or other camping equipment. You can place "want to buy" ads for hard-to-find used equipment in good condition. Often the seller is as happy to get rid of the item as you are to buy it! Perhaps you will find your dream RV languishing unloved in a backyard. Or the perfect tent may be taking up space in the closet of an RV convert! Some radio stations offer free "swap and sell" time, or you can post an inexpensive ad in a community paper. You can also post want ads at local community bulletin boards. Some churches will allow their members to post notices on the church bulletin board or in the weekly bulletin. If your family is traveling to volunteer, mention it in your ads. Some sellers appreciate knowing they are helping with a good cause.

Before you purchase a used canvas tent, take a whiff to make sure that mold or mildew is not embedded in the fabric. It is not only unpleasant but also a health hazard. (Some nylon tents are mildew-proof. Tent canvas is mildew resistant, not mildew-proof.) There is no need to buy a moldy tent; there are plenty of good ones available.

Make Your Own Portable Shelter

Your children can learn useful skills from learning to build a shelter. They can research various types of tepees or other structures built by Native Americans. Southwestern natives built tepees, while eastern tribes, such as the Cherokee, built stationary structures.

It is easy enough to fashion a haphazard tepee with three or four poles and a tarp. Lay the poles on the ground, tie them together near the top, and set them upright. Then cover the frame with your tarp. You may or may not want to sleep in it overnight, but it will be a hit with the kids as a temporary playhouse.

If you cut and sew mildew-resistant canvas into a semicircle, you will make a better tepee. You can find plans for building a tepee or a *yurt*, which is another kind of round, collapsible dwelling. It has vertical walls and a conical apex. Some of the available books and Web sites (listed in the resource guide) include cultural and historical information as well as building directions.

You may also want to study the story of the Israelites, who lived in tents while wandering in the wilderness. Their tabernacle was also a tent. The Arabic word for "tent" means "house of hair," because the tent fabric was made from goat hair, which became waterproof after the first rain. An illustrated article on ancient Israelite dwellings is posted on the Internet (Web address is listed in the resource guide). You may want to learn the answer to questions such as: Why did the Israelites live in tents? How did they build their tents?

Young children can easily understand the concept of a well-built structure. We all remember the story of the three little pigs; however, you can put a new perspective on it. Do you want your structure to be permanent, like the little pig who built his home out of brick? Or do you want it to be portable, such as the little pig who built his home out of sticks? (Watch out for those wolves while you're buying camping supplies and constructing your structure!) Whatever you build, try living in it in your backyard first. Make sure it passes the rain test.

Only the Best Will Do, Inexpensively

In the end, buying inferior or inadequate camping equipment is not cost-effective. Be aware that those cutesy children's sleeping bags with cartoon characters are not designed for warmth. To learn about buying sleeping bags, tents, cookstoves, and other camping paraphernalia, read *The Parent's Guide to Camping with Children* by Roger and Kimberly Woodson.

Generally speaking, the military buys only the best. Check army-navy surplus stores for an eclectic but inexpensive selection of quality camping supplies. Surplus stores stock a variety of common and unusual sporting equipment, usually at bargain prices. Look in the yellow pages under "Surplus and Salvage." These companies purchase from military auctions and pass the savings on to you. You may be able to buy directly from the military, too, but do you want to? The auctions are usually for bulk quantities. Do you need two hundred tarps for camping—or just one?

Your Frugal Recreational Vehicle

There are over nine million RVs in the United States—one for every nine households that own a vehicle of any kind. And many more families dream of owning an RV but assume it is out of their financial reach.

Is an RV really a frugal option? If you want to travel long distances in a short time, you might spend as much or more on gas and other related expenses than you would save on motels, especially if you stay at commercial campgrounds. You will also have to take into account expenses like license plates, insurance, maintenance, and depreciation.

You will need to decide what kind of RV best fits your needs and your budget. On the low end are pop-up tent campers, which often come with a kitchen and sometimes a portable toilet. You need to set it up to use it, but that takes only a few minutes with the modern versions. On the high end are motor homes, which eliminate the hassle of hitching and unhitching and having to go outside to enter your living quarters, which can be a security advantage. But if your vehicle goes in the shop, there goes your bed too. In between are travel trailers, truck campers, and fifth wheels.

Travel trailers weigh less and are cheaper than motor homes. Hitching gets easier the more you do it, but it's very time-consuming to get travel trailers ready to tow. A truck camper has some of the advantages of a motor home, but it allows you to change to a new truck when you need to or unload the camper while your truck is serviced. A fifth wheel has a coupling similar to that of a semitrailer, and it is easier to maneuver than a travel trailer, but its hitch takes up the bed of your pickup truck.

If you are considering the cost and value of an RV, consider how often and how far you plan to travel and how your costs for RV or camping supplies (including the cost of maintenance, gas, and license fees) might compare to paying for other accommodations.

For some people, though, it is not really a question of saving money so much as preferring the camping or RVing lifestyle and finding economical ways to achieve it.

Buying a Fixer-Upper

A typical new RV loses 40 percent of its value in its first year through depreciation. Wow! That alone might be a good enough reason to buy a used one, even if "used" means only a year or two old.

Make it a family project to restore an older RV. Put your elbow grease into cleaning, fixing, and redecorating, and you could discover a hidden gem.

Judith and her husband bought a twenty-year-old twenty-two-foot travel trailer for a thousand dollars in the late 1980s. The family they bought it from did not want to bother unpacking it, so the RV came loaded with towels, bedding, dishes, soap, and matches, among other handy items. After about four years, their tow vehicle (an elderly Ford LTD) bit the dust. They continued using their trailer as a guest cottage in their backyard when they had visitors and as an office when someone needed some peace and quiet for work. They used the refrigerator in the camper for a few months when the refrigerator in their home broke down. Eventually, they traded the RV for a minivan worth about a thousand dollars—meaning that they sold the trailer for very nearly what they paid for it, despite years of use!

RV travel can add versatility to your educational experience. Unlike a hotel, you take your bedroom wherever you have permission to park it—a friend's driveway, a farm, a truck stop, or a campground. Unlike a hotel bill, money spent on camping or RV equipment can be an investment. And a family can sell the equipment at any time if their needs change.

If you do not care if your RV is ugly, you can find great deals. Remember to tell yourself, "Hey, at least it's paid for!"—assuming you're going to pay cash.

Generally you will find your best price from private owners. Look for hot deals on used RVs and secondhand summer sporting equipment in the fall and winter. Shop for winter gear in—you guessed it—the blazing heat of summer. Look in local swap papers or small neighborhood newspapers. Check bulletin boards at supermarkets and community gathering places.

Have a repairperson from a reputable RV center check a used camper before you buy it. It is well worth paying an inspection fee to check out appliances, propane lines, and structural soundness. Older campers may have hidden water damage. Ask your repairperson to check for holding tank and water system leaks. If the person selling the RV will not tow it in for inspection, ask your repairperson about making a house call. As an inducement, Judith paid the seller a small fee for bringing the camper to the RV service center and agreed to let the seller keep that money whether the Allees bought the travel trailer or not. It passed the inspection, and they did make the purchase with more peace of mind.

Another consideration in buying an RV is the tow vehicle. Finding a used car already equipped with a towing package could be a better investment than having your present car equipped for towing. Consult a reputable RV center about requirements for towing, and do not skimp on horsepower, the cooling system, and other requirements. Pop-up tent RVs weigh less than other models, so tow vehicle requirements are less stringent.

If you plan to borrow money for an RV, line up the best deal you can find on a loan before you start shopping for campers. Check *www.bankrate.com,* which posts interest rates available around the country. The interest on an RV loan may qualify as a tax deduction. If the RV has sleeping, toilet, and cooking facilities—and virtually all of them do—you may be able to deduct the interest as a second-home mortgage. You would need to use the RV as security for the loan. For updated tax information, check with your accountant and request publications from the IRS on home-interest deductions and selling your home.

Interested in converting an old step van, truck, Greyhound bus, or school bus into a custom-built camper? This is a labor of love. The number of hours would probably not justify doing it if your only interest is to save money. Indeed, some of the customized vehicles probably cost more than a used commercial RV of a similar size. Some of these babies have inlaid parquet floors and stained-glass windows! Other builders are more interested in functionality and frugality than in looks. Campgrounds sometimes look down on converted buses and other homemade conversions, but the owner-builders are an enthusiastic group.

Judith had a longtime fantasy of traveling in a converted bread truck. After reading Ben Rosander's book *Select and Convert Your Bus into a Motorhome on a Shoestring,* she realized she might be better off converting a commercial vehicle designed for long-distance travel rather than stop-and-go city traffic. Ben's inexpensive book walks you through the advantages and disadvantages of various vehicles—bread trucks, school buses, charter buses, etc. The book is short and sweet, with discussions on many nitty-gritty aspects—like floor plans, tools, and equipment—and it's heavy on illustrations and photographs.

An online discussion list for people who build "housetrucks" (converted buses and trucks), hosted by Canadian Yuri Padowinikoff, is a good way to get specific questions answered. It's a very active community that is fervid about their housetruck lifestyle.

To RV or Not to RV

Some families come up with a cross between tent camping and RVing. The Goza family travels in a van, towing a U-Haul-type trailer for their belongings. As full-time professional storytellers, they travel with props and costumes as well as their personal belongings. Sometimes they set up a tent, other times they simply sleep in the van—"whatever is more convenient," says Kimberly. "We don't always bother to set up the tent, especially if it's raining or we're not going to be there long. The van works well at rest stops, truck stops, and at Wal-Mart parking lots."

The family previously owned two RVs. A big reason for not owning an RV is parking.

It is much easier to get around in something smaller, especially when you have to get to schools and libraries in downtown Washington, D.C., maneuver on the New Jersey turnpikes, or find small schools out in the middle of the Sierra Nevadas in northern California.

When we have a mechanical problem, we don't have to wait for a tow truck to make a four-hour trip to get the RV out of the middle of the street at midnight. (Yes, it happened—luckily we got it started after two hours.) Also we don't have to wait for a week while they order parts. (Yep, that happened too, in the middle of New Mexico.) It doesn't leak either.

Perhaps the biggest disadvantage is not having a toilet. That also means, though, that they don't have to worry about dumping the tanks.

Kathleen, a mother who travels with her son in a truck and a tarp, sometimes stops at truck stops or campgrounds for just a few hours to do laundry and take a shower. Since she is popping money into the washers and dryers, the owners often let her take a shower for no charge or a small fee while she is there.

I purchased a two-bedroom travel trailer two years ago, but I got rid of it. I just did not like hooking up and unhooking and all the trouble. Plus I tended to stay in it too much and not go out and explore wherever I was. I now have a double-cab pickup. We can sleep on the two bench seats, or I take a tent and a large twenty-by-ten-foot tarp that I set up so we live "outside." I *love* it.

Judith's husband, John, towed a travel trailer from Ohio to Texas and back. The trip is a treasured memory—except that John cringes at the idea of hitching and unhitching, or trying to get the vehicle in and out of tight spaces. For future trips, John would like to travel with a camping van. His one requirement: It must fit in a regular parking space.

Needs vary, however. The Allee family tends to visit large cities on their travels, and the family usually only stays a day or two in each place. A family who stays in campgrounds for a week or two might not find those issues as important.

Bedtime in a tent, RV, cabin, or tepee can be cuddly, cozy, and, yes, cramped. It can mean bedtime stories by flashlight and endless "just one more" questions in the dark. For the Morgan family, as well as many other families, it can be the best part of the trip.

Chapter Twelve

Frugal Family Lodging

Getting there may be half the fun, but it can also be exhausting. If your transportation does not provide a place to sleep—such as a train, a house-boat, or an RV—you will need lodging on the way to your destination as well as after you arrive.

Sometimes the best place to stay is with a friend—even one you haven't met yet—or a relative. Sometimes it is a motel or hotel. Or you might want to try out something new, like staying in a hostel, in a college dorm, or on a ranch or farm. It all depends on your preferences, your budget, and your sense of adventure.

PERSON-TO-PERSON HOSPITALITY

Personal contacts provide many opportunities for frugal overnight stays.

FINDING A PLACE WITH FAMILY AND FRIENDS

Not so long ago many grandparents and aunts and uncles and cousins lived in the same neighborhood, if not the same house. Friends were the same people you went to kindergarten and high school with, the people who knew all the embarrassing stories about you from your childhood.

These days it takes effort to maintain close ties with friends and family that are strewn across the land, hundreds or thousands of miles apart. It is easy to talk about the importance of family and friends. Taking the time to travel to renew old friendships and to spend time with your extended family puts your money where your mouth is.

Of course, you also can save money when you practice the time-honored tradition of staying with relatives, but that is not the best reason to do it. Use the opportunity to swap family stories and compare notes on genealogy. As your children learn about your family history, they can see how those events relate to their history books.

When you stay with family and friends, pitch in with chores, buy groceries, and pay for gasoline. Imagine what expenses you would be paying for at home, and find a way to help your host with those costs.

HOST-FAMILY PROGRAMS

If you want to quickly soak up a cultural experience, try living with a stranger. Staying with a host family allows a traveler to experience another culture on a deeper level than as a casual tourist.

When Judith and John traveled to Mexico to adopt their daughter Nancy, they stayed with friends of friends. Their hosts were gracious and generous and, as is the custom in Mexico, they would routinely greet them by saying, *"Mi casa es su casa,"* which means "My home is your home."

"Our new friends helped us navigate through the adoption process, and they shared our joy," says Judith. "We remember the beauty of Mexico, but most of all we remember the generosity of the many people who went out of their way to help us. We learned a lot about hospitality from them."

You can arrange your own home stays. Duke and Sandra Merrion, for example, have visited people in the United States and on their trip to Australia and New Zealand by looking up friends of friends or people connected with organizations they have an affinity with.

Another way to discover "unmet friends" as you travel is to utilize an organization. Home-stay organizations match up travelers with families willing to welcome them. Although home stays can be economical, the purpose of a host-family program is to help you make friendships. A home stay gives you the opportunity to learn about another culture, city, and family.

Even though a host family may not charge a fee, you may or may not save money over staying in a budget motel. You may eat out more (sometimes you will eat out less, though), buy host gifts, and possibly travel out of your way to stay with a host family that is not on your direct route.

If you want to arrive late at night and leave early the next morning, call a hotel, not a host. You must plan to spend time with your host if you want to get to know one another. If you value the journey as much as the destination, as we do, then this slowing down is an advantage. You can cut down the frenetic feeling some vacations have and discover opportunities to see the world from a new friend's front porch instead of a freeway.

When staying with a host family, Judith's family times their arrival for late afternoon or early evening (or whenever is convenient for the host), giving them leisurely time to spend with the host. They usually eat dinner with the host, often providing a covered dish, groceries, or contributing in some other way. Then they leave late the next morning or after lunch. Sometimes the two families do some sightseeing together. If not, the host family usually provides some pointers about cool things to see and do in the area. Sometimes Judith's family stays two days if the area is one where they want to do some sightseeing and it is convenient for the host family. Judith says,

> If we are visiting host families on consecutive days, that means we only get about five to seven hours of driving in per day—which works out fine for us, but I know some people want or need to travel faster. Expecting a traveling guest is a big deal and is a great way to get motivated to clean your house!

Organizations like Servas International and Friendship Force International give you the opportunity to arrange a home stay in your own country or in another country or culture. Both organizations encourage friendship and cultural understanding between nations as a way to work toward world peace. Friendship Force's motto, for example, is, "A world of friends is a world of peace."

True Friendship

"With every true friendship we build more firmly the foundations on which the peace of the whole world rests." —Mahatma Gandhi

Among these organizations, there are three ways to participate: as a traveler, as a host, or as part of the local or national organizations themselves. Local clubs meet to organize friendship activities for travelers. The organizations also meet on regional and international levels.

Friendship Force International, founded in 1977, is active in more than fifty countries. It offers one- or two-week home stays, followed by optional touring in the region. The organization makes many of the arrangements for travelers, which may include airfare, home stays or other lodging, and most meals. Friendship Force includes those arrangements in their fee. Former President Jimmy Carter and his wife, Rosalyn, are longtime advocates of Friendship Force.

Servas International, founded in 1949, has more than fourteen thousand "open doors" (hosts) in 135 countries around the globe. *Servas* means "we serve" in Esperanto, an invented language used worldwide. Volunteers for Servas interview prospective travelers and hosts, and help them connect via a listing published for each country. Travelers who are approved through a personal interview and references then contact each host personally to arrange for home stays. Many Servas hosts allow children, and some of them prefer families with children. Many of the hosts *are* families with children. You can look in the directory for a family with children close to the ages of your own children.

When convenient, Servas hosts may offer accommodations for two nights and invite travelers to share in their evening meal. Hosts are urged to decline a visit if it is not convenient. Hosts who are not able to provide overnight accommodation may wish to join as Day Hosts. A Day Host will find a convenient time to meet the traveler and may provide information, a guided tour, a workplace visit, a meal, or just a chat together. Servas hosts are ordinary people. The only requirement to join Servas as a host is the willingness to offer hospitality to travelers of any race and culture.

Gail Anerine, a Servas host in Florida, lives in a location easily accessible for travelers, so she receives more frequent visitors than more rural hosts.

As a host, I've had more than one hundred visits from Servas members from more than thirty countries. My children (now in their thirties) have benefited from the experience. There is no better way to prepare your children for real life than to have visitors from other countries in your home. Children learn to adjust, learn different ways of thinking and acting, and they learn how to be hospitable and, especially, flexible.

Servas suggests that travelers seek hosts in out-of-the-way places because those hosts usually don't get that many travelers. So I did just that in France and was richly rewarded! One couple from Calais had a summer home in the middle of France in the countryside. The instructions to find them were: "When you get close, ask where we live."

Eventually we found this wonderful couple, who had brought their six foster children south for the summer. The cow was milked in the evening, and a huge bowl of fresh milk was placed on the table. They lived in an old stone building, the kind you see in tourist brochures. The highlight of the visit was sleeping on real linen sheets. I felt like a queen. Such luxury!

One of the families in France we stayed with "in the country" was a German couple who were homeschooling their son. We provided part of his lesson that day by explaining about the denominations of American money, what everything on the coins and bills means, and something about the presidents on them.

The other four French hosts we stayed with were equally gracious and interesting. I simply cannot imagine going to France and staying in a cold, impersonal hotel. This goes for every other country. Yukio, my first Japanese host, and the three other hosts in Japan made Japan such a warm, embracing country. After twelve years, Yukio and I are still corresponding.

In sum, Servas changes the whole idea of travel. I never even think about what there is to see in the area I've decided to visit. What's important is the host. After the trip, it's the personal experiences with the host that dominate the memory. If not for that Dane in New Zealand who told me about all his friends there, I never would have discovered this wonderful world of Servas. And I'll never forget how lonely I felt as I watched him unite with his Servas host at the bus station, each wearing their yellow Servas pin, smiling and talking as if they had been lifelong friends.

A number of home-stay programs have grown out of a special interest. Roger Gravel, an avid bicyclist in Quebec, has identified ten hospitality programs that long-distance cyclists can use. His favorite on the list has a name that will speak to the hearts of bicyclists everywhere: Warm Showers, which was established in 1996 to create a network of friendly stopovers for cyclists. All the programs are linked from Roger's Web site at *http://www.rogergravel.com/wsl.*

Your pastor might know of church-affiliated host organizations you would qualify for. Some of these organizations decline publicity to keep their fellowship from being exploited commercially. They prefer to grow by word of mouth.

Some home-stay organizations are private companies. For example, American International Homestays (AIH) can arrange for you to stay in the home of an English-speaking host family in Western and Eastern Europe and Asia. You get a home-cooked breakfast and dinner, and the host spends four hours a day as your personal guide and interpreter. You pay AIH a fee, which amounts to the cost of a night or two in a nice hotel for a couple. Children are welcome, and fees vary depending on ages and number of children. AIH pays the hosts a fee for their services. For more information, log on to their Web site at *http://www.aihtravel.com.*

You may wish to join Home to Home, which arranges home stays between Christian members. A one-year membership costs less than a typical one-night hotel stay. The other host programs we have discussed so far emphasize friendship rather than low-cost lodging. Home to Home, however, sees their service more as a way for families to avoid motel fees. They ask you not to arrive early in the evening or stay late in the morning unless the host family makes a point of inviting you. Home to Home offers discounts for referring other families and a special discount to pastors and missionary families.

If you want to use Home to Home for lodging but not hosting, you have the option of finding another family to be your substitute as a host. This may sound far-fetched, but Judith has found that more people would rather be a host than be hosted. People who "host only" have a very low membership fee.

Homeschool Home Stays

The Allees have visited homeschool families in sixteen states. They found their hosts through a homeschool magazine called *Growing Without Schooling* (*GWS*). *GWS* was founded by the late John Holt, author of the book *Teach Your Own* and sometimes thought of as the father of the secular "unschooling" movement. As a service to subscribers, *GWS* publishes a directory of families who want to serve as contacts for other homeschool families in their area. Advance notice is required.

Judith usually writes a letter to the host family, telling a little about her family's interests and perhaps including a family photo. "I usually contact the host at least a week or two ahead, and preferably a month. In the letter I ask for a phone number and e-mail address and what time of day would be convenient for a visit."

She also asks if they'd like to share a meal, and if so, if they have dietary restrictions and how the Allees can contribute. Sometimes she arranges to meet a family without staying with them. "When we were traveling without an itinerary," she says, "I have occasionally just looked up a host in the phone book and said, 'I got your name from the *GWS* directory. We're in town—would you like to get together?' Then we might meet at a restaurant—and being local, they will usually know a nice but inexpensive restaurant."

When looking up host families, we find that some of the towns are not listed on our map. If you cannot find a particular town in your atlas, it's usually either a very tiny berg or a town that has been absorbed by a metro area (say, a suburb of Chicago). You can find such places in the commercial atlas at the library.

GWS publishes letters from adults and children about their educational experiences. Judith's daughter wrote an article about clowning a few years ago, and *GWS* used her photo (as Oy-Yoy the Clown) on the cover of the magazine—what a thrill! Perhaps your children would like to have their travel experiences published. You may be able to find *GWS* at your local library. If they do not have it, you can suggest they purchase it. But we recommend subscribing if you can. It is a wonderful resource. (See the resource guide.)

One homeschool family has found it easier to give hospitality than to accept it. Bruce Brown and his wife, Laura, travel extensively across the United States with their sixteen-year-old son Christian and two daughters, eighteen-year-old Rachel and twenty-two-year-old Alyssa. Bruce says,

> One of the precepts in the Bible is to provide hospitality. Providing hospitality to people you might not even know is a foreign concept to most Americans. We've had people stay in our home whom we've never met before. We open our home to them because we get a blessing out of it. At first, it's much easier to open your home to people than to accept hospitality from people. After a while, you realize that you are actually giving others a blessing too. We can travel that way to some extent. Sometimes, however, we want to be just a family, so we'll rent a motel room or stay in a state or national forest campground.

Exchanging Your Home

Want a free, fully furnished vacation home in San Jose? or Italy? Maybe you can trade vacations with another family—they stay in your home while you stay in theirs. Sound unlikely? No old college roommates or cousins in San Jose? In that case, you might consider using a service to help you make just such a connection. When you do, you may find you can trade homes, and possibly cars, with another family in your own country or in another part of the world. If you exchange cars as well as homes, your only major expense will be your transportation.

Two of the oldest home exchange services, Homelink International and Intervac International, have been in existence for forty to fifty years. About half of the exchange families have children at home. Membership fees are roughly the cost of a night in a moderately priced hotel. Both families in an exchange enjoy an inexpensive vacation with all the comforts of home.

With many exchanges, one family arrives before the other leaves. This gives the host a chance to introduce the guest family to their home, neighborhood, friends, and some of the local sights at the end of the vacation. The same can be done when the families switch places on the other end. Many home exchanges result in ongoing friendships and repeated exchanges. If you swap with a family whose children are similar ages to yours, you can swap toys, bicycles, and each other's friends for play dates.

Numerous home exchange services have sprouted up on the Internet. Although home swapping is not a new concept, the Internet has made it easier and more popular. If you are not sure how to get started, Trading Homes International has posted sample letters you can use when contacting a host family and making arrangements for a swap.

Some services offer both a printed listing book and a Web site that members can use to view home listings. Some of the newer companies offer only Web-based listings, which could be a disadvantage if you would like to vacation abroad, since fewer families in other countries have Internet access.

There is a wide range of homes represented, from modest to mansion. Each exchange is worked out privately by the property owners or renters, who may want to exchange letters and references before deciding to make the swap. You can specify no smoking. Pet owners, people who are allergic to pets, those who need wheelchair access, and others with special needs can spell out what they need or prefer. Usually your car insurance and home insurance will cover visitors if no money is exchanged. Indeed, in terms of security, your home may be safer being occupied while you are gone.

You need not live in a tourist destination to participate. After all, if you were to travel to England, you would not necessarily want to vacation in London. You might be happier in a country village cottage. Also, according to Intervac, people visit relatives almost as often as they visit tourist attractions, beaches, and other well-known locations. Having a separate, comfortable home while visiting family members can make your stay more enjoyable for everyone.

If you would like to explore home exchanges, you might enjoy reading *Home Exchange Vacationing* by Bill and Mary Barbour to learn more of the ins and outs.

HOTELS AND MOTELS

A hotel or motel is often just a place to sleep, but it can be a destination as well. Some hotels and motels offer resort-style family facilities—a golf course, tennis courts, a pool, or a recreation room. Holiday Inns designated as Holidomes have a large domed area with an indoor pool, amenities such as miniature golf, table tennis, billiards, and an exercise room. Watch for coupons. Judith recently stayed at a Holidome for about the price of a budget motel, thanks to a coupon from a welcome center on the interstate.

Sometimes location is the attraction. Judith bravely stayed in a lovely hotel across from the beach in South Carolina with her friend, Linda, and *four* teenage boys (that's the brave part)—Linda's two and their two friends. The room cost about sixty dollars a night and included a kitchenette, a fold-out sofa, two double beds, and an all-you-can-eat breakfast buffet (and four teenage boys can eat a *lot*). Before they left, they flew kites on the beach in the sunset one last time, then they packed up the minivan one day before the in-season started—when the price would almost double.

Think twice about package deals that include transportation and the hotel—just where is that hotel? If it is miles from anywhere you plan to go, you may be dependent on their transportation or taxis, which can quickly wipe out any savings on your great deal.

An older hotel or motel can be economical, and it can also be an educational treasure trove. Hotels and motels have their own history. Ask a long-time employee or owner at a slow time. Most will be happy to share the history of their property and illustrate it with some colorful stories. Often you'll find the history of the area intertwined with the history of a building. What type of architecture was used in the building? Was the structure subjected to any earthquakes, fires, floods, or robberies? Has anyone famous ever stayed there? How did the business fare during the Great Depression, the world wars, or more recent times?

Don't forget that people who work at hotels are *people*. In fact, most of them are "people" people. Tell them your family is looking for interesting educational experiences that the whole family can enjoy on a budget. They may be able to steer you to special events you might not otherwise hear about. If your stay has some special significance, mention it—that you are here for an anniversary, a night of comparative luxury after backpacking for a week, so your daughter can visit a nearby college, or to meet a local author. The hotel staff may take a particular interest in your mission and share information about an event or a contact person you would not have stumbled on by yourself.

THE NERVE TO NEGOTIATE: CUTTING HOTEL AND MOTEL COSTS

Whether you want an older hotel with character or a new-from-the-ground-up chain motel, you can find ways to cut costs.

First and foremost, find the nerve to negotiate. Research for this book motivated Judith to try her hand at negotiating for a better rate.

> I've haggled with the best of them at yard sales, but I thought a room rate was a room rate until I began working on this book. When I heard about negotiating with motels and hotels, I felt awkward about it but decided I ought to try it out. My first time, I felt particularly justified, because the motel had signs on the interstate with a special rate. Then it turned out (in the small print on the billboard) that the rate was only for truckers. All it took was asking, "Is that the best you can do?" and I got fifteen dollars off the room rate. That works out to more than two dollars a word.

Ask for the lowest-priced room; they will not always offer it if you do not ask. Be sure you know why the lowest-priced room is priced so low. If there is construction noise or late-night music from the lounge, for example, ask for a better room or a better discount.

Be persistent. Ask several times in different ways. Sometimes the third answer is the one you wanted. You can ask straight out, "Are there any specials that would save us a little money?" or, "Oh, my, I was hoping for a lower rate. Any way to do that?"

Ask if there is any way to qualify for a special rate, such as a weekend rate. If you are traveling on business, ask for the best business rate. If you find a cheaper rate elsewhere but prefer a specific hotel, ask if they would be willing to match the rate.

A hotel or motel may be more open to a lower rate in the evening. By then, most people who are going to cancel their rooms will have done so. The later it gets, the better your chances are. Some folks call before they walk into the lobby, even if they are around the corner. The theory is that you are in a better bargaining position on the phone than you would be standing in the lobby. The desk clerk may think you are less likely to walk off in search of a cheaper room if you are already there.

According to Wendy Perrin in *Condé Nast Traveler,* a lower room rate is not your only bargaining chip. She suggests asking for extras, such as a free breakfast, free parking (if you are in a metropolitan hotel that charges for it), an upgrade to a more expensive room, or a waiver of telephone surcharges. She also suggests joining frequent-guest programs, which are often free and may not require a specific number of stays. A membership may include special benefits, ranging from a free upgrade to late checkout. Also, phone surcharges may be automatically waived.

If you have a problem, complain. No need to be hostile, but an economical room does not justify nonworking facilities. Judith's family looked forward to nice cool showers after many hours of driving in the Texas heat. When they checked into a beautiful, newly constructed motel, the water was hot, hot, *hot*—even water from the "cold" spigot was too hot for showers. And there was no tub, so they could not draw the water and let it cool.

The management was unable to fix the problem or transfer the family to a different room, but the person at the front desk handed them a coupon for a free stay at any of the chain's nationwide sites. Since these coupons were preprinted and in a drawer at the front desk, we assume they are routinely used to resolve various complaints. A less serious snafu might be worth a free meal or a discount.

If you want to find a really cheap motel, the best sources are roadside billboards and the signs at the exit where you see a large assortment of motels. The sincerely cheap motels are so proud of their prices that they advertise them right on the billboard. These motels are usually independently owned rather than part of a national chain. They may be older facilities with small rooms and antiquated bathrooms—or they may be the exact same motel that belonged to one of the chains a year ago. Either way, if you are only there to sleep, the room may be perfectly adequate and may cost 30–40 percent less than budget motel chains. Be aware, though, that the advertised price does not include additional people or taxes, so the bottom line can be quite different from the price on the billboard.

We recommend personally inspecting the room before checking in, a policy that resulted from a night in a musty-smelling room. Worried about having a hard or lumpy mattress? Go ahead, Goldilocks—lie down on the beds while you are inspecting the room.

If you are staying for a longer time and want some privacy and less cramped quarters, consider a suite. Pat Wesolowski, mother of nine, has found that a suite is more affordable than paying for two rooms, and it usually includes a minikitchen. Weekly rates are less expensive, and you may be able to negotiate for extra days.

Phone Last!

Use the Internet for research, but call the hotel yourself. You may get a better price than the lowest Internet price, or you might find that the information on the Internet is no longer valid. (Many small businesses and some large ones find that it is easier to start a Web site than to keep it up-to-date.)

You can cut expenses when you cut down on extra beds or other frills. Book a one-bedroom hotel room and let the kids sleep in their sleeping bags. This saved Melissa's family money and sleep on a trip to Virginia. The family had repeatedly been turned away from inns with no vacancy signs. Finally they found a hotel with one bed. The parents were ready to look elsewhere, but their young son said desperately, "Take it! I'll sleep on my air mattress!" His sister agreed. Just don't expect extra towels.

If you are traveling and find no room at the inn, try local campgrounds. Some rent cabins or tents. If nothing else, a campground gives your family a place to sleep in the car in relative safety.

OFFBEAT PLACES TO STAY

You may want to look into some of the more offbeat places to stay. These options don't have to be expensive, and they can enrich an educational travel experience.

Condos and Vacation Home Rentals

Sometimes parents with larger families have a hard time finding adequate, child-friendly accommodations, and the cost can be prohibitive. "If you have a large family, consider renting a condo or vacation home to save money," says Jennifer Dugan, the mother of two preschoolers and the owner of Dugan Travel, a home-based travel business specializing in family vacations.

"If you are looking at needing more than one room in a hotel, a condo is much cheaper, generally. Plus, in a condo you can make your own meals, which can save a family a lot." Jennifer says your local travel agent has resources for locating rentals. She comments,

> Children are not frowned upon in the condo and vacation home community because they are the whole reason why people want to rent condos and vacation homes. Parents want more space than a normal hotel room can provide. Some units may allow pets. Many of these places have swimming pools or other central locations where people may meet one another, and some have restaurants. Some hotels offer both regular hotel rooms and condos.
>
> Condos and vacation homes are popular in Florida, Mexico, Hawaii, and Arizona. Places that offer skiing tend to have a lot of condos. But condos can be found just about anywhere, and travel agents have connections for both popular and secluded areas. There are several companies that just deal with renting vacation homes and condos.
>
> You can search the Web to find condo rentals or vacation homes, but be careful. Some people advertise their homes on the Web. When the travelers arrive, they can't believe the bad living conditions.

Time-Shares

Buying a time-share can be a good value, but that is much more likely if you buy one being resold rather than if you buy directly from the developer. Look for newspaper ads or search Internet auctions. Resold time-shares often go for a fraction of the original selling price. The disadvantage? Even at a good price, a time-share can lock you into specific dates that may not be convenient for you. You can get around that obstacle with a time-share exchange service, which can match you up with people who want to trade a vacation at their time-share with a vacation at your time-share. Some families never stay in their own unit. If that is your purpose, buy a week during the prime tourist season (often referred to in the industry as a "red week"). Look for a time-share in an area that will be attractive to tourists—and therefore, more desirable to trade. However, if you buy a time-share in a high-cost area, such as the California coast or central Florida, you can expect higher maintenance fees.

The average price of a time-share from a worldwide developer is about $10,500, according to The Shadow, author of *The Shadow Knows,* an online newsletter on time-shares. Prices vary widely according to the location, quality of the facilities, and other factors. While there are stories out there of happy buyers who found a good-quality time-share at an Internet auction for a few hundred dollars, The Shadow says they are rare. You can expect to pay between $1,000 and $2,000 for most time-shares through an Internet auction site, such as eBay.com, where on any given day, about fifty time-shares are auctioned off. The "regular" resale market will be anywhere from $3,000 to $18,000. To get an idea of recent prices, you can search the final prices at Internet auctions for previous time-share sales.

DOWN ON THE FARM

Some farmers and ranchers accept paying guests, which gives your family up-close contact with farm animals, crops, tractors, and farm or ranch folks. We tend to take our milk, broccoli, and hamburger for granted. While some "farms" are commercial bed-and-breakfast operations with farm trappings mainly for show, others really are working farms that are likely to have been farmed by a single family for several generations.

The cost of a farm stay is comparable to most bed-and-breakfasts—more than a discount motel, but less than a luxury hotel. It generally includes one or more meals a day plus activities such as helping with farm chores, fishing, boating or water skiing, horseback riding, or taking a hayride, depending on the farm. Some farms raise specialty animals, such as pheasants, llamas, or ostriches. A day or two may be enough farm for your family. All things considered, the cost is not bad at all.

Farms offer a range of accommodations: a room in the farmhouse with a private or shared bath, or a private cottage or cabin. Others simply offer a campsite.

Contact the state office of tourism for a list of farms that offer vacation stays, or check with the county extension office in the area you want to visit. You can also search the Internet using the keywords "farm stay" and "farm vacation," adding a specific state, province, or country.

HOSTELING YOUR WAY

Hostels provide inexpensive, low-frills lodging. Although known as youth hostels, these facilities welcome all ages. The facilities are usually dormitory style, but some hostels have private family rooms for a higher price. Hosteling gives you a chance to get to know people from around the world, even if you stay in a hostel close to home. American and Canadian hostels are frequented by people from other countries, often college students.

Hostels charge a low per-person fee, sometimes under ten dollars a night. That can add up for a family, though, so hosteling may end up costing about the same as a budget motel. It may be more fun, however. Some hostels have amenities ranging from ski packages to hot tubs, and they have facilities for cooking and common living areas for meeting other hostelers. Chores are shared. (Test the adage that children love doing dishes at someone else's house!)

You are usually responsible for your own bedding and towels, although these may be available for a charge. Bring sheets or a sleep sack—made by folding a sheet in half and sewing it together.

Despite the down-home nature of hosteling, it has gone high-tech, with online reservations at many hostels up to six months in advance. Hosteling International is a worldwide membership organization with minimal dues. HI-affiliated hostels have some policies and standards in common, but they are independently owned. Some hostels are unaffiliated, private facilities.

MORE PLACES TO SLEEP CHEAP

There are some places your travel agent can't help you with. Here are some of the more unusual ideas we've found. If you're adventurous and frugal, one of them may offer the perfect educational experience for your family.

- Retreat centers offer lodging, usually regardless of your religion or denomination. The price range varies and may include meals. You can look up "retreats" in the yellow pages in the area you intend to visit. At Retreats Online, facilities are listed by geographic location or by category, such as spiritual or outdoor retreats. The site includes facilities from all faiths—ashrams to monasteries.

- Intentional communities are rural and urban communities established by people with a common purpose. You can visit an intentional community if you make advance arrangements. *Communities Directory* is a guide to 350 intentional communities in more than fifty countries. The directory lists policies about visitors, fees (if any), dietary restrictions (if any), and religious and environmental orientation (if any). Despite the stereotypes, only a small minority of the communities falls into one of those categories.

- Off-duty and retired military families and Department of Defense (DoD) civilians can sometimes stay in military base lodging, resorts, or camping areas. You may also be entitled to shop at the military store. If your travel is related to your job, you will need to pay for the rest of the family, but the cost is minimal. Policies vary from one facility to the next, and they change periodically. Contact each facility you want to visit. (For contact information, check the resource guide under chapter 2.)

- Dorm space is sometimes available from universities when they are not in session. The price will be cheap for one person (like a traveling student) but might not be as cheap for a family.

- The annual *Christian Bed & Breakfast Directory* by Peggy Hellem lists over fourteen hundred bed-and-breakfast inns, small inns, and home-stay opportunities, with descriptions and state-by-state listings. The author gives you a glimpse of the wide range of experiences you can expect and tells you which listings welcome families with children.

- Colleges and trade schools that teach about the hospitality industry sometimes operate their own hotels or motels and restaurants, which are not necessarily well-publicized but are usually reasonably priced.

No matter how much you've enjoyed your stay, all good things eventually come to an end. In his poem "Stopping by Woods on a Snowy Evening," Robert Frost wrote:

The woods are lovely, dark and deep.
But I have promises to keep,
And miles to go before I sleep,
And miles to go before I sleep.

So you eat a hurried breakfast and check your room for belongings one last time. Family members lug bags and teddy bears outside for the final trip home. Time to hug your friends, old and new.

You can't stay forever. You have promises to keep and miles to go before you sleep in your own bed.

Chapter Thirteen

Transportation on a Budget

Getting there can be half the fun and a big part of the learning. Learning how to find transportation bargains not only saves you money, but it is an educational experience in itself. Let's put it this way: If you pay the published fare for travel, you are probably paying too much.

We'll start with the most basic form of transportation—walking—and then move on to bicycles, automobiles, trains, buses, boats and ships (there is a difference), and airplanes. We already discussed recreational vehicles in an earlier chapter, so we won't repeat that information here, and we're going to skip a few esoteric modes, such as dogsledding and hot-air ballooning. If you want to try them out on your own, go for it.

MOVING WITHOUT MOTORS

Getting there under your own power has its advantages. It's slower, true, but then that's one of the advantages: You see and hear and smell your surroundings and connect with people as you go. There is a sense of achievement and triumph in this kind of travel that is unparalleled.

FEET

You can't beat feet. Most of us arrived in the world with a set already installed, and maintenance costs are minimal. Whether you explore the Appalachian Trail or your own neighborhood, family hiking can conjure up visions of the famous scene out of *The Sound of Music,* with Maria, Captain von Trapp, and the children climbing the mountains into Switzerland to escape the Nazis. Perhaps your walking journey won't be as long, as urgent, or as dramatic, but you can meet more people while you're walking than you will in a car—and you will get a closeup view of the scenery. People of all ages can walk (or be carried), although it is a good idea to check with your doctor and to get in good physical condition if you are making a big change in your activity level.

Communities with interesting downtowns may offer walking tours as a way of taking in the sites. Often these published tours have a theme: historic sites or local architecture, for example. Check with the local visitors center, tourist information center, or chamber of commerce for information on walking tours. If you are in the planning stages, do an Internet search for these offices in the state or area where you want to hike and request information. They often have brochures and maps for the tours.

Some families have adopted a novel way to experience a walking tour by emphasizing the sense of touch while saving money on shoe leather (or rubber soles, as the case may be) in the process. They go barefoot! Melissa can personally vouch for barefoot hiking.

> We welcome barefoot hiking with the kids, although our hikes have been short, so far. We find that we experience God's world more vividly when we explore the ground with our feet. We learn more because we notice everything—acorns, tiny rodent holes, and wildflowers. It is the cheapest form of educational travel possible—totally free. We prefer softer dirt paths—even muddy ones—to pavement! So far, we've had no injuries. You just have to watch where you're going. And that is the point.

It isn't always easy to find comfortable walking trails. If you're just starting out, pack a pair of shoes in your backpack, just in case. For more information, contact Barefoot Hikers or the Society for Barefoot Living. They'll put you in touch with experienced barefoot hikers in your hometown or at your point of destination. Learn to protect your feet and enjoy safe barefoot travel.

Are you considering a long-distance walk? People have walked from the

East Coast to the West Coast, just to give you a sense of scale. You can wing it in a car if you like, stopping when you get tired or when the mood hits you, but on foot you may need more planning. Going an extra ten miles to find lodging is no big deal in a car, but it is a very big deal on foot, whether you plan to hike in your own country or on foreign soil.

When you travel on foot, you will need to be prepared for all kinds of weather. Don't try to outthink the weather forecasters—dress in layers and remove clothing as you warm up.

BICYCLES

In some countries cars are for the wealthy and bicycles are for ordinary folk. In our wealthy society, most people view bicycling as a sport rather than a mode of transportation.

Bicycling is a fun sport, a good way to get physically fit, an excellent form of relaxation, and an inexpensive mode of transportation—all of which can be lifelong assets as opposed to youth-oriented sports like gymnastics or football, which we tend to give up as we get older.

Do not assume that bicycling is only for athletes. Perhaps bicycle racing is for jocks, but people of any age can use a bicycle for transportation. Riding is less strenuous than most people assume. Judith, by no means an athletic person, used her bicycle as her only transportation for a year when she was young and carless. Although friends and coworkers were mightily impressed, she found that riding her bicycle a few miles to work or to other activities took relatively little time. The ride was pleasant, and it got her blood moving in the morning.

They say once you learn to ride a bicycle, you never forget, but if you do not ride regularly, your *muscles* will forget and scream their protest. For extended riding, you will need to get in shape, especially if you want to keep up with a teenager.

Bicycle clubs nationwide have tours and rallies, and their chapters may sponsor local rides and extended trips. If the group rides too hard and too far for your family, the club may be able to put you in touch with other families who ride more casually, so you can set up more gentle rides, or you can offer to host shorter rides yourself.

The League of American Bicyclists *(www.bikeleague.org)* is a national organization that offers information about organized rides, tours at home and abroad, and a selection of cycling-related Web sites. The league advocates a "bicycle-friendly America." Members include 35,000 individuals, 455 recreational clubs, and 50 advocacy organizations. Joining the league costs less than fifty dollars for a family (about half that for an individual). As a member, your bike flies free when you book tickets through the league's affiliate, but some restrictions apply. As with all discounts, shop around to see if your discount is actually the lowest price.

Other club benefits include two publications, which are free to members and available for sale to nonmembers:

- *Tourfinder and Ride Guide* provides a listing and description of commercial bike tours and destinations around the world, from Vermont and California to Vietnam and Belize. The guide lists club-organized rides, including mountain bike rides. It also lists the most scenic rides as well as the most challenging rides.
- The league's *Annual Almanac of Cycling* lists contact information on hundreds of recreational bicycle clubs all over the country and a nationwide listing of instructors in Effective Cycling. Effective Cycling is a league program designed to teach bike safety and handling skills. You may want to consider training for your family, whether you cycle long distances or not.

Check the library for bicycle touring books. In many cases, you will find one specifically for the region you want to visit in the United States and Canada, such as the series Bicycling America's National Parks. If you are traveling overseas, a guidebook such as *Europe by Bike* by Karen and Terry Whithill will help with cycling-specific travel concerns and preliminary route planning. When you contact tourism offices about attractions, ask also for bicycling information.

Bicycling at home instead of driving may also help you save up for your trip. If you save enough, maybe you can head off on a more adventurous itinerary. According to Art Evans, author of *Travel Bargains,* you can travel on a severely limited budget with a bicycle. He favors France for bicycling: "Because of a network of little-used but paved farm roads, France is considered by many to be the best bike touring country."

Buying and Renting a Bicycle

If you don't own a bike, check out secondhand dealers, garage sales, auctions, and flea markets. You can easily find kids' bikes; they are sometimes dumped in the trash when outgrown. The Morgan family was able to purchase a high-quality kids off-road bike for less than ten bucks at a garage sale. Look in your local paper or check grocery stores and retail outlets that post for-sale items, or run your own ad, specifying the sizes and features you want.

Ask police departments in your area when they sell off unclaimed bicycles, usually stolen property whose owners cannot be identified. The police may have an engraver you can borrow to mark some kind of identification on the bicycle so you do not have the same problem later. You can also write identifying information on paper and slip it inside the bike frame tube.

Make sure each bike you choose is in excellent condition or can be economically repaired. If you have a knowledgeable friend, ask him or her to go with you to look at used bicycles. You may not need an expensive bike, but you will need a sturdy bike. Ask an expert to help you understand what kind of bike is best for the terrain at your destination.

You can study topics such as bicycle maintenance and repair to teach physics and to show children how things work. You don't want your two-wheeled steed to break down when you're on a lonely country road or trail. Mistakes in this area will have real-world consequences. Test the bikes you plan to use on your trip (as well as your family's strength, ability, and endurance) by doing some pre-trip training on them.

If you do not want to take your own bicycle on your trip, you may be able to rent one at your destination, especially if you are visiting a metro area or a tourist attraction. Try an Internet search by city ("bicycle rental Toronto") or search by state or province. You can reserve rentals online at Blazing Saddles, a chain rental company that offers bicycles in San Francisco, Seattle, San Diego, Santa Monica, Denver, Washington, D.C., and Gettysburg ("bike the battlefields"). In case you want to purchase a used bike rather than lugging one from home, Blazing Saddles offers one-year-old used bicycles at each store.

Bicycle Camping with Kids

The same lightweight camping equipment that backpackers use can make bicycle touring easier as well. As we mentioned in an earlier chapter, the

Romp family—Billy and Patty and their three children—traveled almost five thousand miles on a custom-built four-seater bicycle pulling a little trailer for their youngest "trailer jockey." They carried only clothing, camping gear, a first-aid kit, a tool kit, and a few choice personal items in waterproof panniers (bicycle saddlebags). As they traveled, they gradually lightened their load as their opinion of what was essential was influenced by the weight of what they carried. Their laptop computer was one of the first things to go.

If you want to bicycle and camp with small children, you might want to use a "sag wagon"—a car that carries tents, food, and other equipment and follows or meets the campers at their campsite. Jim Foreman and his wife travel in an RV with bicycles, and sometimes their grandchildren accompany them. Jim shared with us some of his experiences in bicycling with small children:

> As soon as your children are old enough to ride in a straight line and take instructions, they are old enough to be involved in bicycle camping. It's a completely different experience when they provide their own transportation to the campsite. It can be a somewhat circuitous route that ends up no more than a mile from the starting point, just as long as it has a few rest stops and a variety of things to see along the way to keep it interesting.
>
> The weight of all the gear for an overnight camp builds very rapidly, and a bicycle suitable for loaded touring is necessary. If your bikes lack the racks and panniers to carry all the stuff, it might be a good idea to move the heavier things like tents, sleeping bags, and perhaps a cooler to the camp location before you leave. There may be a certain amount of logistics involved in getting everything in place and the vehicle parked out of sight. Having the family car sitting there will kill the feeling that the children have provided their own way of getting there.
>
> The children should be expected to carry their share of gear. A good rule of thumb for small children is one pound for each year of age. It can be carried in a backpack, since most kids' bikes have no provisions for racks.

Be aware that kids on a trip like this will eat at least twice what they would at home.

Driving

If you can't make the trip under your own power, you will want to consider the economics of automobiles versus airplanes and other forms of travel. The more people in your family, the lower the cost per person to drive—unlike flying, where more people means buying additional expensive tickets.

An auto trip demands a slower pace than air travel. It allows time for unscheduled stops and surprises that would be impossible by bus, train, or air. If you're traveling on a shoestring, some of the "surprises" may be educational but unpleasant.

Bruce, a homeschool dad, travels with his family all over the United States in an aging Suburban, which now has over three hundred thousand miles on it. With the help of a friend, he put a new engine in before a recent trip. "I knew a limited amount about automotive repair," Bruce says. "I know a lot more now than before I started!" His frugal philosophy is this: The best vehicle to buy is one that is two to four years old. Drive it until it drops—and then resurrect it.

Judith's family has taken a number of trips in old cars. Actually, all their trips have been in old cars, sometimes towing an aging travel trailer. If a twenty-thousand-dollar car breaks down, you fix it. If a one-thousand-dollar car breaks down, you have to make a decision about whether to fix it or get another car. Judith comments,

What we decided was, if the car died, we would buy another junker, rent a car, or fly home. That means we had to be financially prepared to do one of those. Fortunately, we have not had to make that decision. Our junkers have always gotten us home.

Sometimes, though, we have had to have repairs done en route. That means finding a trustworthy mechanic. It is best to get a recommendation, even if it is from your waitress. Better yet, contact someone in an organization with which you have some affiliation.

When possible, we call host families, photographers (since my husband is a photographer), or Toastmasters (we are members).

I also think you are a little less likely to get ripped off when you are driving an old car. I can't prove it, but it makes my life easier believing it. As a precaution, we have our trusty mechanic check over our car thoroughly before any long trips. That always brings to the surface a few surprises we would rather experience at home than on the road. Speaking of surprises, if you belong to a travel service such as AAA, check to see if you have used up your emergency road services for the year, as some services have dollar limits. You might as well "know before you go."

Some years I wondered if we should wait to travel until we had a better car. We would have missed a lot if we had waited. We'd still be waiting.

Make believe the halfway mark on your gas tank is "empty." Running out of gas hundreds of miles from home is a real drag. For help finding lower-priced gasoline, Gas Price Watch is an Internet site that posts gasoline prices through over twelve thousand registered "spotters." Spotters are volunteers who pass a gas station during the day and then post the price on the Internet. Not all cities have a spotter, but it might be worth checking out.

Jell-O Planning

"We belong to a group called 'Boomers,'" says Stephanie Bernhagen, "as in 'Baby Boomers.' We're a special-interest group of the Escapees RV Club. Boomers talk about their schedules being carved in Jell-O. This is their way of saying their schedules are flexible and likely to change on the spur of the moment. Recently, we left Oregon for the San Francisco area, but it was raining there and we were looking for sunshine, so we turned toward Palm Springs instead. That is Jell-O planning. You never know where you will end up!" For more of Stephanie's adventures, read her book *Take Back Your Life: Travel Full-Time in an RV*.

Renting a Car

Maybe you want a larger vehicle for the trip, or you don't want to add miles to your own automobile. Perhaps you fear your vehicle will not make the trip, or you don't own a car. In these situations, you may want to consider renting one.

Rental rates may vary widely among various locations and companies. Compare rates months before your trip, if possible. But keep checking, since some of the best deals are last-minute bargains. Let your children do some of the real-life math. Ask if discount rates are available through credit card companies or organizations like AAA or camping clubs. Sometimes you can come out way ahead even after paying club dues.

Find out if your own insurance covers your use of a rental car, including any loss-of-use fees the rental company may charge if you're in an accident and the car has to be repaired. According to conventional wisdom, the "damage waiver" is an expensive form of insurance, especially if it duplicates your own insurance. On the other hand, if you do have an accident and rely on your own insurance, will you get the same coverage? Will your travel be delayed while you sort out the problem? Whatever you decide to do, get it in writing—and read the fine print.

Find out if you will be charged extra for an early return. If the company is out of the economical model you want, ask if you can upgrade to another model without additional charge.

Thoroughly inspect your rental for any damage, however minor, before leaving the lot, so you are not held responsible for existing damage. Check the carpet for stains, including the carpet in the trunk. Also check the spare tire (and tire wrench), radio, and air conditioning. Ask for a signed report listing any damage, the owner's manual, and a twenty-four-hour telephone number to call if you need roadside service.

Find out the company's policy on filling the gas tank. If you bring the tank back less than full, some companies fill it at their pumps and charge you for it, and their price per gallon is often considerably higher than the station a few blocks away.

Transporting a Vehicle for Someone Else

Instead of a standard car rental, you can transport a car or RV for someone else. You'll get a free or low-cost ride through a drive-away company, a car rental company, or a private individual. Most of these arrangements are to or from a "snowbird" destination, like Arizona or Florida. Northerners head there in the fall to avoid snowy winters, then make an exodus in the spring.

Companies offer low rental rates to entice one-way drivers who happen to be taking a car where the rental company wants it to go. This could work well for a family who wants to take a leisurely trip one way and then fly or take the bus home. Beware, though, that one-way airfares are often not significantly cheaper than two-ways, except for "specials." Occasionally a drive-away company can arrange a return trip with another vehicle, but the odds are against it. You can look up drive-away companies in telephone directories under "Auto Drive-Away." Ask about terms and conditions, such as what happens if you spill pop on the seat or grind dirt into the carpet. (Of course, *your* family wouldn't do that, but some people do.)

You might be able to arrange your own drive-away. RV owners sometimes want to use their RV to live in, but they don't want to drive it to and from their destination. They look for someone to transport their RV down south for the winter or up north for the summer. Transporting an RV may allow you sleeping and eating quarters for your trip, but make sure the terms and conditions are spelled out carefully and that the vehicle's insurance policy covers you.

Buying a Car Just for Your Trip

The Merrion family found that buying a car in Australia and selling it at the end of the trip was cheaper than renting one. "We bought a car from a person I knew from a previous business trip," says Duke Merrion, who traveled to Australia for two months with his wife and three children. "We spent some time in Brisbane, because that's where we bought the car, and in Melbourne, because that's where we got rid of the car. We tried advertising it but wound up selling to a dealer." They joined AAA before they left home and bought car insurance offered by the club.

Although the plan saved them some money, Sandra Merrion says there were some disadvantages. "This idea works, but you have to be careful," she says. "We found out when we went to sell the car, due to registration procedures in Australia, we lost five hundred dollars just by trying to sell in another state. When we went to New Zealand for two months after

Australia, we chose to rent a car in that country. One reason is the amount of time it had taken to handle buying and selling the car in Australia."

RIDE SHARING

Have room for another rider? Most colleges have a ride board posted in the student union with notices from students looking for a ride during breaks, holidays, or summer vacation. If you see a notice from a student headed to your destination, consider contacting him or her. Safety concerns arise when traveling with strangers—especially when children are involved. Exchange references and check them out, making sure the person really is a student at the college. Never travel with anyone until you know that they are safe, and always let someone else know where you're going and who you will be with. Train your children to do the same.

Shared expenses are much cheaper for the student than plane fare. You cannot charge for a ride (like a taxi) without a professional license, but you can share expenses.

A single parent or small family might like to share travel and expenses with another compatible family or individual. Often parents find that children will learn more together from the experience—and perhaps behave better—when friends are along for the ride. Compatibility is the primary issue, and sometimes traveling in close quarters puts a friendship to the test. You might want to try a weekend first.

TRAIN, BUS, AND SUBWAY

Even if you travel by car or air, consider using inexpensive public transportation after you arrive at your destination. Buses and subways will surely save you money over taxis. In large cities, driving and parking are a major hassle and expense, and public transportation gives you some of the flavor of city living. (Avoid rush hours to keep from getting too much of a flavor!) The Allees took a train from a "kiss and ride" station in Maryland to do some sightseeing in Washington D.C., which saved them from negotiating city traffic and trying to find a place to park. Train and bus schedules and information on passes are available online these days. (See the resource guide for more information.) You can help your child use math skills to figure out if it would be more economical to buy a bus or subway pass or to rent a car.

For intercity travel, a bus or train might be an option for your family. Trains are especially fascinating to many people, not only kids. Allow yourself time to see the train station and ask about visiting the engineer. Amtrak offers discounts for children accompanied by an adult and runs occasional special discounts.

freebee

Leaders Can Ride Free

Put together a group bus trip, bringing together a busload of people to travel inexpensively to a destination you choose. If you make it a family project, your children could hold positions in a real business enterprise as part of a real "tour company."

To get started, call charter bus companies in your area to compare prices, then negotiate for your best deal. Consider your passengers' needs. Will they want to take a red-eye trip, traveling with few or no stops at night? Or will they enjoy a scenic drive? To find out what each passenger will pay, add up your expenses and divide by the number of other passengers (not including yourself). You get to travel free in exchange for your efforts to make the arrangements.

You can arrange additional freebies if you continue on as a tour guide for your group. Tour guides and drivers may receive free meals, motel accommodations, and admission to attractions. Restaurants sometimes advertise these perks on their highway billboards. Other restaurants may offer freebees only with advanced reservations. For the other places, you would likely need to call ahead and make reservations to get the freebies.

Churches often book group tours. Typically, the person who spends the time coordinating the tour receives a free trip. "I have done this, and the work is extensive if you shop around for the best deals and tours," Melissa says. "The coordinator definitely earns the free trip!"

For more information on guided tours (not just bus tours), see chapter 9 under the section titled "Travel Businesses Equal Travel Discounts."

A bus or train trip will allow you to see the scenery and enjoy the time with your children instead of focusing on driving. On a train or bus ride, your family can experience the gradual changes in climate and geographical features as you travel from flatlands into foothills, cross rivers and creeks, or climb into the mountains. On a plane, you get a good bird's-eye view of your destination from the air as you land, but you see little of the world in between.

When you travel by bus or train, it will take you longer—much longer—to arrive at your destination than if you took a plane. In the United States you will probably spend more for train fare than you would for airfare. Bus travel may be less for one or two people; however, the larger your family, the more it costs to take a bus instead of driving. Even if the fare is cheaper, you have the added expense of meals during the trip and less time to spend at your destination. You may find trains and buses confining, and you do not have the freedom to stop whenever you wish.

If you have never traveled on a modern bus, however, you might be surprised at the comfort level. All Greyhound buses, for example, are smoke-free and equipped with air conditioning, a rest room, and reclining seats with headrests. To avoid stops between cities, ask if express service is available. The bus makes rest stops every few hours and longer stops for meals.

Compare bus companies for features as well as prices. Ask about current discounts for families, such as a free companion ticket (for an adult or a child), or up to three half-price children's fares with one adult fare. Ask about available discounts for students and military personnel. If you work for a large corporation or belong to an organization, ask if you qualify to receive a discount. If you don't ask, they might not tell.

Greyhound and its affiliates offer the Ameripass, an unlimited bus pass for use in the United States on Greyhound Bus Lines and some of its affiliates, valid for up to sixty days. Canada and Mexico have similar programs. Call (888) GLI-PASS for information. With Ameripass, you may stop over as often as you wish and for as long as you wish.

For travel between the United States and Canada, you can use your pass for a few trips from specific U.S. cities to Toronto, Montreal, and Vancouver. Within Canada, Grayline *(http://www.grayline.ca)* currently offers tours to over a dozen locations, from the city lights of Toronto to White Horse in the north.

Travel by Waterways

Traveling by water is another way to journey inexpensively and provides a fascinating education on the way.

Cruises

For many people, cruising is not exactly a vacation on a shoestring; however, *shoestring* means different things to different people. There are also some surprisingly inexpensive deals for cruises, especially when you take into account that all meals are included. A cruise can be a relatively inexpensive way to have some exotic experiences.

Nine Ways to Save on Cruises

Cruise.com (*http://www.cruise.com*) offers this list of the various discounts available and which cruise lines currently offer them:

- twofers—second person's ticket is free
- monetary discount, onboard credit, or discounted air travel
- "added value"—the value could be anything: a free camera, onboard credit, shore excursions
- alumni discounts—available only to past passengers of a cruise line
- "back to back"—get a discount when booking two consecutive cruises
- discount for early booking
- group discounts
- kids sail free or at a deep discount (perhaps 75 percent)
- senior discounts

Some cruises are good values in educational travel. But it can be hard to pin down which ones are inexpensive, since they are difficult to compare feature-for-feature. Packages may include airfare, onshore excursions, meals onshore, and other variables. You may spend less on a vacation package that is all-inclusive than on a trip that sounds cheaper but includes fewer features. Work with a knowledgeable travel agent to make comparisons.

You may wish to barter with cruise lines for passage. Some people earn their passage as entertainers, such as musicians, magicians, or comedians, or by giving workshops on anything from crafts to photography. If a parent-teen couple wants to cruise together, one free passage cuts the cruise price in half.

Adventure Cruising by Don and Betty Martin offers insider information about ships with fewer than a hundred cabins (some with only three cabins) as well as some larger watercraft that primarily offer educational or exploratory voyages.

Expedition cruises are not inexpensive (several hundred dollars a day or more per person), but they are educational. They usually have field guides or speakers aboard who may give lectures or accompany you on shore trips. Some take "the road less traveled," (or "sea" in this case), such as a cruise through Drakes Passage to the Antarctic Peninsula, a tundra hike, or a motorized canoe trip with a native Brazilian up the tributaries of the Amazon for village visits and wildlife hikes. A more luxurious version of expedition cruising is called "soft adventure" cruising. It offers upscale amenities with educational experiences. Some of the better buys include unforgettable shore excursions.

PASSENGER FERRIES

Passenger ferries can save you money on a long trip, especially if they save you hours or days of driving. Some are cheap to start with. Prices range from the cost of a subway token to about the same as a full-service ocean liner. Ferries may be a misleading term, since some have passenger cabins and dining rooms.

Our ferry rides, however, were short ones that local folks use as everyday transportation, a form of mass transit. They were inexpensive and added seagulls, hair whipped in the sea air, and a dramatic arrival to our trip memories. The free Staten Island Ferry gave us a closeup view of the Statue of Liberty, and the inexpensive people-and-car ferry to Galveston Island in Texas cut hours of driving off our route. Washington State Ferries, for example, which has been operating for over fifty years in Puget Sound, makes over five hundred runs a day with commuters and commercial vehicles as well as tourists.

The Alaskan and Canadian ferry system serves coastal areas, including some communities that are inaccessible by land. The regular commuters may read the newspaper. You, on the other hand, will enjoy the breathless view of glaciers, snowcapped mountains, and Alaskan wildlife. Your accommodations may range from a cabin to sleeping bags on the deck of the ferry.

Some ferries (and other boats) carry vehicles so that you can bring your car or RV with you. Fees vary widely, so call for information. You probably will not be allowed to use your RV during transit.

For comprehensive listings and tips, read *Ford's Freighter Travel Guide,* which includes information on ferries.

RIVERBOATS AND BARGES

River and canal boats and barges range from picturesque steamboat replicas to boats that look like ocean liners. Inland water tours can include a variety of shore excursions, and some are less than one hundred dollars a day. Some, not necessarily the cheapest, provide no crew. You and your family are the crew.

FREIGHTERS

Some people have an almost cultlike passion about traveling on freighters, believing that they are the only way to travel. The appeal of riding in a cargo vessel is the lower cost, smoother sailing (since the heavy cargo stabilizes the vessel), and no crowds. In addition, according to *Ford's,* "the freighter, being primarily a cargo vessel, will call at exotic off-the-beaten-path ports the average tourist never has the opportunity to visit." (Two newsletters serve those who want to travel on freighters. See the resource guide for freighter travel resources.)

SAILBOATS AND SAILING SHIPS

Sailboats and sailing ships allow you to be a passenger or a sailor. Some are restored historical vessels that accept volunteer crews. For example, Grays Harbor Historical Seaport in Aberdeen, Washington, sails year-round with volunteers serious about learning to sail. Some ships have auxiliary motors.

If you own your own sailboat, you might be interested in joining the Sailboat Exchange, which offers a database of sailboat owners who wish to exchange the use of their boat for the use of another boat in a different part of the country or world. That saves you the cost of chartering a boat, and you can sail in areas you could not reach with your own boat. You can also get the inside scoop on itinerary and local know-how from the owners. Southern sailors get a chance to go north to beat the summer heat, and northern sailors can extend their cruising season by traveling south.

freebee

Good Old Boat **Magazine**

For a complimentary issue of *Good Old Boat,* write to *Good Old Boat,* 7340 Niagara Lane North, Maple Grove, MN 55311-2655, or request a complimentary issue online at *http:// www.goodoldboat.com. Good Old Boat* focuses on older-model sailboats (ten years and older) and features classified ads, advice on maintaining and upgrading older vessels, and directories of sailing organizations and suppliers for sailboats. With your complimentary issue, you will receive a bill for a subscription, but you can write "cancel" on the bill if you decide not to subscribe. Either way, keep the free issue.

RAFTING, CANOEING, AND KAYAKING

Unless you have some paddling expertise, you might want to try a group excursion with a guide while you learn the ropes. One of the less expensive water excursions is offered by Sierra Mac River Trips, which also conducts whitewater schools up to a week long.

If whitewater is a bit too adventurous for your family, you can start with relatively tame trips on ponds, small lakes, and gentle streams. Inflatable boats can be relatively inexpensive and convenient to transport. Some are surprisingly sturdy and can even support an outboard motor. We go into more detail on canoeing, kayaking, and inflatables in chapter 4.

Falcon publishes the Paddling guidebook series that covers various state or geographical regions, such as Michigan, Northern California, Okefenokee National Wildlife Refuge, and Yellowstone and Grand Teton National Parks. The guides describe the best paddling trips for the region and include detailed maps with access points, flow charts indicating the best seasons, tide information for ocean trips, and a detailed appendix of other resources. Some of them also have information on camping, fishing, wildlife viewing, and other activities that would go well with the trips.

Another useful series for small boat operators is the *Guide to Sea Kayaking* published by the Globe Pequot Press. The series covers various states and geographic areas, with over forty excursions described in each book. Information for each tour includes detailed maps with nautical charts, route courses, towns and landmarks along the way, trip lengths, paddling time, type of experience required, and directions to the launch site. Sidebars throughout the books provide information about local geography, wildlife, history, and legends. The series also offers resource listings for kayak rentals, companies that arrange sailing and kayaking trips, and cabins and bed-and-breakfasts along the way.

The Complete Book of Canoeing, also published by Globe Pequot, includes basic information for beginners on equipment and stroke techniques. For the experienced, it has advanced rescue maneuvers and field medicine. Two sections may be especially helpful for families: tandem paddling and canoeing with children.

GETTING OFF THE GROUND: AIRFARE

You are sitting next to a family on the plane, chatting about your trip. Then you find out you paid three times as much for airfare as they did. It happens!

Chances are your seatmates used a combination of strategies to save on airfare. Perhaps they were able to leave at the drop of a suitcase when a special last-minute deal came up, and they didn't mind leaving and arriving in the middle of the night. Maybe they accumulated frequent-flier miles (also known as bonus program points).

Airfare bargains abound, but they can be complex minefields for the uninitiated. The more you know, the more you'll save. Here are six strategies for airfare savings:

STRATEGY NO. 1: GOOD TIMING AND DESTINATION PLANNING

Save on airfare when demand is the lowest. *Arthur Frommer's Budget Travel Online (http://www.frommers.com)* is a free newsletter that includes worldwide travel deals, up-to-date information and reviews, and access to over a thousand message boards, each with a specific focus related to travel.

Frommer's says,

In the coldest months of the year, bargains are superb to transatlantic destinations, but less so to domestic locations and the tropics.... Clearly, January and February are the time for a transatlantic flight: prices are sharply down at that time, even though the appeal of the various destinations—their generally mild winter weather, their theater and cultural life, their uncrowded museums, the life you witness when most of the population is at home—is at its very peak in these months.

Timing can work two ways:
1. Save by planning ahead. Take advantage of advance purchase excursion fares. You may find a deeper discount if you book seven, fourteen, twenty-one, or even ninety days in advance. Often rates are cheaper if you stay over a Saturday. Make sure you understand any restrictions, such as nonrefundable tickets or a fee for exchanging your ticket.
2. Save by not planning ahead. Be flexible and be ready to travel at a moment's notice.

Unit Study on Air Travel

Elementary-school classes usually spend time studying various forms of transportation from a textbook perspective. You and your family can experience transportation in person with a unit study on air travel. In a unit study, students explore an area of interest, incorporating subjects such as math, language arts, social studies, and science.

If you are taking a plane trip, study the clouds. An airplane is a perfect vantage point from which you can see some incredible cloud formations. For language arts, you could also take turns describing (either orally or in writing) imaginary cloud creatures. Learn about the science of weather and how it can affect your trip. Study economics by comparing the cost of air travel versus automobile travel. Prepare for those inevitable delays at the airport by bringing books about aerodynamics so you can build paper airplanes while you wait. Read about the history of flight, biographies of famous aviators, or stories about early air travel in wartime. With unit studies, a whole family can study the same subject together on different levels.

The world of travel agents is changing rapidly. Not long ago, the airlines encouraged patrons to use a travel agent. Airlines paid a standard commission to the agent, so the agent's service was free to the customer. Now the airlines are encouraging customers to book directly with the airline—by phone or online—and airlines are cutting commissions to local travel agents, making it difficult for some of them to stay in business. Some now charge a service fee. Nonethelesss, knowledgeable travel agents can save you time as well as money. They are experts. An agent can unsnarl any problems that arise. Many are passionate travelers themselves and can share their personal experiences with numerous destinations.

A Smooth Takeoff

When traveling by air, be sure to arrive at the airport early—very early. You would not want to lose a nonrefundable ticket because of a traffic jam or flat tire. Besides, what child does not enjoy watching airplanes take off and land? Find out if there is an observation deck at the airport. If the ticket agent is not busy, perhaps he or she will explain how the reservation system works. Feel free to ask the flight attendant about any strange noises you hear during the flight. Knowing what makes the noises you hear— the lowering of the wheels or the flaps—can make a nervous flier more comfortable. Before your trip you could call a private airport and ask if one of their pilots might be available to show you an airplane cockpit—with its fascinating display of instruments— and answer your questions about flying.

When planning your budget, do not forget taxes and fees. Airfare is usually quoted before these additional charges, which can be an unpleasant surprise.

Be cautious about free vacation offers or ridiculously low packages (like $29) that you will see in the travel section of any newspaper. Read the fine print carefully before you waste your time or money. Often there are numerous restrictions, or you must stay at a specific (very expensive) hotel.

Save by Picking the Right Airport

Sometimes it pays to drive several hours out of your way to depart from a different airport. Compare prices from airports within a few hours' drive. You might also travel by plane to a different, cheaper destination and then rent a car to your final destination, or finish your trip by bus or train. You should consider the extra time and trouble versus the money you would save—which could be hundreds of dollars per ticket.

Wise Destination Tips

For travel in European countries, inquire about discounts and air passes from the tourist board in the specific country. Find the tourist board (the government department in charge of tourism) by searching the Internet with keywords for the country and tourist board (or department or division).

Ask for the lowest fare. Be persistent and keep calling, since discounts change daily. Ask if the rate is cheaper at a different time of day or on a different day of the week. Check to see if you can save by booking on two different airlines—one for the trip out and a different airline for the return trip. Ask if any discounts or promotions are available now or scheduled for the future. Plainly ask for all the discounts that you are entitled to—student, military, travel club, credit card company, hotel chains, auto rental chains, or through certain retailers that offer travel discounts.

Duke and Sandra Merrion found a way to milk a little more vacation out of their airfare dollars. Their ticket broker routed the family with a twelve-hour layover in the Fiji Islands, which was not considered a stop. (Each additional stop on an airline ticket costs extra for each person.) Says Sandy, "We put our luggage in a locker, and for dinner we went to a resort where they had native fire dancing. We got a taste of a South Sea island and got back to the airport by midnight."

STRATEGY NO. 2: FINDING DEALS ON THE INTERNET

You can find up-to-the-minute deals on the Internet. Almost everyone has access to the Internet, either through a home computer, work, school, library, or a friend or relative. If you are a novice, ask an Internet-savvy friend or relative to help you. Don't forget that teens often know more than adults about surfing the Internet, and they enjoy being the experts.

Here are some sites to get you started:

- *http://www.bestfares.com.*
- *http://www.priceline.com.* Name your price first (you must back it up with a credit card number), then Priceline will let you know if anyone will match your price. Check restrictions carefully.
- *http://www.travelocity.com.*
- *http://expedia.com* features promotional offers, such as buy one ticket, get one hundred dollars off a future trip.
- *http://www.lowestfare.com* (includes vacation and cruise packages).
- *http://www.cheaptickets.com* (includes cruises, rental cars, and hotel room deals).

You might want to bookmark the airlines' Web sites and your favorite travel sites and check them regularly. Sometimes discounts do not show up online, though, so you might want to call as well as surf the Internet.

After making your reservation online, you should receive confirmation by e-mail. Be sure to print the e-mail and carry it with you to the airport. In case there is a dispute, you have proof in writing.

Many Internet travel sites allow you to search by date of travel when what you want to know is, Which date is best for getting the lowest fare? Try entering multiple dates or seek offline help from an experienced travel agent.

Strategy No. 3: Award/Bonus Programs or Plans

Air carriers originally started frequent-flier programs to engender loyalty from business travelers who flew often. Now you can accumulate frequent-flier points by shopping at various retail outlets or booking a room at a major hotel chain. One family makes all their purchases through a credit card that offers frequent-flier miles, making sure to pay off the balance every month so they do not incur interest charges. Even grocery store chains, such as Kroger's, offer credit-card reward programs.

Kellogg's currently offers the American Dream program, in association with American Airlines' AAdvantage program. Customers receive one hundred points for each box of cereal. One family can go through many boxes of cereal. Would this be a good deal for your family? You could do the math with your children to find out. How many tickets will you need, and what is your estimated cost per ticket? How many bonus miles would it take to fly to your destination? Would it pay to eat more cereal—or to buy cereal and give it away to the local food bank? What about asking your friends and family to save boxes for you?

You can gather points and exchange them for frequent-flier miles just by visiting certain merchants on the Internet through programs such as MyPoints, Etour, and WebFlyer, which reward you for reading e-mail, shopping online, touring Web sites, or completing surveys. After signing up, you visit sponsored Web sites to accumulate up to twenty-five thousand miles per year with American Airlines. There are trips available worldwide using either American Airlines or a partner airline. Some advertisers offer bonus points for trying out a product or service. Some of these are free, but the bigger bonuses tend to be for paid products or services.

Surfing for Frequent-Flier Miles

The Frequent-Flier Crier is a weekly e-mail newsletter that will keep you up-to-date on frequent-flier offers, available free from *FrequentFlier.com*. Search with the keywords "Free Frequent-Flier Miles" to see what else is out there.

As of 1996 a frequent-flier mile was worth about two cents, according to author Tom Parsons in *Insider Travel Secrets You're Not Supposed to Know*. Use your math skills (or your children's) to figure out when to spend a little extra to get bonus miles from a car rental or ticket upgrade. Sometimes it is worth it—sometimes not. Look for bonus and reward programs that pay you two reward points for every dollar charged. You'll accumulate points twice as fast as programs that only pay you one-for-one.

Consider carefully before spending money to accumulate additional points. Compare the cost of accumulating the points. If you must use a credit card, will you always pay it off every month? If not, you would be better off putting money for your trip in a savings account at a credit union. Interest rates on a credit-card deal can easily outweigh the cost of a "free vacation." Credit card companies know this. That's why they started the programs.

Will you really come out ahead by staying in a more expensive hotel or flying with a more expensive airline just to get points? Think of frequent-flier points as if they are coupons for groceries. Do not look only at how much you "save." Look at how much you spend!

Strategy No. 4: Coupon Books and Cards

You may recoup the cost of an entertainment, travel, or Diners Club coupon book if you use even one of the coupons for a major purchase. The books typically sell for around twenty to fifty dollars and are sold by charities as fund-raisers or offered as premiums. Some employers offer them to their employees free of charge or at a discounted price. Keep a lookout for books that have coupons that are valid nationwide through outlets and chains, or contact someone at your destination to buy a local book for you. Some sources are listed in the resource guide.

There may be travel discounts available through your place of employment or through a credit card company. Check to see if it would pay you to become a member of a club, credit union, or civic organization that offers airfare discounts. Be sure to carry your membership cards with you!

Strategy No. 5: Companion Fares

Ask if a companion fare is available, especially during off-seasons. With a companion fare, the second ticket may be free or discounted, and some companion fares apply to additional family members. You may pay more for the first ticket but less overall. Carefully check twofers (two for one) and discount coupon offers, whether you find them in a coupon book or in your Sunday paper. If the discount is taken off the regular published rates, you may end up paying more with your "discount" than if you shop around for the best price.

Strategy No. 6: Consolidators and Charter Airlines

You may find bargain airfare through consolidators or charter airlines. When researching on the Internet, try using these keywords for your search: "charter airlines," "air travel discount fares tips information," and "travel + consolidator."

A consolidator buys up discounted blocks of unused airline tickets, hotel rooms, cruise tickets, and more and then resells them individually to the public at discounts of 30 to 60 percent. The consolidator makes money, of course, but also passes on savings to customers. Various restrictions may apply. To get the best deal, you may need to travel on the spur of the moment. You may not be able to accrue or use frequent-flier miles.

You can call a consolidator directly or use a travel agent. If you deal directly with the consolidator, you can avoid paying an extra travel-agent fee. However, if you deal with a trusted local travel agent, you can ascertain the reputation of the consolidator, which might make any add-on fees worth your while.

Charter airlines cut costs by cutting service. You can save money if you can put up with some inconvenience and discomfort.

AIRLINE VOUCHERS

When a hotel, tour company, or other travel business owes you money due to a problem of some kind, their first step is usually to offer you a voucher for future services instead of a cash refund. Insist on the cash whenever possible, according to Ed Perkins, a travel columnist for Tribune Media Services. If you have no choice, though, Ed offers some tips for getting the most value from your voucher:

- Ask for an extended expiration date (for two years instead of six months, for example).
- Make sure you can apply the voucher to the best price you can find, not to full retail price. Otherwise, you may actually lose money on the deal.
- Ask for frequent-flier miles or other more desirable compensation.

COURIER FLIGHTS

You have probably heard about people flying free as couriers for important documents or packages. Intriguing as the idea sounds, it is unlikely you can save money by being an air courier, at least when it comes to family travel.

Couriers have to fly on demand with little or no notice. That means family members pay full price, so that "free" ticket may cost a bundle. You also want to be sure to use a legitimate service. The last thing you want is to arrive in another country with contraband. However, if a footloose family member wants to check out courier services as an option, they're listed in the yellow pages.

Chapter Fourteen

Be Prepared: Practical Tips for Parents on the Road

Hours spent cramming belongings into tiny spaces; making arrangements for someone to take care of the cat; draining water pipes in February after everyone uses the "facilities"—then a trip becomes reality. The Allee family's aging station wagon sweeps majestically out of the driveway, and the crunching sound of gravel changes to the steady hum of the paved road. The wagon's fake woodgrain sides groan from the crush of boxes and bags as the car navigates toward Interstate 70, the corridor to an adventure of one kind or another.

"We have reached escape velocity," announces Judith's husband in his official capacity as starship officer of the Oldsmobile. The Allee family has escaped the gravitational pull of home, work, and the details of daily living just as a spaceship must generate enough thrust to escape the earth's atmosphere.

"Even if we drive only two hours on our first day," says Judith, "our trip has officially begun."

A Little More Planning

"The man who goes alone can start today; but he who travels with another must wait till that other is ready." —Henry David Thoreau, 1817–1862

How can we make it easier to reach escape velocity? How can we be better prepared for takeoff and enjoy the rest of our trip? Although parents cannot anticipate every contingency, we can learn what to expect and help our children learn how to deal with the unexpected. Thinking ahead is a skill—an important one—that will benefit our children in every aspect of life. Kids learn that carelessness has a cost—time, money, injury, or even lives.

Planning also reduces the stress level that family travel can bring. Packing light but still having the things we really need, and being able to find what we brought, gives us a chance to get a running start on having a fun time.

Packing for Parents

Do you remember thinking, I meant to bring this or that? As soon as you start planning your travel, assign a box for the trip and start adding items as you think of them. Attach a list for items you cannot pack ahead of time (say, your nighttime dental appliance) but do not want to forget. It helps to keep your packing list to use when you plan your next trip, revising it as you learn from experience.

You do not realize how little you need until you have to carry everything in a backpack. Then the necessities become painfully obvious. Here are some essentials you need no matter what your mode of travel:

- sunscreen (Check the expiration date and read the directions. Most of us use far too little lotion for it to work effectively.)
- a foldable, crushable hat for each person (Ball caps don't cover the back of the neck. Many kids turn them around backward (for fashion) and protect their necks but not their faces. Try to get family members to wear a hat with a wide brim on all sides.)
- a pair of comfortable walking shoes for each person (Don't purchase the shoes at the last minute. Buy them a few weeks before your trip and try them out.)
- moist towelettes for when hand-washing facilities are not available (They are also good for cooling down a hot child.)
- a roll of toilet paper in a plastic bag
- backpacks or fanny packs for each person (You can use them as luggage, then empty them temporarily into plastic bags for outings.)

- a stuffed animal (They're good company, but bringing the most favorite one in the whole world puts it at risk of getting lost. If your child will go for it, maybe a second choice would be better.)
- an extra car key

The Rest Is Optional

"Make a packing list and stick to it. Item #1: Address book. Item #2: Prescription medication. The rest is optional." —Marilyn J. Abraham, *First We Quit Our Jobs: How One Work-Driven Couple Got on the Road to a New Life*

Bring a few extra days' worth of prescription medications and a copy of the prescription from your doctor. Think about any recurrent health problems and be prepared. If someone in your family has migraines or asthma, even infrequently, remember to bring medication and keep something to drink in the car, since the medication works best at the onset of the attack. Like an umbrella, if you do not bring it, you will need it.

Personal items to remember are:

- an extra pair of glasses or contacts and a glasses repair kit
- a night-light (It takes little space and is helpful when staying in strange places, especially if your child is used to one at home.)
- safety plugs for the outlets, if you have preschoolers
- rubber "flip-flop" sandals (They're handy to wear in the shower at a campground.)
- your personal address or phone book tucked under the seat of your car (If you have health, safety, or legal problems along the way, you will be glad you have it with you.)
- your own pillows (They can make for better sleep at night, plus they can be used for comfort and snoozing in the car.)
- insurance information (Contact your health insurance company to make sure of coverage when you travel. You may need to look into supplemental coverage.)

A little red wagon is optional, but if you intend to have lengthy outings and your children are small enough to ride in it, you might want to make room for it. Kids up to seven or eight years of age can easily ride in a wagon, and any resistance to the idea tends to give way when they are tired. The wagon is also handy for carrying a cooler, although some progressive, family-friendly person has invented coolers with long handles and wheels.

Don't Be a Packhorse

Here are some tips from *52 Ways to Make Family Travel More Enjoyable* by Kate Redd:

- "If you're lugging heavy luggage around for the whole family, you'll skip the walking tour and spend extra for the cab ride. Instead, buy each family member an appropriate carry-on piece, preferably a backpack."
- "Consider physical limitations, but be creative. Can you attach an extra (and safe) carrier to the baby stroller? Can a family member in a wheelchair carry the picnic basket, or a toddler, in his lap? Everybody needs to feel useful, and let's face it: we could all use some help. Remember, you're not a packhorse."

BABIES AND TODDLERS ON BOARD

When it comes to walking around with babies and toddlers, you'll likely find yourself pushing a stroller. But Melissa's husband cautions, "Most strollers are not built for taller people. The handles are so low that pushing the stroller for very long kills my back!"

A lightweight umbrella stroller may be easier to lug around than a full-size model. Of course, umbrella strollers don't come with baskets to carry parcels, but you'll probably end up carrying the biggest parcel—your baby—yourself. That means at times you will be pushing around an empty stroller.

A stroller may be more trouble than it is worth. You may want to skip it altogether and look for a baby backpack or carrier. Many nursing moms find that a sling is a handy, private way to nurse in public. Try to find one that adapts to different ages, as you'll be carrying that baby around for a few years.

Instead of checking your stroller with your luggage at the airport, ask for a gate check. You can give it to the flight attendant when you board the plane and get it back when you exit—when you will need it for the long concourses at the airport.

Pet Packing List

Traveling with a pet can make some things easier and other things more complicated. In any event, people who travel with their pets seem to be enthusiastic about it.

Here are some helpful items to bring:

- a bottle of water and a water dish so you can refresh your pet at rest stops
- a pooper-scooper (You can use a plastic bag to pick up droppings and then discard them in the same bag.)
- immunization records and your vet's telephone number

Some animals are content riding in a wire travel crate in the back of a car. They can still see but are confined and less excitable. If you decide to go this route, get your pet familiar with the crate before leaving home. Start by feeding the animal in the crate, leaving the door open. *Never* leave a pet (or a child or anyone else) in a hot car, even with the window cracked.

Check on policies at campgrounds, motels, and hotels to find a place that accommodates pets. The national chains have toll-free numbers and Web sites you can check. Campground guides can be helpful, keeping in mind some guides focus more on this information than others. (The resource guide has additional sources for information.) If you stay with friends or relatives, offer to put your pet up at a kennel. That way you can still travel with your furry friend and not impose on your hosts.

The Organized Packer Strikes Out Against Chaos!

Actually, anyone who sees our car when we set out on a long trip—or particularly when we arrive back home—snickers at the idea that we are organized packers. We do have a few tips to share, however, that help us keep the chaos down to a manageable level.

- You may pack your suitcases and other containers a little at a time, but pack your car all at once. That way you can stick with a master plan for what things need to be easily accessible and what things can be more buried.

- Try rolling your sweaters, jeans, and other bulky items instead of folding them flat. You can find things more easily that way instead of having to root through everything.
- You might consider using boxes instead of luggage for supplies you can keep in the car. Put small items like jewelry or hosiery in a plastic bag.
- Pack some plastic bags in your overnight case for dirty laundry. If you stay at a campground or motel with a washer and dryer, ask about laundry facility hours when you check in and plan on starting a load at a convenient time. This keeps the dirty clothes from piling up and reduces the amount of clothing you need to bring. You might want to pack a few self-sealing plastic bags with premeasured laundry detergent to avoid the hassle of finding laundry soap and the cost of those little premeasured boxes. (True confession: In the time crunch of leaving, Judith once brought dirty clothes along with good intentions of washing them along the way. She ended up bringing them back home again, still dirty, with the family still wearing the few clothes that had started out clean.)
- On hot days, photographers should keep their film in a cooler with an ice pack. Keep the film in its original box or in a sealed plastic film canister. You can also keep your loaded camera in the cooler, wrapped in a plastic bag. To prevent condensation that can damage the film or the camera, remove the bag from the cooler well before you need it—at least fifteen minutes for a roll of film and an hour or so for a camera. Then allow the film to warm gradually to the ambient temperature before opening the bag.
- If you pack any heavy items (Melissa had to pack an apnea monitor and other medical equipment), be sure to secure them so they do not become dangerous projectiles during a sudden stop or accident.

STAYING SAFE

Make sure everyone in your family—including children—carries identification. A "lost-child tag" includes contact information for parents as well as emergency health information that lists any medications the child may be taking. Even an older child can get confused or panicky in an emergency. This is more important than clean underwear in case of an accident or in case your children get separated from you somehow. (It happens!)

When you arrive at a crowded destination, decide on a place to meet if you get separated or stranded. Also talk about where family members should go for help—for example, to a police officer or to shopkeepers.

Keeping each other in sight is easier with matching T-shirts. Judith got her family matching shirts for Christmas that advertised their photography business. Aside from wearing the shirts at certain photography jobs, they used them when traveling and visiting tourist areas. A balloon tied to the wrist of a young child is even better than a T-shirt. It is best not to put your children's names on their clothing. It makes it too easy for a stranger to act like a child's friend—and too easy for the child to believe it.

True Crime

Tourists are inviting, easy marks for criminals because they are often preoccupied and aren't familiar with their surroundings. They also tend to carry cash, credit cards, cameras, and other valuables, or they leave valuables lying out in their motel rooms, cars, or campers. They are less likely to be around to prosecute a thief too. What more could a thief ask?

To protect cameras, computers, and other easily stolen items, engrave them with identification. This makes them less attractive to thieves and makes it possible for you to reclaim the items if they are recovered. Some police offices have engravers available for loan at no charge. Hidden identification can also help you retrieve an item, even if the thief removes the engraving or serial number. You can slip a piece of paper inside the item, like inside your car door, the handlebars of bicycles, or the interior of camera equipment, for example.

Worn, inconspicuous luggage is less inviting to thieves than new designer luggage. Watch for it at yard sales. Keep your junkiest belongings in sight and your valuables hidden or in the trunk. With or without ice, a cooler—especially a shabby one—camouflages cameras and other valuables and makes your car less enticing to thieves.

More important, though, is protecting yourself and your family. If a motel employee unexpectedly knocks on your door, call the front desk before opening the door. Use all of the locking hardware on your door when you are in your room, and keep your room number confidential.

Most of the time, carjackers select victims who are alone. Family travelers tend to pose more complications for a carjacker, plus families are less likely to engage in risky behavior—like parking in isolated, unlit areas. (You don't do that, do you?) Nonetheless, some caution is needed. Since a fake accident is sometimes used as a way to get you out of your car for a carjacking, if you are bumped under suspicious circumstances, wave the other person to follow you and go to a well-lighted gas station, police station, or busy store, where you can more safely exchange insurance information. Carjackers like hanging out at freeway entrance ramps.

If you arrive during daylight, keep in mind what the area will look like at night when you leave. Teach your children not to dawdle when getting in and out of the car, and drive with the doors locked and, if possible, the windows rolled up, especially in high-risk spots.

KEEPING YOUR HOME SAFE WHILE YOU ARE AWAY

Make sure your house looks lived-in while you are gone. Ask the post office to hold your mail, and stop newspaper delivery temporarily, or ask a trusted neighbor to pick up your mail and newspapers. Maybe that neighbor would be willing to park in your driveway at night.

Make arrangements for someone to keep up with lawn mowing or snow shoveling, as the case may be. Maybe you can swap with a neighbor and reciprocate after you get back. If you pull all the blinds, the house will look unoccupied. Set a timer for house lights and a radio—preferably several timers that go on and off at staggered times.

A burglar likes to get in quickly to avoid being spotted. Although good locks will not stop determined burglars, "professionals" usually prefer easier pickings, and there are plenty of them out there. By the way, burglars know all the places to look for hidden keys—in the flowerpot, under the mat, hanging on a nail, on the top of the door jamb. If you leave a note on the door explaining your whereabouts, think of it as a written invitation to a burglar. A message on your answering machine that you are on vacation does pretty much the same thing.

Check with your local police or sheriff's office to see if they offer home inspections with recommendations for making your residence more intruder-proof. If you belong to a Neighborhood Watch program, your police representative can arrange home inspections and a program on crime prevention.

DRIVING SAFELY

Car accidents can happen to even the best drivers. Preventing injuries starts with seat belts and car seats. If you do not wear a seat belt, chances are four-to-one that your children won't either. Set a good example for your children and wear your seat belt—every time, even on short trips. Most accidents happen on short trips.

Adults and teens have a better survival rate with air bags than without them, but you should position your seat as far back as you can to avoid injury from the air bag. Short people might want to consider gas pedal extenders so they do not have to sit as close to the front. Air bags are dangerous for kids. Children under age eleven should ride in the backseat if you have air bags for the front passenger's seat.

Here are some items to bring with you to avoid unnecessary expenses or risks:

- a spare tire (Have it inspected and check the air pressure.)
- a "call police" sign for back car window (You can buy one, usually on the back of a cardboard sunshade designed for car windshields, or make your own with huge letters—large enough for someone to read while driving by at highway speed. "Call police" is better than "Call for help," since someone who is up to no good might assume the police are on their way and keep driving.)
- a flashlight
- jumper cables
- road flares or a battery-operated flashing emergency light, in case of an accident or breakdown
- blankets (to treat shock) or sleeping bags.
- a gas can (It's embarrassing to run out of gas, but it happens to the best of us.)
- a water jug

- a first-aid kit (with thermometer, painkillers, diarrhea medication, and bandages)

At least one flashlight is part of emergency preparedness and handy for finding stuff in your bag, getting organized if you have to leave early and don't want to disturb other people, and reading or looking at a map while traveling. Judith brings a rechargeable flashlight and recharges it using a twelve-volt inverter in the car or by plugging it in at a hotel or campsite.

The combination radio-flashlight made by Freeplay—although a little more expensive in the short run—can be powered during the day with solar energy, making it ready for nighttime use and saving on the cost of batteries. It has an emergency flashing feature and can be powered four ways: solar, hand crank, DC, or AA-size batteries, making it a good backup light for power outages at home as well. It is about twice the cost of a standard rechargeable flashlight. (An interesting side note: The Freeplay hand-crank radio was invented by Trevor Bayliss, who wanted to give people in remote areas of Africa access to independent news sources so they would not be solely dependent on propaganda. According to the *Christian Science Monitor,* Freeplay's radios are made by South African ex-prisoners, battered women, and people with disabilities, who own a stake in the manufacturing end of the business.)

What *don't* you need? Anything you can easily buy anywhere you go. Why load yourself down?

If you are leaving the driving to others, you may find it hard to sleep. If you need to keep your eyes on the road, paradoxically, it can become almost impossible to stay awake. Driving when you're sleepy is as dangerous as driving drunk. Don't do it! If you are getting sleepy, pull over and take a nap. But before you get to that point, here are some drug-free ways to stay safe, awake, and sane on the road.

- Have a "fire drill." Stop your car in a safe place (such as a roadside rest stop) and have everyone get out, run around the car, and get back in, lickety-split. Silly, but fun.
- Take frequent breaks and s-t-r-r-r-r-e-t-c-h.
- Play "Simon Says" for exercise.
- Pack a jump rope. It takes little room. Pack more than one!

- Pack a Hula-Hoop. It is light and lies flat.
- Turn up the radio on a station that you don't like. Sing along.
- Ask the kids to be loud and noisy. (Yes, we have been this desperate, and it really works.)

Are you the kind of person who tries to figure things out first and then reads the instructions as a last resort? If so, you should know that only about one-third of children's car seats are installed properly. A local safety check of over thirty vehicles found that only four baby car seats were installed correctly. All four, by the way, belonged to employees of an insurance company who had received specific safety training!

For children forty to eighty pounds, get a booster seat, especially for a long trip. For one thing, imagine how boring a car ride is when you cannot see out the window. Although many states do not require a booster seat for children over forty pounds, using one greatly improves your child's chances of avoiding injury. Seat belts can cause internal injuries in a small child, and adult-size shoulder harnesses tend to fall right across a child's neck.

MANAGING MONEY AND OTHER MUNDANE MATTERS

Here are some helpful tips for managing your money when you travel:
- Travelers' checks are available with two signatures, allowing either party to cash them. You might have to call around to find a place that carries dual-signature checks.
- You may be able to get cash back when you write a check for purchases at some major chain stores, like Wal-Mart or Target. Check current policies and limits.
- A debit card probably does not have the same protections that a credit card has. If you lose your card, you can get cleaned out—and then some, if you have overdraft protection. However, you can use a debit card to withdraw cash as needed when you travel and don't want to get carried away with credit. Just watch out for ATM charges—they can be vicious!
- If your bank has branches nationwide, you may have cheap or free use of their ATM machines.

- If possible, arrange for direct check deposit of any regular income you expect.
- Bring only the credit cards you need. Thin out your wallet before your trip.

If you want the safety and convenience of credit without the danger of slipping into more debt, you can prepay your credit card. That is what Kay Peterson did. In her book *Home Is Where You Park It*, she tells of traveling full time with her husband, a union electrician, and their children in a recreational vehicle. Kay found that credit cards were a handy, universally accepted mode of handling cash. But she worried that her credit-card bills would not catch up with her, and she had no extra money in her budget for interest fees and late charges. So she sent a check to cover her purchases, bill or no bill. Never once, she says, did the credit card company object to getting money ahead of time! If you like, you can enter credit-card purchases in your checkbook to keep track of them.

One family makes all their purchases with a credit card that offers frequent-flier miles. This can pay off—but only if you are disciplined enough to actually pay the balance each month. Judith fell into the trap of intending to pay off the card immediately after the trip, but she found that to be easier said than done. Be realistic.

There are other options for paying your bills. In many cases, you can pay your bills over the phone using a debit card or credit card. If you travel frequently or for long periods, look into online resources like PayMyBills. Your bills go directly to the service, and the service notifies you by e-mail. You authorize payment from whichever account you prefer.

A last word about credit cards—using your card for a cash advance is *very* expensive. The rules are different than they are for a credit-card purchase through a merchant, which you can pay off when your bill comes with no penalty. With cash advances, interest begins to accrue immediately, and it is usually much higher than the interest you pay on a purchase. If you have a balance on your credit card, the higher interest rates are carried over from month to month, which can make a big difference in how long it takes you to pay off the card. If you use the handy checks the credit card company so considerately sends you now and then, the "checks" will probably be handled as cash advances.

Expect fees for each transaction. Sometimes you are charged a flat fee, which is expensive if you take a small advance, and sometimes fees are calculated on a percentage basis, which is prohibitive if you take a big advance. Some companies snag you either way, by specifying a percentage and a fee, whichever is greater. And that is on top of the ATM fees, if you get your cash advance there. It is best to avoid cash advances except in true emergencies.

COMMUNICATIONS ON THE ROAD

We can journey down the less-traveled road and still stay in touch with the outside world. Communications on the road can prove a lifesaver in an emergency. It also makes travel more convenient, especially for families with home businesses or special needs.

USING THE TELEPHONE

If you are concerned about staying in touch, ask about phone service at your destination before you take your trip. When the Morgan family took their youngest child (who has a chronic medical condition) on her first camping trip, they stayed in a state park. The cabin was equipped with a complete kitchen, cable television, air conditioning, and a gas fireplace—but no phone! What if they had to call 911? Their first priority was to find out how close their cabin was to the phone booth down the street.

Pay Phones

Truck stops along the interstate have made calling easier. If your motel or hotel has a surcharge for using the telephone (sometimes an outrageous one), you might prefer to use the pay phone in the lobby or negotiate with the front desk to waive the fees.

Prepaid Phone Cards

If you need to make phone calls while traveling, you can avoid a big telephone bill when you get home by using a prepaid telephone card. The costs vary enormously, but some of the higher-volume cards (such as the one-thousand-minute ones from Wal-Mart) may be cheaper than your regular home service. Some people have disconnected the long-distance service on their home phones and use prepaid cards exclusively, whether they are traveling or not. Some cards, however, are misleading; they may deduct more minutes than you use as a form of service fee, making the per-minute charge much higher than advertised. Other hidden charges include full-minute billing instead of six-second increments and hookup charges. The cards sold in convenience stores are not usually the best deals.

Call around and keep an eye out for good deals on prepaid telephone cards. Watch out for pay phones that trigger a surcharge on your phone card. If you hear a recording about a hefty surcharge, you can choose to hang up before the call goes through.

Telephone Credit Cards

Telephone credit cards (as opposed to prepaid cards) usually have a surcharge for each call, which can add up fast. Some of the phone credit cards bill directly either to your telephone bill or to your consumer credit card (such as Visa or MasterCard). That lets you see what the specific charges are as you use the card.

Phone Hookups at Campgrounds

A few campgrounds have on-site phone service by just hooking up. Check campground directories to see which campgrounds currently offer this. (Not all directories have this information. Check several.)

Cellular Phones

Even a cell phone with lapsed service will work to call 911. If you have a cell phone, keep it charged and carry it with you, even if you cannot use it to chat.

Just because your cellular plan claims coverage in a certain area does not mean you will have reception there. Your phone may fade in and out in hilly and remote areas. According to Workers on Wheels (WOW), a group for RVers who work and travel, it boils down to this: "There are ways that work for some of the people some of the time in some places." The WOW Web site has a detailed discussion of options and equipment. Judith bought an older "bag phone" at a yard sale for five dollars and keeps it in her car for emergencies. Since she did not activate service, there is no monthly fee.

Cell phone services keep getting cheaper, to the point that some people are getting rid of their home phones altogether and using their cell phones exclusively. That works best for people who make a lot of long-distance calls.

Some cell phone plans offer nationwide calling with no long-distance or roaming charges (a surcharge for when you leave a certain area). Read the plans carefully, though, if you plan to use your phone when traveling. The "no long distance" claim may only apply to calls made within a certain territory, and "no roaming fees" may apply only to a particular carrier. From experience we have learned to require the details of any plans in writing before signing up. What you are told and what you get can be very different.

Watch out for plans that have free access only in digital telephone areas and either do not work at all in analog areas or rack up high roaming charges. Digital service is available in many areas, but it can be spotty as you move away from large cities and major highways. Although cellular phones capable of handling both digital and analog signals are more expensive than their digital- or analog-only counterparts, they may be worth the money if your travels involve a good deal of rural driving.

One last tip: Recharge your cell phone before you leave and while you are traveling. What is the good of an emergency phone if you cannot use it in an emergency?

Prepaid Cell Phones
A prepaid phone will prevent you from charging up a big bill and is ideal for people who want a cell phone primarily for emergencies. The per-minute charge is high, but that does not matter if you use it only occasionally.

Personal Toll-Free Numbers
Because of their photography business, Judith and John need to check messages every day or so, and they like to keep in touch with family members when traveling. A toll-free number is handy and inexpensive if you get the right deal; the service is sometimes free (except for the calls) as a sign-on bonus with your long-distance plan. Judith also uses it locally rather than a pay phone, since the per-minute charge is much cheaper.

COMPUTING

Using a computer may be the last thing you want to do when you are traveling, but for some people it is essential. Using a computer while traveling is getting easier and may be a bonus for extended travelers or families who are self-employed or traveling on business. It can be a convenient way to stay in touch with family, friends, or business contacts. Most travelers use a laptop or notebook computer, but some RVers prefer to install a full-size computer because of the bigger screen and the fact that you can get more computer for your money.

You can power or recharge a laptop computer with your car battery while you are driving. Judith wrote parts of this book as a passenger en route to out-of-state conventions with an aging laptop that would not work on its battery alone. So she looked for an adapter to allow her to plug the computer into the car's twelve-volt system (the "cigarette lighter"). The proprietary cord from the computer manufacturer was over $150, but she found a generic adapter cord with a 12-volt inverter for under $20. Shop around.

If you travel often and want Internet access, you may want to use a national internet service provider (ISP) that provides local access numbers across the country or toll-free numbers.

You can connect to the Internet at motels and hotels, although not all phone lines are up to the specifications of a modem. More and more truck stops (the Flying J, for one) offer free data connections, but you need a calling card or toll-free number to access your ISP. You can also connect from cell phones and pay phones, although currently both methods are slow and cumbersome. If you visit friends, you may be able to check your e-mail using their phone line.

Most campgrounds allow you to plug your modem into their phone line at the office as long as you use a calling card or a toll-free number to connect to your ISP. Some campgrounds have set up a place for this purpose, such as a pavilion or recreation hall.

Many public libraries also provide Internet access, although restrictions vary. Some do not allow you to access e-mail that way. For occasional computer access while you travel, you can go to a Kinko's copy center or to a "cyber café," a coffee shop or restaurant that supplies Internet access as a service to customers.

If all you want to do is check e-mail, look for an ISP that lets you check it by telephone using a toll-free number. If you want to be able to send e-mail as well, you might want to buy a handheld e-mail device (Pocketmail is one), which works with virtually any telephone. A monthly service costs about half the cost of most ISPs, and you access your account via a toll-free number in the United States and Canada. This might be worth considering if you travel frequently or if you can use it when you are back home as well as when you are traveling.

Finding Your Way with Technology

You can get door-to-door directions, mileage, and estimated travel times at Internet mapping sites. Some sites also alert you to road construction, weather updates on your route, and the location of the nearest ATMs, gas stations, restaurants, lodging by type and price, campgrounds, points of interest and attractions, and golf courses. They may print coupons for services along your route, and one site even promises to detour you around tunnels, if that is your wish. Each site has a different combination of services that is updated periodically.

Computers calculate your route using set parameters, so the route could take you out of your way. Your children might get interested in surveying different online services to see which one has the services you need and which map gives you the best route. How about having the kids compare those maps to good, old-fashioned (that is, paper!) road maps?

wiseguy

Some Things Never Change...

Question: Why was Moses in the desert for forty days and forty nights?
Answer: Because even then men wouldn't stop and ask for directions.

You can also use computer software for trip planning. There are a number of programs that offer a searchable road atlas with street directions for any location you specify. Some can locate regions and attractions by area code or ZIP code. The DeLorme company offers both a free online mapping service and mapping software for your home computer.

Beyond Directions

Do you see the sign for the restaurant or service station you were seeking just *after* you pass the exit? *Exitsource.com* is pretty much just what it sounds like—it tells you what you will find if you exit the interstate at whatever exit you want.

If you are accessing the service by wireless Web (available through certain mobile phone providers), you can enter an exit you are approaching and get a listing of services available before and after that exit. Exitsource locates rest stops and emergency services, and you can specify which brand names you want for gas stations, lodging, and restaurants. For RVers and truckers, you can find out what facilities are equipped for large vehicles and where you can buy propane and diesel fuel. Customize your settings to specify the price range you are looking for.

Electronic Travel Gizmos

If the idea of electronic gizmos appeals to you, here's one with a practical purpose on your trip. A GPS (Global Positioning System) is the "ultimate male catnip," according to Anita Dunham Potter, a travel columnist for the SmarterLiving Web site. Our guess is that kids will love it too.

A GPS uses satellites to tell you where you are and how to get where you want to go. Smaller than a cell phone, the receiver-only versions are available for less than a hundred dollars. Use one in the car in conjunction with a laptop computer or a handheld computer like a Palm or a Pocket PC/Windows CE PDA (personal digital assistant). Standalone models (no laptop or palm-top needed) can be considerably more expensive.

DeLorme offers a GPS unit that sits on the dashboard of your car and connects to your laptop or handheld computer. It works in connection with the company's mapping software. For example, you can use drawing tools in the software to put notes on the maps to mark areas of interest, such as a meeting place.

You might consider a handheld electronic gizmo designed for car travelers, such as the AutoPilot, priced at about twenty to thirty dollars. When you enter the milepost number at your current location on one of the interstate highways and other major routes, the device tells you the closest gas stations and lists certain restaurants and motels. You can search by a particular brand name of hotel or gas station or find the closest one. This device also can be handy while you are planning your route.

Technology is fun, sometimes amazing, but don't forget the basics. The day will come when our children will need to know how to read an old-fashioned map, so bring one of those along, too. Speaking of low tech, remember to bring a compass.

Staying Healthy Away from Home

From a doctor's point of view, some patients almost seem to plan on being ill by not taking care of basic needs like sleep, eating healthy food on a regular schedule, and getting enough exercise. When you are traveling, it is easy to get off-schedule. When you are out in crowds and visiting people from different areas, you are exposed to new bugs. And some conditions, like an infected appendix, seem to happen at the worst times.

Bring a thermometer. That can help you decide when a trip to a clinic or emergency room is needed. Judith was especially glad she brought her own thermometer when she had pneumonia in Mexico, which uses metric thermometers. Her hostess took Judith's temperature once with a centigrade thermometer and seemed alarmed, so Judith took it again with her Fahrenheit thermometer so she would know what the numbers meant (103.5!).

If you need to see a doctor while traveling, avoid the emergency room, if possible. You can call the emergency room to find out if there are other options, such as a clinic or urgent care center or a doctor who is accepting patients. Emergency rooms are not only expensive, they provide little treatment for nonemergency illnesses and will usually suggest you see a doctor. Your campground or hotel may be able to give you suggestions for finding a doctor.

If you are visiting people in town, see if they can get you in to see their doctor on a one-time basis. Judith's daughter had chest pain when the Allee family was in Springfield, Illinois, on a Saturday to photograph a conference.

Judith called a homeschool host family whom she had never met, but the family was concerned and helpful about connecting Judith with a local clinic that had Saturday hours.

The Unwritten Rule

"It's an unwritten rule that you must have at least one child throw up in the car while on a family vacation." —Angie Zalewski, *Frugal Family Network* newsletter

MOTION SICKNESS

Some people can enjoy travel time—reading books, drawing, sewing, or playing board games. Then there are those of us who experience motion sickness, which makes travel an ordeal for sufferers and nonsufferers alike. Many people just can't take reading or drawing while in motion, especially if the ride is bumpy or twisty or if a flight has turbulence. While not a serious condition, it can make a vacationer miserable!

Children are most often the ones who get carsick, but adults, too, are sometimes affected. Melissa is one, and Judith is too, if she has a headache. Some people swear by soda crackers, sips of cold water, or sips of carbonated soft drinks. Also, check for carbon monoxide leaks. Sometimes the most sensitive person is affected first, but everyone in the car is being poisoned by this odorless, colorless gas.

Check with your pharmacist about over-the-counter medication. If your child has special medical needs, check with your pediatrician too. Some medications are okay for adults, but not for children under a certain age. Always mention any other medications your child takes to see if there is a chance of ill effects from mixing the medications.

The temptation when you fear nausea is to avoid eating. An empty tummy, however, is more likely to be upset, so a light snack before traveling can be helpful. Try tracking the motion sickness. Is it always in the morning? Maybe you can adjust your travel hours. What seems to help?

Encourage your child to sleep through the trip. It might help if you drive late into the evening or leave *very* early.

Where you sit can make you more or less vulnerable. Sitting over the wings of an airplane tends to be the best spot for those prone to airsickness. The bow and stern of a ship tend to be the worst spots for seasickness.

"My Ears Hurt!"

When you have a cold, pressure changes can cause severe ear pain if you are flying or if you drive through mountainous areas. Small children are especially susceptible. Before your trip, check with your doctor about medications. Prepare for colds even if none are apparent when you leave. An inexpensive device called Ear Planes helps protect sensitive ears during pressure changes when you fly. Ask about it at your pharmacy or at discount stores.

Even without a cold, a baby may have ear pain. Try giving the baby a bottle or pacifier to relieve ear pressure. Some inventive mothers have devised a way to nurse their babies in their car seats. That helps too.

Access-Able Travelers: Accommodating Family Members with Special Needs

Affordable travel can be a challenge for any family. For families with special needs, such as physical or mental challenges, travel can seem almost impossible. Still, many families with children or adults with special needs take long trips in stride.

Sometimes adults or children need to be close to local doctors who know their medical histories well. If someone in your family is medically fragile, consult with your doctor before taking a trip. The MedicAlert bracelet can save the life of a person who needs care. You can also keep an index card in your wallet with key health information—the patient's name, doctor, medical problems, and the names and dosages of any medications. Find out ahead of time about local doctors, hospitals, and the availability of prescription refills. One mother wrote details of her toddler's medical condition on his shoes. Other parents attach stickers to the back of their small child's clothing, with their medical conditions written on the sticker. Several companies offer metal tags that lace into a child's shoes and can be engraved with medical information or identification (available at *www.AwareAbouts.com*).

Sometimes just the right gadget can make all the difference. For instance, you may be able to obtain an electric wheelchair through your insurance policy if you ask your doctor to order it. Your medical supply company may be able to provide you with a more portable suction machine if your child has a tracheotomy. The right equipment may not cost any more. You just need to ask for it.

Sample Magazine

The Society for the Advancement of Travel for the Handicapped (SATH) publishes a magazine called *Open World*. Write or call for a free back issue. The magazine offers information on accessible recreation opportunities in state parks and forests, tours for the physically challenged, and wheelchair trips.

SATH also offers a free information sheet called "How to Travel." It includes advice on accessibility for airlines, railroads, and buses. For example, the information sheet notes Greyhound Bus Lines' policy to allow a free companion for people who require help to remain seated or with personal care.

Search for local programs that provide financial assistance and special equipment to children with physical and developmental challenges. Don't assume that you make too much money to qualify for help. Check into private programs like those offered by the Special Wish Foundation, which provides trips to ill children and their families.

If your child has a life-threatening or chronic illness, he or she can feel pretty isolated and different. Children's Hopes and Dreams Foundation has a free pen-pal service that matches your child (age five to eighteen) with another child who has a similar condition. Perhaps you can visit the pen pal when you travel.

RVers with special needs may want to check out The Enabled RVer column in *RV Companion* magazine. The writer, Hope Sykes, is a seasoned RVer who has traveled extensively, finding ways to accommodate her own disability. Her Web site has information on a wide variety of topics for traveling with special needs, including ways to contribute as a volunteer.

Finding a Helping Hand Away from Home

What do you do when you're at home and need to locate a service or get some help? Let's say you need to find a good mechanic, locate an ear-nose-throat doctor on a Thursday afternoon, track down someone who has moved, or find an ATM machine. On your home turf, you either already know who to call for the services you need, or you have a network of friends, neighbors, and businesses you can count on or who can refer you to someone.

When you're traveling, finding the help you need—when you need it—is a different story. If you're staying at the Waldorf-Astoria, you can simply contact the concierge and cross his or her palm with a little silver. But don't despair if you're not on a Waldorf-Astoria budget. Help may be closer than you realize.

The University of Adversity

"There is no education like adversity." —Benjamin Disraeli, statesman

___

Here are a few helpful resources that are available in virtually every metropolitan area and many small towns as well.

- Ask your waitress or waiter. Waitstaff are a wealth of information, and they tend to enjoy helping people.
- Pass your inquiry by the motel front desk staff.
- Visit a Kinko's copy center. They are an office away from home, offering access to computers, typewriters, fax machines, shipping services, and free use of a telephone for local or credit-card calls. In addition, their staff is often knowledgeable about local resources and business people. A similar resource is Mailboxes, Etc., which provides shipping and copy services.
- Ask the attendant at the gas station (after getting a full tank of gas). That person can often tell you about a good family-owned restaurant nearby, where to find a good mechanic in town, etc.

- Call the chamber of commerce. The staff may personally know someone whose business can help you, and their personal referral may be a ticket to more personal service. They also keep information on community services.

Beyond the businesses you patronize, here are some helpful information sources available (almost) everywhere:

- Call a local information and referral number. These services, which have various names, provide a listing of helpful resources in the community. Look for them in the yellow pages under "Social Services," or try calling 211, which is gradually being instituted across the country as a community information number (similar to the emergency-only 911 number).
- Contact the Travelers' Aid Society.
- Contact a pastor, perhaps one from your own denomination, or the Salvation Army.
- If you belong to a service club or fraternal organization, contact the local chapter.
- Call someone in your own line of business. Judith and John Allee might contact another photographer, explain their predicament, and ask for referrals to local resources.

Reviewing Your Adventures

You pull into your driveway, the kids pile out of the car, and your life resumes its ordinary pattern. But wait. Don't stop yet. Educators know that review is necessary to ensure that a lesson is retained. If we left out this section, we'd be leaving out the most educational part of the trip—preserving, discussing, reliving, and processing your learning.

If family members kept trip journals or took travel notes, you may find that different people noticed different things and that sharing that information can make the experiences more vivid. Here are some questions to use as conversation starters:

- Where did you go and what did you see?
- Who did you meet?
- Do you have unanswered questions? Can we find the answers now?

- What have we learned together as a family about other cultures and other places? What was your favorite part of the trip?
- Did anything about the trip scare you, thrill you, anger you, or make you laugh? Why?
- What have we learned about one another?
- Has your relationship with family members changed? If so, how?

It is not uncommon for individuals in a family to uncover problems that they didn't know they had until they found more time to be together. This is usually a good thing in the long run. Still, facing problems, whether behavioral or relational, is never fun.

In *The Berenstain Bears and Too Much Vacation,* a humorous children's book by Stan and Jan Berenstain, the bear family experiences togetherness through adversity. Even when everything seems to go wrong—a flat tire, a rained-in tent, your food supply raided by raccoons, hotel reservations gone astray—shared memories become part of your family history. It can be the same with our travels. Keeping learning on the front burner means you will find opportunities in the strangest places, whether you are prepared for them or not.

Let the Adventures Begin

There is one more very important item to add to your packing list: Don't leave home without a merry heart.

Travel can be annoying, even maddening at times. Travel snafus can be the acid test for parents. But a lighthearted word can make even a difficult road easier to travel. Pack a joke book in your backpack. Swap silly stories under the stars. And if the old bucket breaks down, try not to get mad. Try to view it as a life lesson in patience.

A father once became quite irritated at the number of times his children requested stops during their trip by car. He decided to add up all the minutes spent in unscheduled stops during the next day—his intention being, of course, to make a well-documented point. He timed each stop to the second and kept a running tally. At the end of the day, the unscheduled stops totaled a half-hour.

His conclusion? His children and wife had enjoyed a merry time traveling.

He had experienced a lousy day keeping track of the time. He decided to go with the flow, and he has been traveling more happily ever since. We can take merriment one step further—to joy. Are we teaching our children to have a joyful heart?

Once you get caught up in the spirit of educational travel and field trips, you begin to look with eager expectation at the maps neatly folded in your car's glove compartment. There in those maps, sometimes just a short distance away, are enticing opportunities to explore the highways and byways that are so cryptically represented on paper by a mass of lines and squiggles. For you and your family, however, the shortest distance between two points is no longer the purpose of your travels. It's the adventure.

Now our maps are not folded so neatly anymore. They are getting worn out from use, which is the secret desire of every map. So let the adventures begin. We hope your travels will be joyful, educational, economical, and fun!

Happy Trails!

Resource Guide

To download the resource guide for a small fee,
visit www.DreamsOnAShoestring.com or www.eaglesnesthome.com.
The downloadable version enables you to search for keywords and link
to any Web site you wish to visit. Updated periodically.

Chapter 1: The Great Adventure

Consumer Information Catalog. Call (888) 878-3256 for a free catalog listing many educational free or inexpensive publications, including information on travel such as *National Wildlife Refuges: A Visitor's Guide, Lesser Known Areas of the National Park System,* and *Washington: The Nation's Capital.* You can also view the printed text of all publications listed in the catalog at http://www.pueblo. gsa.gov.

Just Visiting: How Travel Has Enlightened Lives and Viewpoints Throughout History by George and Karen Grant (Nashville, Tenn.: Cumberland House, 1999).

Planet Talk, a free quarterly print newsletter, contains information about the publisher's products, but the majority of the publication is about exotic destinations and cultures. You can also subscribe to a monthly electronic newsletter, *Comet,* at the Web site. Lonely Planet Publications, 150 Linden Street, Oakland, CA 94607; (800) 275-8555; http://www.lonelyplanet.com/comet.

Strengthening Family Values Through Travel
Answers in Genesis (AIG) offers creation-science seminars for adults and children and tours of natural landmarks. Contact AIG at (606) 727-2222, ext. 506, or (800) 350-3232; http://www.AnswersInGenesis.org.

Discovery Trail: A Pathway to Find Your Spiritual Gifts! is available free from American Tract Society, P.O. Box 462008, Garland, TX 75046; (800) 548-7228; http://www.gospelcom.net/ats.

New Testament Stone Garden is located at Faith Lutheran Church, 170 Mansfield Avenue, Mount Vernon, OH; (740) 393-3666.

Pilgrim's Progress by John Bunyan is perhaps the most famous spiritual journey of all time. Get a free sample of an amplified version (which helps explain the original text) at http://www.orionsgate.org. A free QuickTime movie clip can be found at http://www.whatsaiththescripture.com.

Retreats On Line offers ideas for unusual spiritual destinations; http://www.retreatsonline.com.

Saga of the Pilgrims: From Europe to the New World by John Harris (Chester, Conn.: the Globe Pequot Press, 1990) is out of print but may be available through your library. Check the publisher's Web site for numerous travel books as well as books to research the history of your destination. The Globe Pequot Press, Box Q, Chester, CT 06412; http://www.globe-pequot.com.

Sandy Cove Ministries offers Christian conferences, recreation, and camping. Visit them on the Web at http://www.sandycove.org.

HOMESCHOOLING INFORMATION
Books
And What About College? : How Homeschooling Can Lead to Admissions to the Best Universities and Colleges by Cafi Cohen (Cambridge, Mass.: Holt, 2001). Cohen's Web site includes a free chapter from her book and other resources; http://www.homeschoolteenscollege.net.

Big Book of Home Learning by Mary Pride (Chandler, Ariz.: Alpha Omega, 2000); different editions cover specific age levels and include comprehensive curriculum reviews.

The Complete Idiot's Guide to Homeschooling by Martha Ransom (Indianapolis: Alpha Books, 2001) includes a look at various homeschool styles and methods, legal issues, and other common concerns.

Home Schooling from Scratch: Simple Living—Super Learning by Mary Potter Kenyon (Bridgman, Mich.: Gazelle, 1996).

Homeschooling Almanac, 2000–2001 by Mary Leppert and Michael Leppert (Rocklin, Calif.: Prima, 2000) is a subject-by-subject directory of educational materials, including listings of state laws, organizations, and explanations of various teaching and learning styles. Contains over $1,000 worth of coupons.

The Homeschooling Book of Answers: The 88 Most Important Questions Answered by Homeschooling's Most Respected Voices by Linda Dobson (Rocklin, Calif.: Prima, 1998). A new edition is forthcoming.

Homeschooling on a Shoestring by Melissa L. Morgan and Judith Waite Allee (Wheaton, Ill.: Shaw, 1999).

Real Lives: Eleven Teenagers Who Don't Go to School, edited by Grace Llewellyn (Npp: Lowry House, 1993).

The Relaxed Homeschool: A Family Production by Mary Hood (Cartersville, Ga.: Ambleside Educational, 1994) provides a Christian perspective on interest-based learning.

The Successful Homeschool Family Handbook: A Creative and Stress-Free Approach to Homeschooling by Raymond S. Moore and Dorothy Moore (Nashville, Tenn.: Nelson, 1994).

The Unschooling Handbook: How to Use the Whole World as Your Child's Classroom by Mary Griffith (Rocklin, Calif.: Prima, 1998).

Magazines and Newspapers
Growing Without Schooling magazine and the John Holt Bookstore. The January issue of *GWS* includes an annual directory of homeschool families worldwide, some of whom host traveling homeschool families. Credit-card orders: (888) 925-9298; questions: (617) 864-3100; http://www.holtgws.com.

The Link: A Homeschool Newspaper. Write for free subscription to bimonthly printed version; 587 N. Ventu Park Road, Ste. F-911, Newbury Park, CA 91320; (888) 470-4513; e-mail: the.link@verizon.net; http://www.homeschoolnewslink.com.

The Teaching Home, a Christian magazine for home educators; online articles, listings, and links for state and national organizations, and homeschool suppliers. Box 20219, Portland, OR 97294; (503) 253-9633; http://www.teachinghome.com.

Internet Resources
Allee, Judith; http://www.DreamsOnAShoestring.com.

Homeschool.com includes a travel page and frequently asked questions about homeschooling; http://www.homeschool.com.

Homeschool Zone offers book excerpts and interviews with a variety of homeschool authors and authors of books about parenting children with special needs, such as autism, bipolar disorder, ADHD, and learning disabilities. They also offer crafts, recipes, frequently asked questions about homeschooling, and various online support group communities for the topics mentioned; http://www.homeschoolzone.com.

Morgan, Melissa; http://www.eaglesnesthome.com.

Organizations and Resources
Clonlara School, home-based education program enrolls families worldwide; Web site has hundreds of interesting educational links; 1289 Jewett, Ann Arbor, MI 48104; (734) 769-4511; http://www.clonlara.org.

GED (General Education Equivalency Diploma) hotline is a referral service for GED classes and tests; (800) 626-9433.

Homeschool Legal Defense Association lists state-by-state laws and regulations that affect homeschool families. Annual membership dues include legal representation in case you encounter problems with your school district; http://www.hslda.org.

National Home Education Network is a clearinghouse of information about home education and support group referrals; P.O. Box 41067, Long Beach, CA 90853; http://www.nhen.org.

Chapter 2: Researching Your Destinations

AARP is an organization for those age fifty and over. Membership includes a monthly magazine; discounts on motels, prescriptions, and other services; and political lobbying on issues involving seniors; 601 E St., NW, Washington, DC 20049; (800) 515-2299; http://www.aarp.com.

ABCentral, lists special-interest clubs and organization worldwide. Click on "societies" and then on whatever topic interests you to find local, national, or international groups; http://www.my-edu2.com/index.html.

Adventuring with Children: An Inspirational Guide to World Travel and the Outdoors by Nan Jeffrey (Ashland, Mass.: Avalon House, 1995) is devoted to "developing an unassailable *joie de vivre.*"

All the Best Contests for Kids by Joan M. Bergstrom and Craig Bergstrom (Berkeley, Calif.: Ten Speed Press, 1995).

American Amateur Press Association is an organization that promotes writing and printing; members submit short samples of their writing, and AAPA distributes packets of submitted work monthly to the membership; c/o Leslie Boyer, 535 Kickerillo Dr., Houston, TX 77079; http://members.aol.com/aapa96.

American Automobile Association (AAA) provides emergency roadside assistance, maps, airline reservations, and other services to members. Check your telephone book for a local office or go to http://www.aaa.com.

Blueprint for Paradise: How to Live on a Tropic Island by Ross Norgrove (Chico, Calif.: Moon, 1986).

Cheap Talk with the Frugal Friends by Angie Zalewski and Deana Ricks (Lancaster, Pa.: Startburst, 2001).

Consumer Information Center Web site offers inexpensive ($ .50 to $3.00) travel booklets, such as "Lesser-Known Areas of the National Parks System" and "Your Trip Abroad," and a consumer information catalog. Order booklets at (888) 8-PUEBLO or visit the Web site at http://www.pueblo.gsa.gov.

Consumer Reports Travel Letter provides information on travel deals and scams. Call for a sample copy or ask at your public library. Consumer's Union of United States, Inc., 101 Truman Ave., Yonkers, NY 10703-1057; (800) 234-1970; http://www.consumerreports.org.

The Directory of Alternative Travel Resources, One World Travel Network, Lost Valley Center, 81868 Lost Valley Lane, Dexter, OR 97431; http://www.transabroad.com.

Encyclopedia of Associations (Gale Research Group, annual) is available in the reference section at most public libraries.

Families on the Road; http://families on the road.com.

Fodor's, a publisher of travel guides. The online guide lets you select the information you want about Washington, Los Angeles, San Francisco, Chicago, and New York to create your own miniguide online. Let the kids navigate with Fodor's book series *Around the City;* http://www.fodors.com.

Home Is Where You Park It by Kay Peterson (Livingston, Tex.: RoVers, 1990).

The North American Vexillogical Association; PMB 225, 1977 N Olden Ave. Ext, Trenton, NJ 08618-2193; http://www.nava.org.

Smart Vacations: The Traveler's Guide to Learning Adventures Abroad, edited by Priscilla Tovey (New York: St. Martin's, 1993).

Thomas Register of American Manufacturers (Thomas Publishing annual) lists manufacturers by product. It is available in the reference section at most public libraries.

Thrifty Traveling: Your Step-by-Step Guide to Bargain Travel in the U.S., Canada, and Worldwide by Mary VanMeer (editor and publisher of the *Thrifty Traveler* newsletter) offers forms, checklists, and hundreds of resources and travel tips; P.O. Box 8168; Clearwater, FL 33758; http://www.thriftytraveling.com.

The Through the Back Door series of books by Rick Steves (*Europe Through the Back Door*, etc.); also Rick Steves's Europe television show on PBS; http://www.pbs.org; http://www.ricksteves.com.

Worldmark Encyclopedia of the States provides state-by-state information, including photos of parks, museums, and points of interests. *The Junior Worldmark Encyclopedia of the States* is written for grades four to ten. For travel outside the United States, check the *Worldmark Encyclopedia of the Nations* (Worldmark/Gale).

The Traveler's Reading Guide: Ready-Made Reading Lists for the Armchair Traveler edited by Maggy Simony (New York: Facts on File, 1994); Facts On File, Inc., 132 W. 31st St., 17th Floor, New York, NY 10001; (800) 322-8755; fax (800) 678-3633; e-mail: CustServ@factsonfile.com; http://factsonfile.com, or check the reference section of your public library.

COLLEGE AND CAREER EXPLORATION

Best College Picks; http://www.Petersons.com.

Peterson's Guide to College Visits (annual) is a digest of information for selecting a college; http://www.petersons.com.

ShawGuides, Inc., lists more than four thousand career programs and learning vacations, including camps, workshops, trips, and specialty schools. With 164 listings under archaeology alone, there are lots of ideas here for possible vacations; P.O. Box 231295, Ansonia Station, New York, NY 10023; (212) 799-6464; http://www.shawguides.com.

DESTINATIONS, EVENTS, AND ACTIVITIES

68 Great Things to Do Together series (Fodor) includes nine cities with "great things" like the five-stories-tall dinosaur fossil exhibit at the American Museum of Natural History in New York City.

101 Things for Kids in Las Vegas by Carol Anne Stout (Indianapolis: 101 Things, 1999).

101 Things for Kids in New Orleans by Carol Anne Stout (Npp: Journey Publications, 1999).

Canadian and U.S. Food Co-op Directory provides an online directory of co-ops you can visit as you travel to learn about their operation, volunteer, or meet like-minded people; http://www.prairienet.org/co-op/directory.

Christian Heritage Tours offers tour, books, and videos, including resources such as *God's Signature over the Nation's Capital*, *The Rewriting of America's History*, *A Children's Companion Guide to America's History*, and *Great American Statesmen and Heroes;* http://www.christianheritagetours.com.

Hershey, Pennsylvania; home of Hershey Chocolate; (800) HERSHEY; http://www.hersheypa.com.

Kids Culture Catalog: A Cultural Guide to New York City for Kids, Families, and Teachers, edited by Randall Bourscheidt and Maria Asteinza (New York: Alliance for the Arts, 1998).

LEGOland; (877) LEGOLAND; http://www.legoland.com.

Lobster Kids series by destination, including *The Lobster Kids' Guide to Exploring Montreal* by John Symon (Montreal: Lobster, 2000).

National Scenic Byways map and directory (free); (800) 4-BYWAYS; http://www.byways.org.

Newsgroups: bit.listserv.travel-l; recreational groups such as rec.travel.use-canada, rec.travel.asia, rec.travel.air, rec.travel.cruise, rec.travel.marketplace, rec.travel.misc; sociology groups such as soc.culture.latin-america. (You can post and read articles, questions, and comments on virtually any subject through computer newsgroups. To learn about newsgroups and how to use them, access the help (F1) feature on a personal computer that is equipped with a recent version of Windows, or check out materials on the subject at the library. You may wish to read a newsgroup's FAQs (Frequently Asked Questions) before posting material, or you can use a newsgroup service such as http://www.squeakycleannews.com to help you filter your newsgroup content before posting it.)

Peabody Museum of Natural History at Yale University is home to an outstanding permanent collection of dinosaur fossils; P.O. Box 208118, 170 Whitney Avenue, New Haven, CT 06520-8118; (203) 432-5050; http://www.peabody.yale.edu.

Peterson's Learning Adventures Around the World by Peter S. Greenberg (Npp: Peterson's, 1997).

The Pilgrim's Guide to the Sacred Earth by Sherrill Miller (Stillwater, Minn.: Voyageur, 1991).

Road Trip U.S.A.: Road Traveler's Complete Guide to America's Best Scenic Drives by William Herow (Aurora, Colo.: Roundabout, 1994).

Road Trip USA by Jamie Jensen (Emeryville, Calif.: Avalon Travel Publishing, 1999).

Rodale Experimental Farm, 611 Siegfriedale Road, Kutztown, PA 19530; (610) 683-1482; http://www.rodaleinstitute.org.

Two-Lane Roads is a quarterly newsletter about traveling America's back roads. For a free issue, send three first-class stamps or $1.00 and mention this book. Allow four to six weeks for delivery. A sample issue is posted online. P.O. Box 23518, Fort Lauderdale, FL 33307-3518; http://www.two-lane.com.

Watch It Made in the U.S.A. by Karen Axelrod and Bruce Brumberg (Santa Fe: N.Mex.: John Muir Publications, 1997).

Fairs and Festivals

Fairs, Festivals, and Other Oddities, a free e-mail newsletter from the CoolTravelMail Web site; http://www.cooltravelmail.com.

Festivals.com lists festivals and events by country, state, city, or type of festival; http://festivals.com.

International Festivals and Events Association catalogs festivals around the world; http://www.ifea.com.

Military Installation Tours and Resources

Department of Defense (DoD) links to each of the U.S. service branches. Look up a specific base to find contact information for the Public Affairs Office at that installation for tour and facilities information; http://www.defenselink.mil/faq/pis/sites.html.

Military.com offers a travel section that includes a military installations guide with a clickable map. The site offers military adventures from the ordinary to the truly adventurous (driving a tank on a firing range); http://www.military.com/Travel/FrontDoor.

Navy; www.navy.mil. For base access http://www.chinfo.navy.mil/navpalib/bases/navbases.html.

AVOIDING FRAUD AND SETTLING DISPUTES WITH TRAVEL SERVICES

The American Society of Travel Agents. If you are working with a member agency, the society may be able to mediate any disputes; 1101 King St., Suite 200, Alexandria, VA 22314; (703) 737-2782; http://www.astanet.com.

Angie's List is a membership consumer service available in many large cities and offers referrals to reputable businesses, including travel agencies and auto repair companies. To be listed, a company must be recommended by satisfied customers; http://www.angieslist.com.

The Better Business Bureau (BBB) offers brochures (in print and online) for evaluating travel and vacation offers. Send $2.00 and a self-addressed envelope to Council of Better Business Bureaus, Department 023, Washington, DC 20042-0023; http://www.bbb.org (look under the "Resource Library, Publications" section).

Consumer Reports Travel Letter is published by Consumers Union and contains information on travel deals and scams; 101 Truman Ave., Yonkers, NY 10703-1057; (800) 234-1970.

Consumer World is a noncommercial resource with more than two thousand consumer resources; http://www.consumerworld.com.

National Fraud Information Center offers a free booklet, *Telemarketing Travel Fraud;* P.O. Box 65868, Washington, DC 20035; (800) 876-7060; http://www.fraud.org.

ONLINE RESOURCES
Internet Service Providers (ISPs)
Family Connect currently charges a $29 setup fee. After that, the service is free if you complete an information survey every month. If you don't fill out the survey, you will be charged $19.95 per month. Service includes Internet access, a pornography filter, and unlimited e-mail with five addresses; (888) 398-8899; http://www.familyconnect.com.

Free Stuff Center offers a long list of free e-mail services at http://www.freestuffcenter.com.

Juno.com; http://juno.com.

NetZero, (800) DEFENDER; http://www.netzero.net.

Internet Travel Newsletters and Web Sites

ABCentral; http://www.my-edu2.com/EDUSOCS.

Cheapskate Monthly offers travel tips at Mary Hunt's Web site: http://www.cheapsk8.com/tiptionary/plane_travel.html.

The Christian Traveler provides information on travel sites of interest to families and individuals seeking spiritually enriching vacation destinations; P.O. Box 1736, Holland, MI 49422; (616) 494-0907; http://Christiantraveler.com.

CoolTravelMail offers eight free travel newsletters; http://www.cooltravelmail.com.

Crosswalk is a Christian travel information source and offers many references to other resources; http://www.trip.com/trs/crosswalk/home/index_01.xsl.

Expedia.com includes a "Family Travel" section; http://www.expedia.com.

Family Travel Newsletter; http://www.smarterliving.com/family.

Fodor's "Family" section; http://www.fodors.com.

Frugal Family Network offers cost-cutting ideas for traveling with children; http://www.frugalfamilynetwork.com.

LifeMinders Travel is a free e-mail newsletter; http://www.lifeminders.com.

Shoestring Travel Guides from Lonely Planet at http://www4travelguides.com.

Smarter Living. Subscribe to free newsletters and receive travel discounts from various services and agencies; http://www.SmarterLiving.com.

Trip Advice provides online travel resources, chat, forums, and free advice via e-mail; http://www.TripAdvice.com.

News from Around the World

Online Newspapers links you to several newspapers' Web sites around the globe; http://www.onlinenewspapers.com.

Worldwide News Letter offers a selection of newspapers from all over the world. It also provides free sample newsletters online with news tidbits from around the world; http://www.worldwidenewsletter.com.

Search Engines and Directories

Ask Jeeves; http://www.ask.com.

Christian Search Engines; http://www.topsites.org.

Copernic searches a variety of search engines and saves the results to your computer so you can work through the results over several sessions instead of having to do a new search each time. You specify how many results you want so your hard drive is not swamped; http://www.Copernic.com.

Dog Pile searches a variety of search engines at once; http://www.dogpile.com.

The Education Place Activity Search; http://www.eduplace.com.

GCN Search; http://www.gcnhome.com/asp/search_srchrslt.asp.

Google; www.google.com.

HotBot; www.hotbot.com.

Infoseek; http://www.go.com.

The Internet Sleuth; http://www.isleuth.net.

New Rider's Official World Wide Web yellow pages; http://www.mcp.com.

Research-It!; http://www.iTools.com/research-it.

Search the Net includes detailed instructions and explanations for various search engines; http://www.trussel.com/f_search.htm.

Webcrawler; http://webcrawler.com.

Yahoo; http://www.yahoo.com.

Yahooligans is designed for kids; http://www.yahooligans.com.

Software for Educational Travel

AAA Trip Planner, Compton's New Media; (800) 862-2206.

Jumbo facilitates searches for freeware and shareware travel, language, and geography programs; http://www.jumbo.com.

Map'n'Go (DeLorme) is a road atlas program designed to locate regions and attractions by area code or ZIP code; (207) 865-1234.

Travel Planner Gold (Expert Software) addresses trip planning, attractions, airport, and airline information; (800) 759-2562.

Unbeatable Deals offers free (not counting the $5 shipping charge) travel and language software on CD-ROM; members are entitled to hundreds of full-version CD-ROM titles; http://unbeatabledeals.com.

World of Reading contains a free demonstration reading program; Box 13092, Atlanta, GA 30324-0092; (800) 729-3703; http://www.wor.com.

Virtual Trips

Clipper Cruise Line. Take a virtual cruise and find out if cruising is for you. For a free twenty-five-minute videotape, contact: (800) 325-0010; http://www. clippercruise.com.

Columbia Queen offers cruises on the Columbia River Gorge (http://www.
columbiaqueen.com) and Hawaii cruises on the *SS Independence* (http://www.
cruisehawaii.com). Call (800) 215-7940 for free brochures for either cruise.

The Delta Queen Steamboat Company provides paddle-wheel boat cruises on the
Mississippi and Ohio Rivers. Check out the free sixty-five-page steamboat vacation
brochure. They also sell an inexpensive video, if you'd like a video trip. Robin
Street Wharf, 1380 Port of New Orleans Place, New Orleans, LA 70130-1890;
(800) 533-3098; http://www.deltaqueen.com.

The Odyssey is an interactive Web site sponsored by Worldtrek, a nonprofit
educational organization. The site is designed for classrooms but is open to
anyone. Worldtrek has a team of five educators traveling the world. They post
photos, video, audio, and text for students to follow along. Students can interact
with the team and with prominent local figures through chats, e-mail, polls, and
discussion boards; http://www.worldtrek.org.

Video Placement Worldwide provides free "on loan" videos and teacher guides
for educators, including homeschool families. Other families may want to ask
their school, library, or other educational organization to show the videos. You
are able to pick and choose between various choices of virtual trips, such as a
video tour of the Jelly Belly factory that includes free sample Jelly Bellys.
25 Second St. North, Suite 120, St. Petersburg, FL 33701; (727) 823-9595;
http://www.vpw.com.

Miscellaneous Online Resources
Consulates may be located online at http://travel.state.gov. Many countries
have consulates in major U.S. cities. Most maintain an embassy in Washington,
D.C. Contact any consulates that interest you and ask them for free tourist
information.

Jay Computer Services ZIP and Area Code Lookup is a great resource for U.S. ZIP
codes, area codes, cities, states, time zones, and county information; http://nt.jcsm.
com/General.asp.

Travel Industry Association of America. Click on "Discover America," which provides links to tourism offices in every state and territory. Discover America also offers a links page with an assortment of travel sites to explore; http://www. tia.org.

U Seek U Find. Includes transportation links; fare information for air, rail, ship, and subway travel; home exchange programs; an adventure-travel database; travelogues; and language study through worldwide chat rooms; http://www. useekufind. com/trqindex.htm.

Yahoo's government information; http://www.yahoo.com/Government/Countries.

TELEPHONE INFORMATION

Canada Toll-Free; http://CanadaTollfree.com.

Free long-distance service is available via the Internet: http://phonefree.com; http:// www.dialpad.com.

Smart Pages; http://SmartPages.com.

Switchboard; http://www.switchboard.com.

Toll-free information (United States): (800) 555-1212. This number does *not* work with other toll-free area codes, such as 855, 866, 877, and 888.

MAPS, FREE AND CHEAP

MapBlast; http://www.mapblast.com/myblast.

Mapquest (U.S. maps and directions); http://www.mapquest.com.

Rand McNally; http://www.randmcnally.com

Refdesk.com includes atlas and maps; http://www.refdesk.com/facts.html.

Smart Travel: Total Planning on Your Computer (New York: Ziff-Davis, 1995).

Chapter 3: Low-Cost Learning

Earn College Credit for What You Know by Lois S. Lamdin and Susan Simosko (Dubuque, Iowa: Kendall/Hunt Publishing, 1997).

College Degrees by Mail & Internet by John Bear, Mariah P. Bear (Berkeley, Calif.: Ten Speed Press, 2001).

52 Ways to Make Family Travel More Enjoyable by Kate Redd (Nashville, Tenn.: Nelson, 1994).

Fitness
Project Fit America; http://www.projectfitamerica.org.

History
African American Heritage Directory, Howard Johnson International, 1 Sylvan Way, Parsippany, NJ 07054. Enclose a self-addressed, stamped envelope.

American Historical Fiction: An Annotated Guide to Novels for Adults and Young Adults by Lynda G. Adamson (Phoenix, Ariz.: Oryx, 1998). Check the reference section at your library. Provides geographical listing, state by state and city by city, of historical fiction.

America's Best Historic Sites: 101 Terrific Places to Take the Family by B. J. Welborn (Chicago: Chicago Review Press, 1998).

Amistad, a full-size reproduction of the slave ship; Interactive's Video on Demand documentary Webcast; http://www.amistadamerica.org and http://www.mysticseaport.org.

The Christian Traveler's Companion: Western Europe by Amy S. Eckert and William J. Peterson (Grand Rapids, Mich.: Revell, 2001).

The Civil War News: For People with an Active Interest in the Civil War Today, 234 Monarch Hill Rd., Tunbridge, VT 05077; http://www.civilwarnews.com.

Dear America series; historical fiction for girls (New York: Scholastic). (See also My Name Is America series.)

Freedom Trail Foundation, (617) 227-8800; or the Greater Boston Convention and Visitors Bureau, (888) 733-2678; http://www/bostonUSA.com.

Institute of Outdoor Drama offers a low-cost directory of historical dramas, or view the directory online at their Web site. The institute's home page has audio soundtracks for a few of the shows and photographs from about fifty shows. Sponsored by the University of North Carolina at Chapel Hill, 1700 Airport Road, CB #3240, Chapel Hill, NC 27599-3240; (919) 962-1328; http://www.unc.edu/depts/outdoor.

Living History Web site includes links to more than one hundred living-history museums; http://www.alhfam.org/alhfam.links.html.

Pilgrim's Progress by John Bunyan is perhaps the most famous spiritual journey of all time. Get a free sample of an amplified version (which helps explain the original text) at http://www.orionsgate.org. A free QuickTime movie clip can be found at http://www.whatsaiththescripture.com.

My Name is America; historical fiction series for children (New York: Scholastic). (See also Dear America series.)

World Historical Fiction: An Annotated Guide to Novels for Adults and Young Adults by Lynda Adamson (Phoenix, Ariz.: Oryx, 1998). Contains a place and time index.

Family History, Heritage

Ancestry.com offers access to an extensive network of family history resources, including genealogical databases; http://www.ancestry.com.

Irish Times contains listings of St. Patrick's Day parades and festivals worldwide as well as other Irish events. Annual contest for photos about St. Patrick's Day festivities; http://www.ireland.com.

LANGUAGE ARTS

All the Best Contests for Kids by Joan M. Bergstrom and Graig Bergstrom (Berkeley, Calif.: Ten Speed Press, 1988); http://www.tenspeed.com.

The Penny Whistle Traveling with Kids Book by Meredith Brokaw and Annie Gilbar (New York: Simon & Schuster, 1995).

World Pen Pals, P.O. Box 337, Saugerties, NY 12477; (845) 246-7828; http://www.world-pen-pals.com.

LANGUAGES

Help Your Child with a Foreign Language by Opal Dunn (Princeton, N.J.: Berlitz Kids, 1998) teaches useful words and phrases in French, Italian, German, and Spanish through songs, games, and rhymes. It also includes lists of embassies, cultural centers, and foreign language centers for more information.

Learnables is a self-teaching foreign language program recommended for ages seven and up. International Linguistics Corporation, 3505 East Red Bridge Road, Kansas City, MO 64137; (800) 237-1830; http://www.learnables.com.

American Sign Language, Grace Works Ministries offers a "Special Signs" video for Christians. 1617 Briggs, Wichita, KS 67203; (316) 269-3013. Order through Timberdoodle and receive a free book with every order: (360) 426-0672; http://www.timberdoodle.com.

Virtual travel language phrase book; http://www.travelang.com.

MATHEMATICS

Math Is Everywhere series is available from Christian Book Distributors and includes workbooks such as *Math on a Trip* by Bob DeWeese and *Math in Geography* by Tom Nelson. Christian Book Distributors, P.O. Box 7000, Peabody, MA 01961-7000; http://www.christianbook.com. For help choosing homeschooling products, contact their homeschool assistance line, (978) 977-5045.

Math Play: 80 Ways to Count and Learn by Diane McGowan and Mark Schrooter (Charlotte, Vt.: Williamson, 1997).

Pigs Will Be Pigs math series by Amy Axelrod (New York: Simon & Schuster, 1994).

SOCIAL STUDIES

Ask your librarian to help you find fiction books set in various geographical settings that include foreign words. Look for books set in your destination country or city. A few examples of book series set in various countries: the Tintin series of comic books from Europe (Hergé), the Hardy Boys (Franklin W. Dixon), or the Ruby Slipper books (Stacy Towle Morgan).

Canadian and U.S. Food Co-op Directory is an online directory of co-ops you can visit as you travel. Learn about their operation, volunteer, or meet like-minded people; http://www.prairienet.org/co-op/directory.

The Elijah Company issues an educational resource catalog; 1053 Eldridge Loop, Crossville, TN 38558; (888) 2-ELIJAH; http://www.elijahco.com.

State Unit Studies

50States.com has an information sheet for each state. You will find links for each president who came from that state, tourism links for each large city, genealogy links, and other information. (Don't use http://www. when logging on this site.)

The Home School is a free catalog with numerous resources; P.O. Box 308, North Chelmsford, MA 01863; call for free homeschool advice, (800) 788-1221; http://www.thehomeschool.com (the homeschool section of http://www. Christianbook.com.)

Homeschooling.about.com offers a printable map of the United States (color in each state as you study it). Print a state information sheet for each state you wish to study; http://homeschooling.about.com/education/homeschooling/library/blstate-unit.htm.

Performing Arts

Activated Storytellers is the performance name of the Goza family. Their Web site offers stories and activities for families and provides a performance schedule; http://www.activated-storytellers.com.

Henson International Festival of Puppet Theatre is held every other year in September (2002, 2004) and features puppet companies from more than a dozen countries on stages throughout New York City. The Jim Henson Foundation, an affiliated organization founded by the creator of The Muppets, offers puppetry workshops and grants to puppet artists. The Web site offers a free e-mail newsletter that lists puppetry events in the New York area and nationwide. Both organizations are at 117 East 69th Street, New York, NY 10021; (212) 439-7556, but they have separate Web sites: www.hensonfestival.org and www.henson.com/foundation.

The National Storytelling Festival is a three-day event in early October in Jonesborough, Tennessee. (800) 952-8392; http://www.storytellingfestival.net.

Puppeteers of America is a national organization with affiliated guilds. The Web site includes a guide to puppet festivals and puppetry guilds, along with a bookstore and a magazine called the *Puppetry Journal*. P.O. Box 29417, Parma, OH, 44129-0417; (888) 568-6235; http://www.puppeteers.org.

Story Net details storytelling events; http://www.storynet.org.

Tellabration is a worldwide storytelling event on the third weekend of November each year; http://www.tellabration.org.

Chapter 4: Discovering the Great Outdoors

Airboat Rides at Boggy Creek, Central Florida Everglades; (407) 933-4337; http://www.bcairboats.com.

Creation: Ex Nihilo magazine supports the theory of intelligent design of the universe, P.O. Box 6330, Florence, KY 41022; (800) 350-3232.

Dawes Arboretum, 7770 Jacksontown Rd. S.E., Newark, OH 43055; (800) 44-DAWES; http://www.dawesarb.org.

Dig-for-a-Day program: Wyoming Dinosaur Center, 110 Carter Ranch Road, P.O. Box 868, Thermopolis, WY 82443; http://www.wyodino.org.

Hostelling International—American Youth Hostels offers a free listing of hostels in ski-accessible areas. 733 15th St. NW, Suite 840, Washington DC 20005; (202) 783-6161; e-mail: hiayhserv@hiayh.org; http://www.hiayh.org.

Family Matters volunteer line: (800) VOLUNTEER.

National Arbor Day Foundation, 100 Arbor Avenue, Nebraska City, NE 68410; (402) 474-5655; http://www.arborday.org.

The National Audubon Society publishes the Pocket Guides, a series of 31 guides on topics ranging from cacti to clouds; To join the society, write 700 Broadway, New York, NY 10003, or call (800) 274-4201; For general information: (212) 979-3000; http://www.audubon.org.

National Geographic Magazine, P.O. Box 96095, Washington, DC 20090-6095; (800) 647-5463; For a free catalog call (800) 447-0647; http://www.nationalgeographic.com.

USDA Wildlife Habitat Council: (888) LANDCARE.

The Wilds is a southeast Ohio nature preserve; (740) 638-5030; http://www.thewilds.org.

ANIMALS
Lindsay's Backyard Wildlife Web site teaches about critters from butterflies to raccoons, with instructions on how to build nest boxes, bat boxes, and bird feeders to help with the loss of natural habitats, how to rescue orphaned animals, and how to get rid of pesky animals without hurting them (the Webmaster is eleven years old); http://www.lindsaysbackyard.com.

The Natural Heritage Program; http://www.nature.org.

Wild Horse and Burro Adoption Information, Bureau of Land Management, P.O. Box 12000, Reno, NV 89520-0006; (775) 861-6583 or (866) 4-MUSTANGS; http://www.wildhorseandburro.blm.gov.

Birds

America's 100 Most-Wanted Birds: Finding the Rarest Regularly Occurring Birds in the Lower 48 States by Steven G. Mlodinow and Michael O'Brien (Helena, Mont.: Falcon, 1996).

The Bird Almanac: The Ultimate Guide to Essential Facts and Figures of the World's Birds by David Michael Bird (Buffalo, N.Y.: Firefly, 1999).

The Bird Finder's 3-Year Note Book by Paul S. Eriksson (Middlebury, Vt.: Ericksson, 1989).

A Bird-Finding Guide to Mexico by Steve N. G. Howell (Ithaca, N.Y.: Cornell University, 1999).

Bird Watching for Dummies by Bill Thompson III (Foster City, Calif.: IDG, 1997).

The Birder's Guide to Bed and Breakfasts: United States and Canada by Peggy van Hulstey and Roger Tory Peterson (Santa Fe, N.M.: John Muir Publications, 1995).

Families on the Road newsletter is for families who RV. Subscribe at 2601 S. Minnesota Ave., Ste. 105 #191, Sioux Falls, SD 57105; e-mail: RovinUSA@ aol.com.

Birds: Peterson Field Guide Coloring Book by Roger Peterson, Peter Alden, and John Sill (Boston: Houghton Mifflin). Includes full-color pictures and detailed information about birds. Designed for children who can color in small areas.

The Purple Martin Conservation Association publishes a free catalog with insert about purple martins. Write to Edinboro University of Pennsylvania, Edinboro, PA 16444.

Traveling Birder: 20 Five-Star Birding Vacations by Clive E. Goodwin and Roger Tory Peterson (New York: Doubleday, 1991).

ASTRONOMY ORGANIZATIONS AND RESOURCES

ABCentral Web site: click on "societies," then on "astronomy." The site lists twenty-five clubs in Canada, more than two hundred in the United States, and hundreds more worldwide; http://www.my-edu2.com/index.html.

Astronomy Picture of the Day; http://antwrp.gsfc.nasa.gov/apod/astropix.html.

Boy Scouts of America; http://www.scouting.org.

Exploring the Moon Through Binoculars and Small Telescopes by Ernest H. Cherrington Jr. (New York: Dover, 1984).

Exploring the Night Sky with Binoculars by David Chandler (Npp: Chandler, 1995).

Fourmilab provides earth and moon viewing from your computer and free software in the public domain for astronomy; http://www.fourmilab.ch/earthview/vplanet.html.

Heavens Above; http://www.heavens-above.com.

The International Dark Sky Association is an organization concerned with reducing urban light pollution. 3225 N. First Ave., Tucson AZ 85719; (520) 293-3198; http://www.darksky.org/ida/index.html.

Kids Astronomy is a free e-mail newsletter; http://kidsastronomy.about.com.

NASA; http://spaceflight.nasa.gov.

Night Sky Planisphere or the Night Reader penlight; to order by mail or phone: P.O. Box 33303, San Diego, CA 92163; (800) 993-2993. To search for a different retailer or Internet source, check out http://www.DavidChandler.com.

Sky and Telescope, 49 Bay State Rd., Cambridge, MA 02138; (800) 253-0245 or (617) 864-7360; http://www.skyandtelescope.com.

Sky Atlas for Small Telescopes and Binoculars: The Beginners Guide to Successful Deep Sky Observing by David Chandler and Billie Chandler (Npp: Chandler, 2000).

Space Weather for day-by-day information on solar activity and its effect on the earth; http://www.spaceweather.com.

Telescopes; http://www.telescope.com.

CAMPING AND HIKING WITH CHILDREN

All Outdoors; http://www.alloutdoors.com.

Appalachian Trail Conference, 799 Washington Street, P.O. Box 807, Harpers Ferry, WV 25425-0807; (304) 535-6331; http://www.atconf.org.

Backpacker's Start-Up: A Beginner's Guide to Hiking and Backpacking by Doug Werner (Chula Vista, Calif.: Tracks, 1999).

Best Hikes with Children is a series published by Mountaineer Books, a nonprofit conservation club; (800) 553-4453.

The Boy Scout's Hike Book by Edward Cave (Dallas, Tex.: Stevens, 1992).

Bureau of Land Management, Office of Public Affairs, 1849 C Street, Room 406-LS, Washington, D.C. 20240; (202) 452-5125; http://www.blm.gov/nhp/index.htm.

Camping and Backpacking with Children by Steven Boga (Mechanicsville, Pa.: Stackpole, 1995).

The Essential Guide to Nature Walking in the United States by Charles Cook (New York: Holt, 1997) includes a state-by-state guide of walking trails.

Forest Service, U.S. Department of Agriculture, P.O. Box 96090, Washington, DC 20090-6090; http://www.fs.fed.us.

Gorp.com provides advice on wilderness survival, fishing, adventure stories, travel information, links, expert advice, and shopping; http://www.gorp.com.

Kids Outdoors: Skills and Knowledge for Outdoor Adventurers by Victoria Logue, Frank Logue, and Mark Carroll (Camden, Maine: Ragged Mountain Press, 1996).

National Park Service; http://www.nps.gov.

The Parent's Guide to Camping with Children by Roger Woodson and Kimberly Woodson (Cincinnati: Betterway Books, 1995).

Trails.com provides skill level, topography, and weather information for each trail; http://www.trails.com.

Wilderness with Children: A Parent's Guide to Fun Family Outings by Michael Hodgson (Mechanicsville, Pa.: Stackpole, 1992).

EARTH SCIENCE

52 Nature Activities by Lynn Gordon (San Francisco: Chronicle, 1996).

American Federation of Mineralogical Societies lists rock shows, demonstrations, and other events nationwide; P.O. Box 891208 Oklahoma City, OK 73189-1208; (405) 682-2938 http://www.amfed.org.

Bottle Biology: An Idea Book for Exploring the World Through Plastic Bottles and Other Recyclable Materials by Mrill Ingram, illustrated by Amy Kelley (Dubuque, Iowa: Kendall/Hunt Publishing Co., 1993).

Classroom Direct offers discounted hands-on educational supplies, including social studies, science, and nature resources; P.O. Box 830677, Birmingham, AL 35283-0677; (800) 248-9171; http://www.classroomdirect.com.

Geologic Records Center provides free rock and mineral sets. Shipping is free if you request one set; 4383 Fountain Square Dr., Columbus, OH 43224; (614) 265-6576 or e-mail, geo.survey@dnr.state.oh.us.

Weather

National Weather Service features education pages with resources for teaching meteorology; http://www.nws.noaa.gov.

Weather.com is sponsored by ABC News and provides worldwide weather information that is searchable by city, state, and country; http://www.weather.com.

Weatherwise is a weather magazine published six times a year; http://www.weatherwise.org.

YOUTH PROGRAMS

Boy Scouts of America has a Lone Scouting program for youth who cannot participate on a regular basis with a local scouting troop; http://www.scouting.org/factsheets/02-515.html.

Junior Ranger Program; http://www.nps.gov/interp/jrranger.html.

Keepers of the Faith, a Christian youth program; P.O. Box 100, Ironwood, MI 49938; (906) 663-6881; http://keepersofthefaith.com.

CHAPTER 5: FREE AND FRUGAL FIELD TRIPS AND DAY TRIPS

Constitution Finder allows you to read the Constitution or charter of countries around the world; http://www.urich.edu/~jpjones/confinder/const.htm.

Culture Finder lists arts and culture in cities around the world; http://www.culturefinder.com.

Downloadable world map; http://daniel.aero.calpoly.edu/~dfrc/World.

Explore Your World offers a free lesson booklet; http://www.esri.com/k-12.

Fellowship of Christian Magicians has twenty-five chapters in the United States and Canada as well as an international convention; 7739 Everest Court North, Maple Grove, MN 55311-1815; http://www.gospelcom.net/fcm.

Geography Place provides maps, games, and quizzes; http://www.geography-games.com.

Government resources; http://www.whitehouse.gov/government/services/educate.html.

"History Is Fun" is a Jamestown Settlement Museum teacher's resource packet; http://www.historyisfun.org.

The Jason Project is the scientific expedition site of explorer and oceanographer Robert Ballard; http://jasonproject.org.

"Learn To" has a travel section that allows you to post a question and receive a variety of answers from participants; http://www.LearnTo.com.

Musee is a virtual trip to museums of art, science, history, archaeology, and zoos; http://www.musee-online.org.

Story Net lists storytelling events; http://www.storynet.org.

Torpedo Software offers free European geography games and a U.S. puzzle; http://www.torpedosoftware.com.

Unbeatable Deals offers full-version CD-ROMs (free after shipping charge), including language and reading programs; http://www.unbeatabledeals.com.

Virtual World Surfari; http://www.supersurf.com.

WebMuseums offers virtual field trips; http://www.ibiblio.org/wm.

World Factbook contains information from the CIA on countries of the world; http://www.odci.gov/cia/publications/factbook/index.html.

World Strides (formerly American Student Travel); 2000 Holiday Drive, Charlottesville, VA 22901-2823, (800) 999-7676; http://www.WorldStrides.com.

BOOKS AND MAGAZINES
The Cockroach Hall of Fame: And 101 Other Off-the-Wall Museums by Sandra Gurvis (Secaucus, N.J.: Carol, 1994).

Family Fun Activity Book by Bob ("Captain Kangaroo") Keeshan (Minneapolis: Fairview, 1994).

The Frugal Family Network is a newsletter published six times a year. A free sample can be requested by mailing a legal-size self-addressed stamped envelope to: Frugal Family Network, P.O. Box 92731, Austin, TX 78709; http://www. frugalfamilynetwork.com.

Glove Compartment Scavenger Hunt publishes travel games, available from God's World Book Club, P.O. Box 20003, Asheville, NC 28802; http://www.gwbc.com.

Raising a Modern-Day Knight: A Father's Role in Guiding His Son to Authentic Manhood by Robert Lewis (Colorado Springs, Colo.: Focus on the Family, 1997).

RECIPROCAL MEMBERSHIPS FOR MUSEUMS AND OTHER EDUCATIONAL ORGANIZATIONS
American Horticultural Society, 7931 East Boulevard Drive, Alexandria, VA 22308-1300; (703) 768-5700 or (800) 777-7931; http://ahs.org.

The American Zoo and Aquarium Association offers a search engine to locate a zoo or aquarium in the state you plan to visit; http://www.aza.org.

The Association of Science Technology Centers Web site allows visitors to locate a science center from among over five hundred members in forty countries. Members include not only science-technology centers and science museums but also nature centers, aquariums, planetariums, zoos, botanical gardens, space theaters, and natural history and children's museums; 1025 Vermont Avenue NW, Suite 500, Washington, DC 20005-3516; (202) 783-7200; http://www.astc.org.

The USDA Wildlife Habitat Council offers a free backyard conservation packet; (888) LANDCARE.

CHAPTER 6: "ARE WE THERE YET?"

FAMILY TRAVEL RESOURCES

AudioMemory Publishing offers audiotapes and workbooks; 501 Cliff Dr., Newport Beach, CA 92663; (800) 365-SING; http://www.audiomemory.com.

Christian Book Distributors (CBD) offers bargain packs of Christian activity books and fiction and has a special catalog of educational materials, including historical fiction, science projects, games, and textbooks; P.O. Box 7000, Peabody, MA 01961-7000; (978) 977-5050; http://www.Christianbook.com.

Lakeshore Learning Store, 2695 E. Dominguez St., P.O. Box 6261, Carson, CA 90749; (800) 421-5354; http://www.lakeshorelearning.com.

Lauri Toys offers travel activity packs for ages two to ten. P.O. Box F-e, Phillips-Avon, ME 84966; (800) 451-0520; http://www.lauritoys.com.

The Learnables is an audio series for learning Chinese, Czechoslovakian, French, German, Hebrew, Japanese, Russian, Spanish, or English as a Second Language; published by International Linguistics Corporation, 3505 East Red Bridge Road, Kansas City, MO 64137; (800) 237-1830; http://www.learnables.com.

INTERNET FAMILY TRAVEL TIPS

20ish Parents; http://www.20ishparents.com.

Family Travel: Tips and Advice for Families Who Travel Together is a free newsletter; http://www.cooltravelmail.com.

Freebies4U, offers educational freebies; http://www.freebies4u.com.

LEGO lesson plans; http://www.weirdrichard.com/activity.htm.

My Sheet Music lists free songs; http://www.dalymusic.com.

Smarter Living offers family travel articles by columnist Kyle McCarthy; http://www.smarterliving.com/columns.

How to Make a Mankala Game
Supplies:
   1 egg carton
   2 rubber bands
   48 small, smooth stones or pennies or seeds or buttons or marbles.
Directions: Mankala, a game for two players, has a game board of twelve small bowls, six on each side—just like the bottom part of an egg carton. First, use the bottom half of an egg carton. You will also need two storage banks, which you make by cutting the top part of the egg carton (the part without the twelve egg bowls) into two pieces, width-wise. These two storage banks are placed at each end of the game board during play. To make the game easier to transport, attach the storage banks to the top of the egg carton with a rubber band. You can store your stones or other movable pieces in the egg carton.

   If you want to decorate your game, you can spray paint it. You may wish to use a color to contrast with your stones or to simulate a natural wood look. Use decorative designs from Egypt, Ethiopia, or Nigeria for your game. Ask a librarian to help you find books on African art. You may also wish to study how Mankala games vary in different areas of the world.

   There are several versions of Mankala. Find Mankala rules at: http://www.elf.org/mankala/Mankala.html and http://www.ahs.uwaterloo.ca/~museum (provides instructions for dozens of games, from ABC Spelit [a Finnish card game] to Yoke Puzzles).

Printing Paper Dolls from the Internet
For help making paper dolls using the Internet, check out the following sites:

- http://www.ameritech.net/users/macler/paperdolls.html
- http://www.foxhome.com/shirley/html/doll/dollf.html
- http://www.ushsdolls.com/paperdoll/pdarc.htm

Speeches to Read or Memorize

Indian Oratory: Famous Speeches by Noted Indian Chieftains compiled by
W. C. Vanderwerth (Norman: University of Oklahoma, 1971).

The History Place has a Great Speeches Collection; http://www.historyplace.
com/speeches/joseph.htm.

Public Broadcasting System; http://www.pbs.org/greatspeeches.

FAMILY TRAVEL TIP BOOKS

AAA Travel Fun Book (New York: Simon & Schuster, 2000).

A Simple Choice: A Practical Guide to Saving Your Time, Money, and Sanity
(Vancouver, Wash.: Champion, 2000) includes "Keep a Straight Face" game and
other ideas for traveling families.

Car Smarts: Activities for Kids on the Open Road by Ed Sobey (New York: McGraw-
Hill, 1997).

Fun on the Run: Travel Games and Songs by Joanna Cole and Stephanie Calmenson
(New York: Morrow Junior Books, 1999).

The Guinness Book of World Records (New York: Mint, 2000).

Just Plane Smart: Activities for Kids in the Air and on the Ground by Edwin J. C.
Sobey (New York: McGraw-Hill, 1998).

Kids on Board: Fun Things to Do While Commuting or Road Tripping with Children
by Robyn Freedman Spizman (Minneapolis: Fairview, 1997).

The Penny Whistle Traveling with Kids Book by Meredith Brokaw and Annie Gilbar
(New York: Simon & Schuster, 1995).

The Usborne Book of Air Travel Games by Moira Butterfield (Tulsa, Okla.: Usborne, 1986).

Chapter 7: Family Volunteering

America's Second Harvest is the largest domestic hunger relief organization in the United States. Links with nearly two hundred food banks or food-rescue programs; http://www.secondharvest.org.

The Christian Connector offers free information on Christian colleges and universities, Bible colleges, short-term missions, ministry opportunities, Christian music, Christian teen publications, and Christian teen events and conferences. You can access their Web site at http://www.christianconnector.com.

Christian Freedom International (CFI) is dedicated to helping persecuted Christians around the world; they offer a one-year subscription to their monthly magazine and an eighteen-minute video about the persecution of Christians in Burma; P.O. Box 16367, Washington, DC 20041-6367; (800) 323-CARE; http://www. christianfreedom.org.

Deep South is a ministry organization that uses families to carry out the work of repairing houses in Appalachia. Contact: Pam Ianni, 11900 Morse Rd., Pataskala, OH 43062; (740) 927-9438.

EarthWise Journeys is a membership organization promoting socially responsible tourism for ecological and cultural preservation; P.O. Box 16177, Portland, OR 97292; http://www.teleport.com/~earthwyz/tourism.htm.

Family Matters is a project of the Points of Light Foundation; 1400 I Street, Suite 800, Washington, DC 20005; call (800) VOLUNTEER and enter a ZIP code to be linked automatically with a volunteer center in your area or the area you wish to visit; all other calls: (202) 729-8000; http://www.PointsOfLight.org.

The Green Pages is an online directory of socially responsible "eco-travel" sources, both domestic and international; http://www.coopamerica.org/travel.htm.

Habitat for Humanity is a coalition of homeowners and volunteers who build affordable houses for people worldwide, under trained supervision; 121 Habitat St., Americus, GA 31709; (229) 924-6935; http://www.habitat.org.

National Registration Center for Study Abroad, P.O. Box 1393, Milwaukee, WI 53201; (414) 278-0631; http://www.nrcsa.com.

Random Acts of Kindness Foundation offers suggestions for people of all ages for performing small kindnesses that make the world a better place; http://www.actsofkindness.org.

U.S. Army Corps of Engineers Volunteer Program, Nationwide Volunteer Clearinghouse; (800) VOL-TEER.

Volunteer: The Comprehensive Guide to Voluntary Service in the United States and Abroad is available from the Council on International Educational Exchange.

Volunteer National Center maintains a list of books on volunteering; 1111 N. 19th St., Suite 500, Arlington, VA 22209; (703) 276-0542.

Volunteer Match is a nationwide matching service for nonprofit agencies and volunteers; www.volunteermatch.org.

FAMILY VOLUNTEERING BOOKS, MAGAZINES, AND VIDEOS

"54 Ways to Help the Homeless" is an online article by Rabbi Charles A. Kroloff; http://www.earthsystems.org/ways.

2001 Guide to Adoption is an annual publication from *Adoptive Families* magazine with listings of local and national parent organizations and state-by-state listings of adoption agencies. Available from bookstores or by calling (800) 372-3300; http://www.adoptivefamiliesmagazine.com.

Adoptive Families of America provides adoption resources for families; http://www.adoptivefamiliesmagazine.com.

American Girl series, including *Felicity* books, by various authors (Middleton, Wis.: Pleasant Company).

Environmental Vacations: Volunteer Projects to Save the Planet by Stephanie Ocko (Santa Fe, N.Mex.: John Muir Publications, 1992).

Gladys Aylward: The Adventure of a Lifetime by Janet Benge and Geoff Benge (Seattle, Wash.: YWAM, 1998).

The Lady in the Box by Ann McGovern (New York: Turtle Books, 1997) is a children's story about a homeless woman and how a family reaches out to help her.

Revolution in World Missions by K. P. Yohannon is available free of charge from Gospel for Asia, 1800 Golden Trail Ct., Carrollton, TX 75010-9907; (800) WIN-ASIA.

The Road to Reality: Coming Home to Jesus from the Unreal World by K. P. Yohannan (Altamonte Springs, Fla.: Creation House, 1988); (214) 416-0340.

Saga of the Pilgrims: From Europe to the New World by John Harris (Chester, Conn.: Globe Pequot, 1990).

Six Months Off: How to Plan, Negotiate, and Take the Break You Need Without Burning Bridges or Going Broke by Hope Dlugozima, James Scott, and David Sharp (New York: Holt, 1996).

Uncle Willie and the Soup Kitchen by Dyanne DiSalvo-Ryan and Mira Reisberg (Mulberry Books, 1997).

Vacations That Can Change Your Life: Adventures, Retreats, and Workshops for the Mind, Body, and Spirit by Ellen Lederman (Naperville, Ill.: Sourcebooks, 1998).

Volunteer Vacations by Bill McMillon (Chicago: Chicago Review, 1999).

International Volunteer Opportunities

Adventures Abroad, Suite 2148, 20800 Westminster Highway, Richmond, British Columbia, V6V2W3 Canada; (800) 665-3998; http://www.adventuresabroad.com.

Archaeological fieldwork opportunities are available from Archaeological Institute of America, 675 Commonwealth Ave., Boston, MA 02215; (617) 353-0361.

Global Volunteers (GV) offers volunteer projects worldwide to families with children of all ages; 375 Little Canada Road, St. Paul, MN 55117; (800) 487-1074; http://www.globalvolunteers.org.

Go M.A.D. (Go Make A Difference) needs help with Web site development, brochures, letter writing, grant proposals, etc.; http://www.gomad.org.

Goshen Ministries; index of Christian organizations; http://www.goshen.net.

Idealist helps you search for internships, jobs, or volunteer opportunities with nonprofit organizations worldwide; http://www.idealist.org.

Intercristo is a Christian placement network for mission work; 19303 Fremont Ave. N., Seattle, WA 98133; (800) 251-7740; http://www.jobleads.org.

King's Kids/Mercy Ships; Mercy ships encourages involvement of whole families, offering ministry opportunities for teens and leadership opportunities for adults. Apply online. Mercy Ships is a division of Youth with a Mission and is a sponsor of King's Kids International; P.O. Box 2020, Garden Valley, TX 75771; (903) 882-0887; e-mail: kingkids@mercyships.org.

Mama Terra provides volunteer opportunities at orphanages in Romania; http://www.motherearth.org.

The Mennonite Central Committee is the relief and development arm of the North American Mennonite and Brethren in Christ churches; http://www.mcc.org.

World Vision offers useful information about how to raise financial support for a mission trip and includes links to other mission organizations; http://www.wvi.org.

RV Volunteers

Care-A-Vanner is a network of RVers who travel as a group to work on Habitat for Humanity home-building projects; (800) HABITAT, ext. 2446; http://www. habitat.org/gv/rv.html.

The Enabled RVer; for travelers with disabilities; http://maxpages.com/enabledrver.

Families on the Road newsletter; 2601 S. Minnesota Ave., Ste. 105 #191, Sioux Falls, SD 57105; online e-mail discussion list: RovinUSA http://www. familiesontheroad.com.

RV Lifestyle newsletter; 1020 Brevik Place, Unit 5, Mississauga L4W 4N7, Ontario, Canada; (905) 624-8218.

The RVing Volunteer; http://maxpages.com/rvingvolunteer.

Take Back Your Life: Travel Full-Time in an RV by Stephanie Bernhagen (Livingston, Tex.: Berham-Collins, 2000).

Virtual Volunteer Project; http://www.serviceleader.org/vv.

Volunteers on Wheels (VOW) promotes mobile volunteering among RVers; http://maxpages.com/rvingvolunteer/Volunteers_on_Wheels.

Jobs with Nonprofit Organizations

Charity Village lists Canada-based jobs; http://www.charityvillage.com

Community Career Center; http://www.nonprofitjobs.org.

Idealist; http://www.idealist.org.

OpportunityNocs; http://www.opportunitynocs.org.

Teen Resources

The Council on International Educational Exchange sponsors study, work, travel, and volunteer programs in Europe, Asia, Africa, and Latin America; http://www. councilexchanges.org.

Acquire the Fire is a series of conventions in twenty-six cities across North America with intense gatherings of thousands of young people and youth pastors. Sponsored by Teen Mania, the convention uses modern technology in audio, lighting, video, drama, and pyrotechnics for a powerful presentation. Honor Academy, sponsored by Teen Mania, offers a one-year ministry internship for teens; e-mail: info// www.teenmania.org.

National Registration Center for Study Abroad allows you to search for programs by country, language, or type of educational program; P.O. Box 1393, Milwaukee, WI 53201; (414) 278-0631; http://www.nrcsa.com.

Project Vote Smart offers internships and volunteer work to research the background and voting record of political candidates—regardless of their party affiliation—to assist voters in making informed choices. The goal is to create an extensive, continuously updated database available to all. Financial assistance is sometimes available for both students and volunteers. Contact: One Common Ground, Philipsburg, MT 59858; (406) 859-8683; http://www.vote-smart.org.

The Student Conservation Association sponsors high-school conservation work crews; P.O. Box 550, Charlestown, NH 03603; http://www.sca-inc.org.

Studyabroad.com lists thousands of study abroad programs in more than one hundred countries throughout the world; http://www.Studyabroad.com.

Touch America Project (TAP) is a volunteer program of the U.S. Department of Agriculture that gives youth, ages fourteen to seventeen, work experience and environmental awareness while working on public lands. Write or call the volunteer coordinator of your nearest Forest Service office (look it up in the online Forest Service directory at the TAP Web site, or look for it in your phone book under

"U.S. Government" and "Department of Agriculture, Forest Service") for information and to volunteer; http://www.fs.fed.us/people/programs/volunteer.htm#tap.

"Travel Tips for Youth"; http://www.geocities.com/TheTropics/4979/who.html.

U.S. Forest Service, U.S. Department of Agriculture, P.O. Box 96090, Washington, DC 20090-6090; http://www.fs.fed.us.

Books

And What About College? How Homeschooling Can Lead to Admissions to the Best Universities and Colleges by Cafi Cohen (Cambridge, Mass.: Holt, 2000).

The High-School Student's Guide to Study, Travel, and Adventure Abroad, Council on International Educational Exchange (New York: St. Martin's, 1995).

Smart Vacations: The Traveler's Guide to Learning Adventures Abroad, edited by Priscilla M. Torey, Council on International Educational Exchange (New York: St. Martin's, 1993).

Teenagers' Guide to Study, Travel, and Adventure Abroad (New York: St. Martin's, 1991).

Work, Study, Travel Abroad, edited by Max Terry and Lazaro Hernandez, Council on International Educational Exchange (New York: St. Martin's, 1994).

CHAPTER 8: BUDGETING AND LIFESTYLE CHANGES

Eagle'sNestHome.com, Melissa Morgan's Web site, offers information on wise stewardship, homeschooling, and freebies; http://www.eaglesnesthome.com.

The Frugal Gazette; http://www.frugalgazette.com/samplearticles.htm.

The Frugal Life is a free newsletter featuring tips, articles, recipes, links, and a contest; http://www.thefrugallife.com.

Homeschooling on a Shoestring by Melissa L. Morgan and Judith Waite Allee (Wheaton, Ill.: Shaw, 1999) contains numerous resources and information on frugal living.

Miserly Moms; http://www.miserlymoms.com.

The Simple Times, edited by Deborah Hough, is a free twice-monthly e-mail newsletter. It features frugal and simple living ideas, make-ahead cooking, family educational ideas, and message boards; http://members.aol.com/DSimple/index.html.

Extended Travel

Center for Interim Programs guides people planning sabbaticals or other alternatives to school or work; P.O. Box 2347, Cambridge, MA 02238; (609) 683 4300; http://www.interimprograms.com.

Headfirst into America by Marlene Smith-Graham (Colcourt, 1998), the journal of a year-long fifty-state adventure for a family of four traveling in a van.

MoreTimeOff.com, Web site of Dana Nibby, author of online articles on world travel and taking extended time off from work, includes the article "Take This Job and Love It: Leisure-Friendly Workplaces"; http://www.MoreTimeOff.com.

My American Adventure: Big Things Happen When You Reach Really High by Amy Burritt (Grand Rapids, Mich.: Zondervan, 1998) is a twelve-year-old home-schooler's journal about completing her dream to travel through all fifty states and interview all fifty governors.

Road School by Jim, Kaitlin, Jordin, and Janet Marousis (Tempe, Ariz.: Blue Bird, 1995) is the journal of the Marousis family as they traveled for eight months with a tent and pickup truck.

Six Months Off: How to Plan, Negotiate, and Take the Break You Need Without Burning Bridges or Going Broke by Hope Dlugozima, James Scott, and David Sharp (New York: Holt, 1996).

INTERNET SERVICES

Address.com (http://www.address.com) provides free Web access and Internet service.

Family Connect includes Internet access, a pornography filter, and unlimited e-mail with five addresses; (888) 398-8899; http://www.familyconnect.com.

MONEY MANAGEMENT

Big Ideas, Small Budget is both a book and a newsletter by Pat Wesolowski. For current subscription and book information, e-mail: bisb@juno.com.

Rich Dad, Poor Dad: What the Rich Teach Their Kids About Money That the Poor and Middle Class Do Not by Robert Kiyosaki (New York: Warner Books, 2000).

Your Money or Your Life: Transforming Your Relationship with Money and Achieving Financial Independence by Joe Dominguez and Vicki Robin (New York: Viking, 1992).

Budgeting for Living in a Foreign Country

Expatriate Exchange provides inside information on costs and other advice; http://expatexchange.com.

Overseas Digest catalogs overseas positions, classifieds, forums, etc.; http://www.overseasdigest.com.

Personal Finance for Overseas Americans by Barbara Frew (Sterling, Va.: GIL Financial, 2000).

Credit

Christian Financial Concepts is Larry Burkett's financial ministry to help families get out of debt and practice good stewardship; P.O. Box 2377, Gainesville, GA 30503-2377; (770) 534-1000; http://www.cfcministry.org.

Consumer Alert is a nonprofit membership organization that encourages a free market and offers a free copy of the "Consumers Take Charge Budget Worksheet." Send a self-addressed, stamped No. 10 envelope to Consumer Alert, 1001

Connecticut Ave., N.W., Suite 1128, Washington, DC 20036; or download it from
their Web site: http://www.consumeralert.org/pubs/commonsense/Budget98.htm.

Consumer Credit Counseling Service; (800) 388-CCCS.

Cornerstone Christian Counseling helps with budgeting and debt consolidation;
(888) PLAN4ME; e-mail: Debtbustr@AOL.com; http://www.cornerstonecredit.com.

Chapter 9: Working Vacations, Portable Businesses, and Fund-Raisers

Fundcraft offers free recipe-creation software that can be used for fund-raising; P.O.
Box 340, Collierville, TN 38027; (801) 853-7070; http://www.fundcraft.com.

Associations and Organizations

Campus Crusade for Christ lists opportunities for evangelistic Christian outreach
worldwide; 100 Lake Hart Dr., Orlando, FL 32832; http://www.ccci.org.

*Encyclopedia of Associations: International Organizations, Encyclopedia of Associations:
National Organizations,* and *Yearbook of International Organizations* are available at
most public libraries.

Intercristo is a Christian ministry/job opportunity placement network; 19303
Fremont Ave. N., Seattle, WA 98133; (800) 251-7740; http://jobleads.org.

National Christmas Tree Association lists seasonal jobs selling Christmas trees,
often for nonprofit organizations; 1000 Executive Parkway, Suite 220, St. Louis,
MO 63141-6372; (314) 205-0944; http://www.realchristmastrees.org.

Preferred Chiropractic Doctor is a membership club for discounted chiropractic
healthcare; http://www.bewell2.com.

SCORE (Service Core of Retired Executives) offers free counseling for starting or
running a small business; http://www.score.org.

Small Business Administration sponsors workshops and counseling for starting or running a small business; P.O. Box 15434, Fort Worth, TX 67119.

Small Business Resource Center provides useful information to small business entrepreneurs; http://www.webcom.com/~seaquest.

Trans World Travel, Inc., works with individuals who put together tours in exchange for free travel; 734 Central Ave, Highland Park, IL 60035; (800) 323-8158; http://www.transworldtravel.com.

Travel Industry Association of America. Click on "Discover America," which provides links to tourism offices in every state and territory. Discover America also offers a links page with an assortment of travel sites to explore; http://www.tia.org.

The U.S. Agency for International Development (USAID) lists contracts, grants, and cooperative agreements with universities, businesses, and nonprofit institutions; http://www.info.usaid.gov.

BUSINESS TRAVEL WITH CHILDREN

BusinessTravel provides ideas from a variety of online travel sites and includes additional helpful tips; http://businesstravel.about.com/business/businesstravel/mbody.htm.

"Taking Kids Can Be Child's Play" by Marilyn Adams; http://www.usatoday.com/life/travel/business/1999/t0518kc.htm.

JOBS AND SELF-EMPLOYMENT, INCLUDING MINISTRIES AND BUSINESSES THAT INVOLVE TRAVEL

Overseas Digest Employment Guide: How to Find a Job Overseas with Half the Hassle, in Half the Time is an electronic book by the editors of Overseas Digest (YEAR). The Web site also features Teaching Jobs Abroad and Live and Teach in Spain; countries in the series include Germany, France, and Italy. Order and download books at http://www.overseasdigest.com.

Jobs That Travel

Bizy Guide to Operating a Home-Based Travel Agency by Jennifer Dugan (Npp: Bizy Moms, 2001) is an electronic book (e-book) available at the Bizy Moms' Web site, which features a variety of e-books on home-based businesses; http://www.bizymoms.com.

The Caretaker Gazette lists rent-free positions around the world for property caretaking or housesitting on estates, mansions, farms, ranches, resort homes, hunting or fishing lodges, and private islands; P.O. Box 5887-M, Carefree, AZ 85377-0887; (480) 488-1970; http://www.angelfire.com/wa/caretaker.

Caretaking; http://www.workersonwheels.com/working/caretaking.html.

Digital Women is an international online community and information resource for women in business around the globe; http://www.digital-women.com.

Dugan's Travel, started by Jennifer Dugan, offers commission opportunities for travel-agent families; http://www.onlineagency.com/duganstravels.

Home Parents; http://homeparents.about.com/parenting/homeparents/msub3.htm.

How to Make Money Performing in Schools: Definitive Guide to Developing, Marketing, and Presenting School Assembly Programs by David Helflick (Orient, Wash.: Silcox Productions, 1997).

Jobs for People Who Love to Travel: Opportunities at Home and Abroad by Ronald L. Krannich and Caryl Krannich (Manassas Park, Va.: Impact, 1999).

Monster.com is a large job-search Web site; http://www.monster.com.

NoBoss.com profiles entrepreneurs, including "parent-preneurs"; http://noboss.com.

RV Lifestyle newsletter and *RV Lifestyle* magazine, 1020 Brevik Place, Unit 5, Mississauga, ON L4W 4N7, Canada; (905) 624-8218; http://www.rvlifemag.com.

There are temporary staffing agencies in towns of all sizes (check local telephone directory), with workers doing everything from day labor to professional work.

"Working Vacations for Photographers: Selling Photos on Spec at Conferences" by Judith Allee (Npp: Allee Photography, 2001) is a short report for professional photographers on booking conferences, handling orders, and including your children in the fun and profit; http://www.DreamsOnAShoestring.com.

Jobs in Campgrounds and Parks

Camphosts links people who want to work at campgrounds with campgrounds that are looking for either paid or volunteer help; http://www.camphosts.com.

CLM Campground Managers coordinates forest service concessionaires; (800) 959-6956.

Road Work: The Ultimate RVing Adventure by Arline Chandler includes job tips for working at amusement parks, campgrounds, Army Corps of Engineers facilities, and resorts, plus earning money by delivering RVs or leading RV caravans. The book also contains information on how to become a certified RV technician and mechanic; (501) 362-2637(information); (800) 446-5627(order); http://www.workamper.com.

State and federal park jobs: To find a listing of jobs or volunteer positions in a federal or state park, contact the national forest where you are interested in working and ask for the name of the concessionaire that takes care of their campgrounds. Check out http://usparks.about.com. You'll find job listings and links to national and state parks as well as links to state travel and tourism offices.

Workamper News is a newsletter and Web site featuring thousands of job openings that range from part-time volunteer positions to full-time careers at campgrounds, theme parks, motorsports, resorts, etc. Subscribers may also place free situations-wanted ad in both the magazine and on the Web site; 201 Hiram Road, Heber Springs, AR 72543-8747; (501) 362-2637; (800) 446-5627 (order); http://www.workamper.com.

Workers on Wheels provides advice for those who want to work while traveling, especially RVers. The Web site includes profiles, information on mobile self-employment opportunities, and job listings; http://www.workersonwheels.com.

Jobs in Other Countries

Alternative Travel Directory: The Complete Guide to Work, Study, and Travel Overseas by Clayton A. Hubbs (Transitions Abroad, updated periodically); Transitions Abroad, P.O. Box 1300, Amherst, MA 01004-1300; http://www.transitionsabroad.com.

Overseas Digest Employment Guide; http://www.overseasdigest.com/findajob.htm.

Transitions Abroad is a bimonthly magazine with practical information on affordable alternatives to mass tourism: living, working, studying, or vacationing alongside the people of the host country. Web site resources include information on searching for overseas jobs, Internet resources, permits, and the opportunity to interact with other site visitors; P.O. Box 1300, Amherst, MA 01004-1300; http://www.transitionsabroad.com.

Travel & Teach eNewsletter is a free monthly guide to living and teaching overseas; register at http://www.transitionsabroad.com.

Work Abroad: The Complete Guide to Finding a Job Overseas (Transitions Abroad, annual) provides information on international work, including work permits, short-term jobs, volunteer opportunities, planning an international career, and starting your own business. Order from Transitions Abroad, P.O. Box 1300, Amherst, MA 01004-1300; http://www.transitionsabroad.com.

ONLINE AUCTIONS TO EARN MONEY

Amazon.com; http://amazon.com.

AuctionWatch.com; http://www.auctionwatch.com/company/about.html.

eBay.com; http://ebay.com.

Official Guide to Online Buying and Selling by Dennis Prince (Npp: AuctionWatch.com, 2000).

Yahoo; http://yahoo.com.

TELECOMMUTING AND TELEWORKING

AT&T Telework Webguide; http://www.att.com/telework/getstart.

International Telework Association and Council; http://www.telecommute.org.

Telecommuting Knowledge Center links to articles and Web sites on telecommuting; http://www.telecommuting.org.

CHAPTER 10: FRUGAL FOOD FOR THE ROAD

Fit for Life by Harvey Diamond and Marilyn Diamond (New York: Warner Books, 1987).

Big Ideas, Small Budget by Pat Wesolowski (self-published, 1995). To order the book or subscribe to the newsletter of the same name, e-mail: bisb@juno.com. The newsletter is available bimonthly for a yearly subscription fee of $12.

The Book of Sandwiches by Louise Steele, Paul Grater (photographer), and Julia Ransome (New York: Berkley Publishing Group, 1989).

L'Ecole, the restaurant of the French Culinary Institute; 462 Broadway, New York, NY 10013-2618; (212) 219-3300; http://www.frenchculinary.com.

Mardi Gras School of Cooking; (504) 362-5225; e-mail: chefbond@att.net; http://www.mardigrasschoolofcooking.com.

Mountain Safety Research is a maker of lightweight equipment for camping and backpacking; P.O. Box 24547, Seattle, WA 98124; (800) 877-9677; http://www.msrcorp.com.

Stalking the Wild Asparagus by Euell Gibbons (Chambersburg, Pa.: Alan C. Hood & Co., 1987).

COOKBOOKS AND INSTRUCTION BOOKS

52 Ways to Make Family Travel More Enjoyable by Kate Redd (Nashville, Tenn.: Nelson, 1994).

Armadillo Pie by Jim Foreman (Npp: Jim Foreman, 1989) is out of print, but most of the recipes are posted at http://www.geocities.com/jimforetales/cookbk1.htm.

The Big Book of Preserving the Harvest by Carol W. Costenbader (Pownal, Vt.: Storey Books, 1997).

Catfish: An All-American Restaurant and Recipe Guide contains recipes for cooking the catfish you catch as well as a list of restaurants that serve catfish. It's free from the Catfish Institute, P.O. Box 247, 118 Hayden Street, Belzoni, MS 39038; http://www.catfishinstitute.com.

Dehydrating foods information from Susan Reynolds is available at http://edis.ifas.ufl.edu/scripts/htmlgen.exe?MENU_HE:Drying_Foods.

Manifold Destiny: The One! The Only! Guide to Cooking on Your Car Engine by Chris Maynard and Bill Scheller (New York: Villard, 1998).

The Penny Whistle Traveling with Kids Book by Meredith Brokaw and Annie Gilbar (New York: Simon & Schuster, 1995).

Solarcooking.org provides general and technical information, resources, and discussion groups on solar cooking as well as information on solar water distillation and pasteurization; http://www.solarcooking.org.

Whole Foods from the Whole World by Virginia Sutton Halonen; La Leche League International members from all over the world contributed their favorite recipes; La Leche League International, P.O. Box 4079, Schaumburg, IL 60168-4079; (800) 525-3243; http://LaLecheLeague.org.

Cooking in an RV

MotorHome, 2575 Vista Del Mar, Ventura, CA 93001; (805) 667-4100; http://motorhome.tl.com.

Trailer Life Campground Directory; http://www.goodsamclub.com.

Coupons

Entertainment Publications offers discount coupon books for restaurants, attractions, and services, along with location maps; http://www.entertainment.com.

Freebie Coupon Corner is a source for discount coupons anywhere in the country; http://www.couponcorner.net.

Search the Internet with the keywords "restaurant coupons" and the state or province you will be visiting to see if you can print coupons for any restaurants at your destination.

Restaurant Locators

CuisineNet Menus Online for sixteen major American cities (so far); http://www.menusonline.com.

Diner City, Online Guide to Classic Diners and the American Roadside; http://www.dinercity.com.

Exitsource.com tells you what restaurants, gas stations, and accommodations are available at specific highway exits; http://www.exitsource.com.

Chapter 11: Camping and RVing

Building Your Own Shelter

The Indian Tipi: Its History, Construction, and Use by Reginald Laubin (Norman: University of Oklahoma, 1990) provides detailed historical and cultural information and plans.

Israelite houses; http://webstu.messiah.edu/~sg1168/home.htm.

Make Your Own Tipi by James E. Jones (Portland, Oreg.: Living History Publishers, 1999).

Smocks and Kisses provides an inexpensive pattern to build your own tepee in various sizes (from model to full size); P.O. Box 334, La Jolla, CA 92038-0334; (858) 457-0045; http://www.smocksandkisses.com.

Tipis & Yurts: Authentic Designs for Circular Shelters by Leslie Dierks (Asheville, N.C.: Lark Books, 2000).

CONVERTING A TRUCK OR BUS INTO AN RV

MrSharkey.com provides information on homemade "truckhouses" (motor homes), solar energy, book reviews, and photographs; http://www.mrsharkey.com.

Online discussion lists at http://www.groups.yahoo.com. Search under "house-trucks" or other keywords to access various forums on technical issues and aspects of living a mobile lifestyle.

School bus conversion; http://www.schoolbusconversion.com.

Select and Convert Your Bus into a Motorhome on a Shoestring by Ben Rosander (self-published); http://www.rv-busconversions.com.

RVNetLinx.com contains technical information and tips on where to camp; http://www.rvnetlinx.com/buses.htm.

CAMPING INFORMATION

A Simple Choice: A Practical Guide for Saving Your Time, Money, and Sanity by Deborah Taylor-Hough (Beverly Hills, Calif.: Champion, 2000).

Be Like Christ Foundation provides an opportunity for needy youth to attend a residential Christian summer camp; 1001 S. Perry St., Suite 109, Castle Rock, CO 80104; http://www.belikechrist.org/scholars.htm.

Big Ideas, Small Budget by Pat Wesolowski (self-published, 1995). To order the book or subscribe to the newsletter of the same name, e-mail: bisb@juno.com.

Camping; http://camping.about.com.

Camping on the Internet by Loren Eyrich (Elkhart, Ind.: Cottage, 2000). A sample chapter is posted at http://www.two-lane.com.

Two Lane Roads is a quarterly newsletter about America's back roads. Subscribe at http://www.two-lane.com.

Workamper News is a newsletter and Web site featuring thousands of job openings that range from part-time volunteer positions to full-time careers at campgrounds, theme parks, motorsports, resorts, etc. Subscribers may also place free situations-wanted ad in both the magazine and on the Web site; 201 Hiram Road, Heber Springs, AR 72543-8747; (800) 446-5627 (order); (501) 362-2637; http://www.workamper.com.

Campgrounds and Free Parking Spots for RVs

American Camping Association; http://www.acacamps.org.

Christian Camping International; http://www.cci.org.au. Christian Camping International USA is an affiliate; http://www.gospelcom.net/cci/#.

Don Wright's Guide to Free Campgrounds by Don Wright; (800) 272-5518.

Free Campgrounds of the West: Free RV Parks, Boondock Areas, Rules and Regulations, edited by Chuck Woodbury. The author also publishes *Out West,* a newsletter about off-the-beaten-track America. The Web site includes listings of free camp-sites and links to sites about boondocking (camping without hookups) and RV information. The book includes an extensive listing and updates, including city parks, fraternal lodges with camping facilities, military campgrounds, camping at independent truck stops, casinos, and rest areas. Order from Out West, 9792 Edmonds Way #265, Edmonds, WA 98020. Available in print form or as a down-loadable file; http://www.freecampgrounds.com.

Gypsy Journal offers a list of over five hundred free and low-cost overnight parking places. Send $5 to *Gypsy Journal*, 1400 Colorado Street C-16, Boulder City, NV 89005-2448; http://www.gypsyjournal.net.

Kampgrounds of America (KOA); request a directory: (406) 248-7444; http://www.koa.com.

Trailer Life Campground Directory; http://www.goodsamclub.com.

Woodall Campground Directory (annual), and other directories; http://www.woodalls.com.

Public Lands Available for Camping
Bureau of Land Management, Office of Public Affairs, 1849 C St., Room 406-LS, Washington, DC 20240; (202) 452-5125; http://www.blm.gov/nhp/index.htm.

Fodor's Complete Guide to America's National Parks, edited by Ellen Browne (New York: Random House, 2001).

National Forest and Army Corps of Engineers; http://www.reserveusa.com.

National Park Service's ParkNet allows you to make online reservations at campgrounds in national parks. Visitor information: (209) 372-0200; http://www.nps.gov.

Office of Surface Mining pinpoints reclaimed strip mines that are available for recreation; http://www.osmre.gov/map.htm.

State campground and cabin guides, links to national and state parks, and also links to state travel and tourism offices; http://usparks.about.com.

CAMPING WITH CHILDREN
Cradle to Canoe: Camping and Canoeing with Children by Rolf Kraiker and Debra Kraiker (Erin, Ont.: Boston Mills, 1999).

The Joy of Family Camping by Herb Gordon (Short Hills, N.J.: Burford Books, 1998).

The Parent's Guide to Camping with Children by Roger and Kimberly Woodson (Cincinnati: Betterway, 1995).

MOTORIST RESOURCES

For the American Automobile Association (AAA), check your local telephone book or go to http://www.aaa.com.

Mountain Directory East for Truckers, RV, and Motorhome Drivers (Baldwin City, Kans.: R&R Publishing, 1999) details locations and descriptions of mountain passes and steep grades in eleven Eastern states (and eleven Western states for the Western edition, which is also available); P.O. Box 941, Baldwin City, KS 66006; (800) 594-5999.

RVING

Camper and Recreation, Inc., can manufacture canvas for any folding trailer if the old canvas is available; W2299 Highway 98, Loyal, WI 54446; (800) 232-2079; http://www.canvasreplacements.com.

Home Is Where You Park It by Kay Peterson (Livingston, Tex.: RoVers, 1990); available through Life on Wheels Bookstore, P.O. Box 9755, Moscow, ID 83843; (208) 882-7388; http://www.lifeonwheels.com.

Motorhome magazine offers information about driving and maintaining a motorhome; http://motorhome.tl.com.

Movin' On: Living and Traveling Full-Time in a Recreational Vehicle by Ron Hofmeister and Barb Hofmeister (Livingston, Tex.: R&B Publications, 1999).

RV Doctor is a collection of advice and articles for RV owners; http://www.rvdoctor.com/faqs.html.

Take Back Your Life: Travel Full-Time in an RV by Stephanie Bernhagen (Livingston, Tex.: Bernham-Collins, 2000).

Trailer Life; http://www.trailerlife.com

Buying and Selling an RV

Bankrate.com; check bank rates and research your bank; http://www.
workamper.com.

Check with the Internal Revenue Service for information on the tax deductibility
of RV loan interest. Copies of "Publication 936: Home Interest Deduction" and
"Publication 523: Selling Your Home" are available by calling (800) 829-3676 or
visiting http://www.irs.gov.

The National Automobile Dealers Association publishes lists of the resale value of
used vehicles, including RVs; http://www.nadaguides.com.

News-Journal Online posts classified ads for RVs; (386) 255-6735; http://www.
news-journalonline.com/class/870.htm.

RV Consumer Group; http://rv.org.

RV Lite focuses on used RVs, towing guide, and information on weights and
hitches; 10600 S. Freeway, Fort Worth, TX 76140; (800) 725-5190; http://
www.rvlite.com/used.htm.

RV Network Swap Forum has free listings of used RVs for sale. The forum is
sponsored by the Escapees RV Club; http://207.70.132.68/wwwboard/
wwwboard.html.

RV Trader Online; http://www.rvtraderonline.com/adsearch.html.

Clubs

Escapees RV Club is for full-time or long-term RVers; 100 Rainbow Drive,
Livingston, TX 77351; (888) SKP-CLUB; http://www.escapees.com.

Good Sam is an RV club that offers a magazine, campouts, and activities; P.O.
Box 6888, Englewood, CO 80155-6888; (800) 234-3450; http://www.
goodsamclub.com.

Chapter 12: Frugal Family Lodging

100 Best Family Resorts in North America by Janet Tice and Jane Wilford (Chester, Conn.: Globe Pequot, 1998).

Bed-and-breakfasts; http://BedandBreakfast.com.

The Birder's Guide to Bed and Breakfasts: United States and Canada by Peggy Van Hulsteyn (Santa Fe, N.M.: John Muir Publications, 1995).

The Christian Bed & Breakfast Directory by Peggy Hellem (Ulrichsville, Ohio: Barbour Publishing, annual).

Communities Directory (updated periodically) is a guide to over six hundred intentional communities worldwide; Fellowship for Intentional Community, RR 1 Box 156-ET, Rutledge, MO 63563-9720; (800) 995-8342; http://www.ic.org.

The Complete Guide to Bed and Breakfasts, Inns, and Guesthouses in the United States and Canada by Pamela Lanier (Berkeley, Calif.: Ten Speed, 2000); http://www.tenspeed.com.

Condé Nast Traveler is a monthly magazine available in most libraries or by subscription at http://www.condenet.com.

PlacesToStay.com; http://www.PlacesToStay.com.

Retreats Online lists religious retreats; Adventure Guides, City Square P.O. Box 47105, Vancouver, Canada V5Z 4L6; (604) 872-1185; e-mail: connect@retreatsonline.com; http://www.retreatsonline.com.

Timeshare Users Group posts reviews and ratings of more than eighteen hundred timeshare resorts and discussions with other timeshare owners; http://www.tug2.net.

Home Exchanges

Home Exchange Vacationing by Bill Barbour and Mary Barbour (Nashville, Tenn.: Rutledge Hill, 1996).

Homelink International USA; Karl Costabel, P.O. Box 47747, Tampa, FL 33647; (800) 638-3841; e-mail: usa@homelink.org; http://www.homelink.org.

Homelink International Canada; Jack Graber, 1707 Platt Crescent, North Vancouver, BC V7J 1X9; (604) 987-3262; e-mail: exchange@homelink-canada.ca.

Intervac International publishes home-exchange listings; Box 12066, S-291, 12 Kristianstad, Sweden; (800) 756-HOME; http://www.intervacus.com and http://www.intervac.com.

Teach Your Own: A Hopeful Path for Education by John Holt (New York: Delta Seymour, 1982).

Trading Homes International is an Internet-based home swapping service; P.O. Box 787, Hermosa Beach, CA 90254; (800) 877-TRADE (USA) or (310) 798-3864 (international); http://www.trading-homes.com.

Hotels

Budget travel, http://budgettravel.about.com.

Concierge offers a selection of articles and tips, a "Worldwide Airport Guide," insider guides on hotels, shops, and restaurants; http://www.concierge.com.

EXITInfo's Traveler Coupon Guide offers printable online coupons for hotels and motels; http://www.exitinfo.com.

Roomsaver provides hotel discount coupons you print from your computer (up to 50 percent off thousands of hotels) via the Web; http://www.roomsaver.com.

"Special Report on Priceline.com" by Jens Jurgen is a sixteen-page report on bidding strategies for Priceline's air tickets, car rentals, and hotel rooms. Order from

Travel Companion Exchange, P.O. Box 833, Amityville, NY 11701; http://www.WhyTravelAlone.com.

The Travel Buddy contains a variety of regional publications distributed at welcome and information centers; http://www.interstatetravelbuddy.com.

Travelscape claims to guarantee the lowest hotel rates; http://travelscape.com.

TravelWeb offers a hotel searchable hotel database with availability information, prices, deals, maps, etc.; http://www.TravelWeb.com.

Warm Showers List; http://www.rogergravel.com/wsl.

Home-Stay and Host Organizations

American International Homestays, P.O. Box 1754, Nederland, CO 80466; (303) 258-3234; e-mail: ash@igc.apc.org; http://www.aihtravel.com.

Friendship Force, 34 Peachtree Street, Suite 900, Atlanta, GA 30303; (404) 522-9490; http://www.friendship-force.org.

Growing Without Schooling publishes an annual directory of homeschool families interested in hosting overnight travelers. For orders: (888) 925-9298. For questions: (617) 864-3100; http://www.holtgws.com; see also http://www.fun-books.com.

Home to Home; P.O. Box 629D, Kiowa, CO 80117; (888) 57-4HOME; e-mail: home2home@aol.com; http://www.christianhospitality.com.

Servas International; 11 John Street, #407, New York, NY 10038; (212) 267-0292; http://www.usservas.org.

Hostels

Hosteling International Guide to North America (Washington, D.C.: Hosteling International, updated periodically) and other hostel guides are available free to members and for sale to the general public; (202) 783-6161; http://www.hiayh.org.

Hostels.com is independent of all hosteling organizations. It provides the *Worldwide Hostel Guide,* an on-site resource with a clickable world map for locating hostels on your route. You can also read the stories of travelers and interact with other hostelers on the Hosteler's virtual bulletin board. The organization publishes a book, *The World Awaits: How to Travel Far and Well* by Paul Otteson (Emeryville, Calif.: Avalon Travel, 2001); http://www.hostels.com.

International Youth Hostels; http://www.iyhf.org.

Youth hostels; http://home.concepts.nl/~oprins/yh.html.

MILITARY AND DEFENSE DEPARTMENT LODGING

Army lodging regulations are posted for military and Department of Defense civilians; (800) GO-ARMY-1; http://trol.redstone.army.mil/mwr/lodging/new.

Guide to Military Installations by Dan Cragg (Mechanicsville, Pa.: Stackpole, 2001).

Military.com has a travel section with information on lodging for active and retired military personnel, civilians, and their families, including Armed Forces Recreation Centers, camping, and hotels; http://www.military.com/Travel/FrontDoor.

Off Duty Travel posts information and travel services for military and Department of Defense civilians; http://www.offdutytravel.com.

MISCELLANEOUS LODGING

10,000 Vacation Rentals will assist you in renting someone else's cabin or vacation home; (888) 369-7245; http://www.vacationrentalsonline.com and http://www.10kvacationrentals.com.

Christian College Coalition lists Christian colleges in the area you wish to visit and provides contact information to see if they offer low-cost lodging; http://www.gospelcom.net/cccu.

Maine Farm Vacation Association; http://www.mainefarmvacation.com.

Pennsylvania Farm Vacation Association; http://www.pafarmstay.com.

Ranch Vacations by Gene Kilgore (Emeryville, Calif.: Avalon Travel, 1999).

Rural Information Center lists ranch and farm vacation information; National Agricultural Library, Beltsville, MD 20705-2351; (800) 633-7701.

CHAPTER 13: TRANSPORTATION ON A BUDGET

AIR TRAVEL

Best Fares; http://www.bestfares.com.

Biztravel; http://www.biztravel.com.

Cheaptickets lists airfare, cruises, rental cars, and hotel rooms; (800) OKCHEAP; http://www.cheaptickets.com.

Expedia provides updates on current promotional offers from airlines; http://expedia.com.

Frequent Flier Crier is a weekly e-mail newsletter; http://FrequentFlier.com.

Frommer's Online is a newsletter and provides message boards as well as travel book series; http://www.frommers.com.

International Association of Air Travel Couriers offers information about courier travel and available flights for members; http://www.courier.org.

LastMinuteTravel.com is a listing service where providers post their travel packages at discounted prices; http://www.lastminutetravel.com.

Lowestfare.com posts airfare and vacation and cruise packages; http://www.Lowestfare.com.

MyPoints.com has guides to earning frequent-flier points; http://www. MyPoints.com.

WebFlyer allows you to enroll in multiple airline programs simultaneously; http:// www.webflyer.com.

Auctions and Searches

Bid for Vacations is an auction house that offers travel packages and hotel rooms; http://www.bidforvacations.com.

Cheap Fares offers tickets at unpublished discounts; http://www.cheapfares.com.

FareChaseSearch; http://www.farechase.com.

Priceline; http://www.priceline.com.

Qixo; http://www.Qixo.com.

Sidestep; http://sidestep.com.

Travelocity offers online reservations for airlines, hotels, and rental cars; http:// www.travelocity.com.

Airline Web Sites

American Airlines offers the AAdvantage program for accumulating frequent-flier miles through an alliance with Citibank credit cards; (800) 882-8880; http:// americanair.com.

British Airways has limited time promotional offers, such as a frequent-flier program travel club; (800) 211-1248; http://britishairways.com/tryclub.

Continental; (800) 525-0280; http://www.continental.com.

Delta Airlines; (800) 323-2323; http://www.delta.com.

Northwest Airlines; http://www.nwa.com.

Southwest Airlines: http://www.southwest.com.

United Airlines; (800) 421-4655; http://ual.com.

Canadian Airfare Resources
Air Canada; http://www.aircanada.ca.

Department of Foreign Affairs and International Trade of Canada sponsors a Web site with thousands of links to help Canadian travelers plan a journey; http://www.lcnd.com/travel/links/agents.htm.

Exit is a Canadian airfare and travel resources; http://www.exit.ca.

Tripeze posts articles from Canadian travel writers and facilitates airfare searches and a free e-mail newsletter that offers special deals on Canadian airfare; http://www.tripeze.com.

Auto Drive-Away and Vehicle Rentals

All American Auto Transport; American and overseas information for shipping your car; (800) 942-0001; http://www.aaat.com.

Allstates Worldwide Delivery Systems; (800) 822-SHIP; http://www.aswd.com.

Auto Driveaway; (800) 346-2277.

Gas Price Watch posts gasoline prices through over twelve thousand registered "spotters"; http://www.gaspricewatch.com/AboutUS.asp.

Kelley Blue Book lists retail and trade-in values for virtually any vehicle as well as dealer invoice information; http://kbb.com.

Quality Driveaway; (800) 695-9743.

Tn'T Auto Transport; 6352 Corte del Abeto, Suite A, Carlsbad, CA 92009; (800) 624-2021; http://www.tnt-inc.com.

BICYCLING

Bicycling America's National Parks series, and other books about outdoor recreation published by Countryman Press, P.O. Box 748, Woodstock, VT 05091; (800) 245-4151; http://www.countrymanpress.com.

Bicycling Magazine's Bicycle Touring in the '90s by Bicycling Magazine Editors (Emmaus, Pa.: Rodale, 1993).

Blazing Saddles offers bicycle rentals in seven cities in the United States; http://www.blazingsaddles.com.

Europe by Bike by Karen and Terry Whithill (Tucson, Ariz.: Mountaineers Books, 1993). Mountaineers Books publishes resources for climbers, hikers, skiers, bicyclists, and paddlers; (800) 553-4453; http://www.mountaineersbooks.com.

The League of American Bicyclists publishes an annual *Almanac of Cycling* and the *Tourfinder & Ride Guide;* 1612 K St. N.W., Suite 401, Washington, DC 20006-2082; (202) 822-1333; http://www.bikeleague.org.

BUS AND TRAIN TRAVEL

Ameripass is an unlimited bus pass for use in the United States on Greyhound Bus Lines and some of its affiliates; (888) GLI PASS; http://www.greyhound.com.

BusAbout Network focuses on transportation in European cities and inexpensive lodging; http://www.busabout.com.

Grayline offers tours to over a dozen locations in Canada; http://www.grayline.ca.

International bus routes; http://www.routesinternational.com.

Online travel includes information on European trains as well as air travel, Middle Eastern destinations, and student discounts; http://euroair.com.

United Motorcoach Association locates charter bus operators; http://www. uma.org.

USA by Rail; http://www.usa-by-rail.com.

CRUISES

Adventure Cruising by Don Martin and Betty Martin (Columbia, Calif.: Pine Cone, 1996); P.O. Box 1494, Columbus, CA 95310; e-mail: pinecone@ sonnet.com.

Cruise.com reviews various ships and provides discount information, price quotes, and online booking; http://www/cruise.com.

FREIGHTER AND FERRY TRAVEL

Ford's Freighter Travel Guide by Judith A. Howard (Northridge, Calif.: Ford's Travel Guides, updated semiannually) covers commuter and commercial ferries as well as other freighters. Ford's Travel Guides, 10520 Reseda Blvd., Northridge, CA 91326-3129; (818) 701-7414.

Freighter Space Advisory is published by Freighter World Cruises, 180 S. Lake Ave., Suite 335, Pasadena, CA 91101; (818) 449-3106.

Freighter Travel News is published by Freighter Travel Club of America, 3524 Harts Lake Rd., Roy, WA 98580.

Freighter World Cruises (FWC) specializes in placing passengers on freighter ships; http://www.freighterworld.com.

"Poor Man's Cruise" is an online article by Richard Bangs about inexpensive travel by ferry; http://www.msnbc.com/news/367804.asp.

TravLTrips Magazine provides information about freighters and other long and unusual cruises; Cruise and Freighter Travel Association, P.O. Box 580188, Flushing, NY 11358; (800) 872-8584; http://www.travltips.com.

Foot Travel

Backpacking with Babies and Small Children: A Guide to Taking the Kids Along on Day Hikes, Overnighters, and Long Trail Trips by Goldie Silverman (Berkeley, Calif.: Wilderness, 1998).

The Barefoot Hiker by Richard Frazine (Berkeley, Calif.: Ten Speed, 1993); http://www.tenspeed.com.

Best Hikes with Children: San Francisco's North Bay by Bill McMillon, Kevin McMillon (Seattle, Wash.: Mountaineers Book, 1992). Separate guides (different authors, various publication dates) are also available for a variety of other states.

Society for Barefoot Living; http://www.barefooters.org.

Small Watercraft: Sailing, Rafting, Canoeing, Kayaking

Canoeing: The Complete Guide to Equipment and Technique by David Harrison (Mechanicsville, Pa.: Stackpole, 1996).

Good Old Boat Magazine; 7340 Niagara Lane North, Maple Grove, MN 55311-2655; http://www.GoodOldBoat.com.

Grays Harbor Historical Seaport has a replica of a two-hundred-year-old sailboat and operates year-round with a crew of volunteers serious about learning to sail; P.O. Box 2019, Aberdeen, WA 98520; (800) 200-LADY.

Guide to Sea Kayaking series by Globe Pequot; http://www.globe-pequot.com.

Houseboating Magazine; 360 B St., Idaho Falls, ID 83402; (800) 638-0135; http://www.houseboatmagazine.com.

Paddling series by Falcon; http://www.falcon.com.

The Sailboat Exchange offers a database of sailboat owners who wish to exchange the use of their boat for the use of another boat in a different part of the country; http://www.sailboatexchange.com.

Sierra Mac River Rafting Trips; P.O. Box 366, Sonora, CA 95370; (800) 457-2580.

Additional Resources for Budget Transportation

Adventurous Traveler Bookstore; http://AdventurousTraveler.com.

American Automobile Association; http://www.aaa.com.

The American Society of Travel Agents, Consumer Affairs, 1101 King St., Alexandria, VA 22314; http://www.astanet.com.

Family Travel Forum; http://familytravelforum.com.

Gomez rates travel Web sites for consumers; http://www.gomez.com.

Smarter Living posts weekly airfare e-mail notices; Smarter Living, Inc., 432 Columbia St., Suite B-4, Cambridge, MA 02141; http://www. SmarterLiving.com.

Travel Information Center; 12th St. and Tabor Rd., Philadelphia, PA 19141; (215) 329-5715.

Travel with Kids, http://www.travelwithkids.about.com.

Books and Magazines

Arthur Frommer's Budget Travel posts online information on travel destinations, hotels, restaurants, etc.; http://www.frommers.com.

Discount Travel Handbook edited by Mary Lu Abbott (Houston: Vacation, 1996).

The Frugal Globetrotter: Your Guide to World Adventure Bargains by Bruce T. Northam (Golden, Colo.: Fulcrum Publishing, 1996).

Insider Travel Secrets You're NOT Supposed to Know by Tom Parsons (Arlington, Tex.: Best Fares USA, Inc., 1998); http://www.bestfares.com.

Take Back Your Life: Travel Full-Time in an RV by Stephanie Bernhagen (Livingston, Tex.: Bemham-Collins, 2000), two chapters on traveling with children.

Travel Bargains: How to Pay Less and Travel More by Arthur G. Evans (Redondo Beach, Calif.: Photo Data Research, 1997).

CHAPTER 14: BE PREPARED: PRACTICAL TIPS FOR PARENTS ON THE ROAD

The Berenstain Bears and Too Much Vacation by Stan and Jan Berenstain (First Time Books, 1989).

Home Is Where You Park It by Kay Peterson (Livingston, Tex.: RoVers, 1990).

Magellan's travel supply catalog; (800) 962-4943; http://Magellans.com.

Solarsense distributes solar-powered products; http://www.solarsense.com.

The Vermont Country Store offers comfortable travel shoes and serviceable hats as well as other hard-to-find items; P.O. Box 6999, Rutland, VT 05702-6999; (802) 362-8440; http://www.vermontcountrystore.com.

Workers on Wheels offers advice to those who want to work while traveling, especially RVers. Includes profiles of travelers, jobs for entertainers, and information on mobile self-employment opportunities; job listings include concessionaire or campground positions in government or private parks; http://www.workersonwheels.com.

BABIES AND SMALL CHILDREN
Baby Bargains by Denise and Alan Field (Boulder, Colo.: Windsor Peak, 1999) includes a buyers' guide; 1223 Peakview Circle, Suite 600, Boulder, CO 80302; (800) 888-0385; http://www.windsorpeak.com.

Consumer Products Safety Commission provides information on baby equipment recalls; (800) 638-2772.

Safety Belt Safe USA offers advice for checking the safety of your used car seat, recalls, car seat inspections, etc.; http://www.safekids.org.

COMMUNICATION ON THE ROAD

Camping on the Internet by Loren Eyrich (Elkhart, Ind.: Cottage, 2000) has helpful hints on the economical use of telephones, cell phones, computers, and the Internet while traveling in an RV; order from bookstores or from (800) 272-5518.

Internet Travel Planner by Michael Shapiro (Chester, Conn.: Globe Pequot, 2000).

Layover.com includes a listing of computer-friendly truck stops where you can plug in your laptop and log on to the Internet; http://www.layover.com.

Travel Planning Online for Dummies by Noah Vadnai and Julian Smith (Foster City, Calif.: IDG Books, 2000).

HEALTH AND SPECIAL NEEDS

EarPlanes (made by Cirrus) are an inexpensive (under $5) device that prevents ear pain during flying by equalizing pressure. They are available at most discount stores.

Internet Health Library is a children's page that has links to Web sites dealing with children's health; http://www.healthlibrary.com.

MedicAlert Foundation sponsors MedicAlert bracelets for emergency medical information; P.O. Box 1009, Turlock, CA 95381; (800) 432-5378.

Accessibility and Funding for Travelers with Disabilities

Aaron's Trach Web page; http://www.tracheostomy.com.

At About.com, search the site with the keywords "disability travel." You can also search for specific special needs (wheelchair, cerebral palsy, diabetes, etc.); http://about.com.

Access-Able Travel Source provides information on special-needs travel; LLC, P.O. Box 1796, Wheat Ridge, CO 80034; (303) 232-2979; http://www. access-able.com.

Armchair World provides information about handicapped-accessible tours, including a variety of water sports; http://armchair.com/tour/hc/handcap.html.

Children's Hopes and Dreams Foundation offers a free pen-pal service that matches children ages five to eighteen with another child who has a similar medical condition; 284 Route 46, Dover, NJ 07801-9964; (201) 361-7348.

Flying Wheels Travel facilitates wheelchair-accessible tours, mostly to other countries with tours originating in the United States; 143 W. Bridge St., Owatonna, MN 55060; (507) 451-5005; http://www.FlyingWheelsTravel.com.

Mobility International USA, P.O. Box 3551, Eugene, OR 97403.

Open Directory Project lists many "disabled travel" links; http://dmoz.org/ Society/Disabled/Travel.

Society for the Advancement of Travel for the Handicapped, 26 Court St., Brooklyn, NY 11242; (718) 858-5483.

"Tips for Disabled Travelers"; http://www.tips4trips.com/Tips/distips.htm.

RVing for People with Disabilities
About.com has many links to accessibility and RVs; http://rvtravel. about.com/cs/ accessibility/index.htm.

Base Camps of America—RV Services, Disabled Travelers; http://www. rvlinks.org/disabled.html.

"The Enabled RVer" column appears in the *RV Companion* magazine. Subscribe at http://www.rvcompanion.com.

Road Trips: The Enabled RVer; http://maxpages.com/enabledrver.

Wheelchair ramps for RVs; http://www.alumiramp.com.

Help for Stranded Travelers

Public libraries often have guides that list local social service agencies.

The Salvation Army is usually listed in local phone directories or ask at a church; http://www.salvationarmy.org.

Travelers' Aid Society; check local telephone directory or inquire at airport, train station, or bus station information kiosks.

Mapping and Trip Planning

AAA Map'n'Go (DeLorme) is road atlas software designed to locate regions and attractions by area code or ZIP code; (800) 452-5931; http://www.delorme.com/cybermaps.

Excite; http://maps.excite.com.

Expedia; http://www.maps.expedia.com.

Free Trip has online trip planning services called Autopilot and TruckPilot to plan your route and check gas prices along the way; e-mail: ft-webmaster@freetrip.com; http://www.freetrip.com.

MapBlast; http://www.mapblast.com/myblast.

MapQuest; http://www.mapquest.com.

Rand McNally; http://www.randmcnally.com.

Travel Planner Gold (Expert Software) is an aid to trip planning, attractions, airport and airline information; (800) 759-2562.

PACKING

52 Ways to Make Family Travel More Enjoyable by Kate Redd (Nashville, Tenn.: Nelson, 1994).

First We Quit Our Jobs: How One Work-Driven Couple Got on the Road to a New Life by Marilyn J. Abraham (New York: Dell, 1997) includes information on paring down belongings to move from a house to an RV.

The Packing Book: Secrets of the Carry-On Traveler by Judith Gilford (Berkeley, Calif.: Ten Speed, 1998); http://www.tenspeed.com.

TRAVELING WITH PETS

American Animal Hospital Association has an online listing of animal hospitals across the country as well as pet-care advice. If your pet becomes sick while traveling, you can call for a referral to the nearest affiliated clinic; (800) 252-2242; http://www.healthypet.com.

Dog Friendly can help you research all the great places you can go with your dog; http://www.DogFriendly.com.

Pet Vacations allows you to post questions about travel arrangements, find accommodations, listings, and jokes; http://www.petvacations.com.

PetsWelcome.com lists over twenty-five thousand hotels, bed-and-breakfasts, ski resorts, campgrounds, and beaches that are pet-friendly. The site also lists emergency vet contact information, pet sitters, and boarding kennels; http://www.petswelcome.com.

TravelDog.com offers lists of accommodations and information about choosing kennels and pet sitters; http://www.traveldog.com.

TraveLodge is a motel chain, and its Web site offers a list of cat- and dog-friendly locations in the TraveLodge chain and a page of helpful hints for traveling with a pet. Follow the pet links; http://www.travelodge.com.

INDEX

About the Authors

Judith Waite Allee has visited families in sixteen states and Mexico through host exchanges, along with her husband, John, and daughter, Nancy, now a college student. Judith and her husband own a home-based photography business that gives them opportunities to take their livelihood on the road as they photograph conferences and reunions. Judith's Web site, *www. DreamsOnAShoestring.com,* offers a free e-mail newsletter for educational family travelers. As former foster parents, the Allees have traveled with up to three children.

Judith speaks on a variety of topics, including parenting, family literacy, mental health, advocacy for children in foster care, and homeschooling. As a parent education coordinator for a mental health association, Judith facilitates a support group and presents workshops for parents under stress. As a volunteer, she performs victim-offender mediations and parent-teen mediations for the local juvenile court.

Melissa L. Morgan's three children are thirteen, ten, and two. The family travels with Melissa's husband, Hugh, on business, on treks across the country to visit family members, and on numerous field trips. No matter why they travel or what route they follow, the family takes advantage of educational opportunities in the real world.

Melissa has served as a college-level instructor and managed several commercial and nonprofit Web sites. She currently writes an online newsletter, *Parents Are Teachers,* and manages a Web site, *www.eaglesnesthome.com,* to provide a forum and resources for Christian writers and homeschoolers. She has taught groups ranging from preschoolers to adults, including seminars for writers, the Twelve Steps for Kids program, and homeschool support-group classes.

Judith and Melissa are the authors of *Homeschooling on a Shoestring: A Jam-Packed Guide for Parents* (Harold Shaw Publishers).